MW01644475

British History

A Captivating Guide to the Story of Britain, the Britons, and the Battle of Britain

Free Bonus from Captivating History (Available for a Limited time)

Hi History Lovers!

Now you have a chance to join our exclusive history list so you can get your first history ebook for free as well as discounts and a potential to get more history books for free!

Simply visit the link below to join.

captivatinghistory.com/ebook

Or, Scan the QR code!

Also, make sure to follow us on Facebook, X, and YouTube by searching for Captivating History.

Table of Contents

Part 1: History of Britain

A Captivating Guide to Events and Facts You Should Know about the Story of England, Wales, Northern Ireland, and Scotland

Introduction: Back When Britannia Ruled the Waves

Today, it is almost hard to fathom that Britain was once the largest empire on the planet. We see the island of Britain, which is home to Scotland, England, and Wales, and wonder how this minuscule piece of real estate gave birth to such a juggernaut. As far as islands go, Britain is quite large; it is the ninth-largest in the world. But when compared to massive nations like China and Russia, it is easy to fall into the trap of seeing Britain as a small island that could not hold its own when faced with the threat of larger powers.

Nevertheless, for centuries, the island of Britain stood as both a lighthouse and a fortress. Since the days of the Magna Carta, Britain shined as a beacon of what a nation could achieve if only its citizenry were given the proper opportunity.

Britain brought us the plays of William Shakespeare and the first locomotives to hit the railroad tracks. In many ways, Britain was well ahead of its peers. Even so, Britain had a long history of fending off adversaries. The British Isles, which primarily consist of Britain proper and the island of Ireland (home to Ireland and Northern Ireland), were waylaid by Vikings and then subject to a Norman invasion. (As a note, the term "British Isles" is sometimes seen in a negative light due to the British Empire's dominance of Ireland. The term is still used by most scholars, which is why we have elected to use it at times in the book.)

The Anglo-Saxons were subdued in 1066 by William the Conqueror, one of the most famous men in history. However, the Norman newcomers were more likely to co-opt what they found in Britain rather than replace it with their own modes of living. William is often credited with "introducing" feudalism, but this is not entirely accurate. It has been noted that some forms of feudalism were already in existence in England prior to his arrival. However, William placed a heavier emphasis on feudalism and greatly sped up the process of making it an enshrined state institution.

Once in force, the feudal system better streamlined the control of land, allotting whole sections to various members of the elite. Most of these "elite" were William's fellow Normans who had fought alongside him to subdue England. The French-speaking Normans established castles throughout the realm, further solidifying their grip on their many landed estates.

The greatest shock of William's takeover was felt by prominent Anglo-Saxon nobility who were stripped of their land and titles. For them, the change was tremendous. But for the landless peasants, who were already landless before the invasion, the immediate impact on their daily lives was not so great. At most, they could look forward to new landlords who spoke a new language. No matter who the landed elite might have been, the general character and spirit of the British masses remained mostly the same.

Britain has long had a spirit of originality—some might even say defiance—which makes it stand on its principles without interference from others. One could say this independent streak came to prominence during Henry VIII's reign. This monarch is often lambasted for being reckless and self-centered due to his falling out with the Catholic Church over his wishes to pursue another wife and thereby produce a male heir for his throne.

But whatever you might think of this Tudor king's motives, you have to hand it to him—even when the status quo of the Roman Catholic Church refused to give him what he wanted, he was unwilling to just take no for an answer. When the Roman Catholic Church indicated that it was against their rules and regulations for him to annul his marriage, Henry VIII simply created a church of his own, the Church of England, and put himself at its head.

People might argue about whether he was right or wrong for doing so, but we can all agree that the stiff upper lip of British defiance showed itself. And it did so in countless other epochs of British history. Britain stood practically alone against the Axis Powers at the outset of World War Two after France fell, yet it stood ready to defend its way of life at all costs.

Even after British troops had been driven off the shores of Dunkirk, the bold and courageous prime minister, Winston Churchill, stood in the gap, declaring the British would fight their foes every step of the way and "never surrender."

These bold words sum up Britain's history in its entirety. From the Anglo-Saxons to Brexit, Britain has dared to be different, and the whole world has continuously stood in awe.

SECTION ONE: ENGLAND

Chapter 1: The Arrival of the Anglo-Saxons

"I hope for nothing in this world so ardently as once again to see that paradise called England. I long to embrace again all my old friends there."

-Cosimo III de' Medici

The Anglo-Saxons' arrival to Britain dates back to the middle of the 5th century. Just as Roman influence over Britain was coming to a close around 410, new arrivals from the European mainland known as the Anglo-Saxons began to make their presence known in large numbers. The Anglo-Saxons, which consisted of the Angles, Saxons, and Jutes, were a Germanic people group who arrived in several waves of migration. These migrants would come into direct contact (and conflict) with the Romanized Britons of southern England, which at that time is said to have been quite large.

When we say "Romanized Britons," it is important to understand these people hailed from various backgrounds and tribal groups. Among them were, of course, the Celts (at least those who chose to submit to Roman rule), Bretons, Caledonians, and Brigantes. These tribal groups were early adopters of Romanization and now found themselves in direct conflict with the Anglo-Saxon newcomers.

The Anglo-Saxons initially established their enclave in England's eastern corner—East Anglia—which is named after them. The influx of the Anglo-Saxons has been likened to a slow-moving invasion. Unlike the Roman invasion of Britain and the later Viking and Norman invasions, the

Anglo-Saxons' arrival occurred in a piecemeal fashion over the centuries. According to at least one account by a monk named Gildas, there were some more overt episodes of takeover as well. Around 540, Gildas compiled a brief history of events said to have occurred in the 440s, right at the tail end of Roman influence in western Europe.

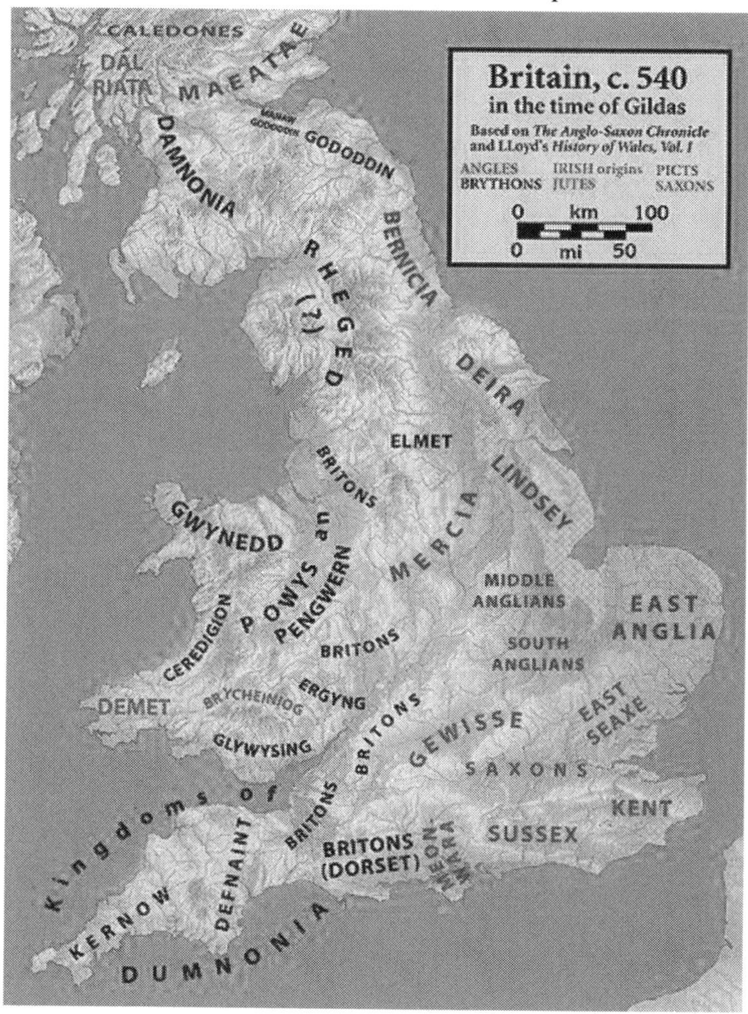

Britain in 540.[1]

According to Gildas, in the 5th century, a British warlord named Gurthigern, better known as Vortigern, attempted to hold his own in eastern England but decided to make use of an old Roman tactic of recruiting mercenaries. This strategy led to one of the most massive influxes of Anglo-Saxons. Some question Gildas's account, saying

Vortigern was not even real. However, the general consensus is that he did exist, and it is not out of the realm of possibility that he hired foreign mercenaries. And as was often the case with the Romans themselves, it would not have taken long for these hired hands to turn on their employers and attempt to seize lands outright.

As Anglo-Saxons more aggressively seized British real estate, the inhabitants of Roman Britain were pushed farther north and west in hopes of avoiding the recklessness of the Anglo-Saxons. And while the Anglo-Saxons would change the cultural landscape of Britain over time, they would also be influenced by those who had come before.

Even after the fall of the Western Roman Empire, the civil structure of Roman Britons who spoke Latin and adhered to various aspects of Roman customs would remain intact, at least for some time. Most importantly, the Latin alphabet would be adopted by the Anglo-Saxons around the year 600. The Anglo-Saxons had no written language of their own save for their symbolic runic script. This merger produced the first Anglicized literature, with Latin script, bright artistic lettering, and an Anglo-Saxon flair.

The Romans themselves had become increasingly Christian ever since Emperor Constantine's fateful Edict of Milan in 313 CE approved of Christianity. When the last Western Roman emperor, Romulus Augustus, was overthrown in 476, the Roman Catholic Church became a guiding light, with the pope taking on the guise of an ideological emperor ruling over all of the Catholics scattered throughout the former Roman Empire.

As the last remnants of Roman thought flowed into Anglo-Saxon circles, the Anglo-Saxons eventually adopted the Christian religion, as well as many aspects of Roman culture. Countless Christian missionaries played a major role in the Anglo-Saxons' conversion. They fearlessly risked life and limb to preach to warlike tribes throughout the former provinces of the Roman Empire.

As the Romanized Britons and Anglo-Saxons began to merge, their cooperation became clear. By the end of the 6th century, leading Briton and Anglo-Saxon figures were more or less in sync with each other. The Anglo-Saxon period of England created seven kingdoms: East Anglia, Essex, Sussex, Wessex, Mercia, Northumbria, and Kent. Wales was divided into the states of Gwynedd, Gwent, Dyfed, and Powys.

The Welsh maintained a strong confederation and were able to keep Anglo-Saxon encroachments at bay. But the Anglo-Saxons' inexorable push northward would eventually deprive the Welsh of their most arable farmlands, with the Anglo-Saxons moving into the Welsh Lowlands. From this point forward, the Welsh would be pigeonholed into a much more hardscrabble existence in the Welsh Highlands. Around this time, Scotland was facing some territorial changes as well.

In the late 6th century, Scotland boasted the Kingdom of Rheged, which ran from the Solway Firth all the way toward Cumbria. At this time, the northernmost reaches of Scotland were controlled by a tribal group called the Picts. Not a whole lot is known about the early history of the Picts, although we know they thrived during the British "Dark Ages." They were observed as far back as the Roman era, as the Romans appreciated their fierceness while simultaneously deriding them as barbarians. The Romans called them Picts since their warriors were covered in tattoos. "Pict" is derived from the Latin word *pictus*, which means "painted." The Romans were both awed and repulsed by these people who painted their bodies and resisted them at every turn.

By the 5th and 6th centuries, the Picts were on the rise. They had formed a confederation between several of their larger tribes. However, they were forced to become a tributary for the more powerful neighboring kingdom to their immediate south: Northumbria.

Formed in northern England and southeastern Scotland in the early 600s, Northumbria would become one of Britain's strongest, most consolidated kingdoms in the Early Middle Ages. Its starting point was just north of the Humber, an estuary, hence the name (north of the Humber). The Northumbrians descended from the Germanic tribes who had arrived in Britain during late antiquity. Northumbria is said to have been founded by a warrior king named Æthelfrith, who built up a powerful army to subdue his neighboring rivals.

Æthelfrith would ultimately perish on the battlefield in 616. He was succeeded by his brother Edwin. As king of Northumbria, Edwin, though from a pagan background, eventually turned to Christianity and used it to ideologically unify his kingdom. Northumbria officially adopted the faith in 627. Northumbria was home to Christian focal points like the majestic monastery of Lindisfarne. Here, monks laboriously compiled the Lindisfarne Gospels. This was a painstaking work of biblical scripture showcased in illuminated lettering. It would be finished sometime between 715 and 720.

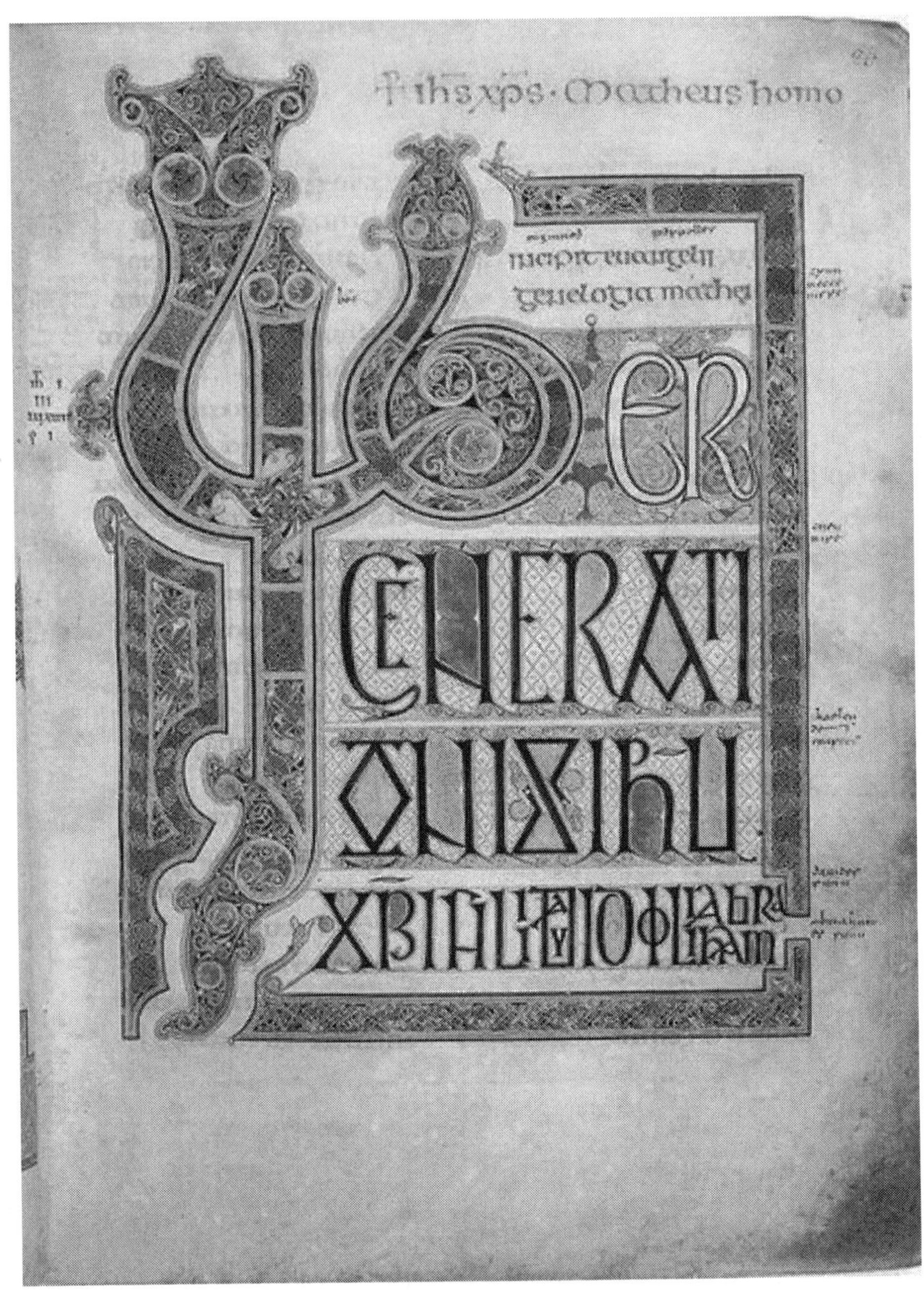

A page from the Lindisfarne Gospels[2].

King Æthelfrith was succeeded by his son, who ruled for a few years. Oswald, another one of Æthelfrith's sons, ruled next, coming to power in 634. He greatly expanded Northumbria during his reign. His brother,

King Oswiu, would succeed him and go even further by absorbing the nearby Kingdom of Mercia, making Northumbria the most impressive kingdom in Britain. However, the greatest thorn in the Northumbrians' side would remain the Picts.

After relations between the two had broken down, the Picts are said to have lured the Northumbrians into an ambush, which resulted in the disastrous Battle of Nechtansmere (also known as the Battle of Dun Nechtain) in 685. The Northumbrians were terribly defeated, even losing their king, Ecgfrith. They would never rally the strength they previously had. From here on out, the Kingdom of Northumbria would go into decline. The Picts' efforts are said to have helped ensure the northernmost regions of Britain would be too difficult for any later English ruler to conquer them.

By 750, the Picts still reigned over much of what we now call Scotland. Yet in the turbulent backdrop of the Dark Ages, the Picts would be no more. By the end of the 10th century, the Picts disappeared from the record. This in itself presents a mystery, and there is much debate as to what might have befallen the once-mighty Picts.

Some have laid the blame for the demise of the Picts on Viking incursions from Scandinavia. This theory makes a lot of sense since this would have been around when Scandinavian Vikings invaded and explored northern Britain, spreading havoc as far south as Lindisfarne Priory. Lindisfarne had one of the most memorable encounters with the Vikings, as it was the first recorded encounter of a Viking attack on Britain. In 793, the pagan invaders desecrated the monastery and ruthlessly put its monks to the sword.

Could it be then that the Vikings decimated the once-strong buffer state to the north—the kingdom of the Picts? If so, it seems the Vikings who descended from their longboats onto Britain's northernmost shores were able to do one of two things. Either they managed to catch the Picts entirely off-guard or were able to poke and prod their weakest flanks and deal devastating knockout blows, decimating the Picts' ability to fight. Neither the Romans nor the Northumbrians were ever able to do this.

As devastating as the Viking attacks were, the Viking raids proved more transitory in nature, and the Vikings did not put down permanent roots in Scotland on a large scale. In 843, a powerful leader whose name comes down to us as "Kenneth MacAlpin" sent a large force into the shattered remnants of Pict territory to establish his authority over a patchwork conglomerate, which would eventually come to be known as Scotland. Not a whole lot is known about MacAlpin's background, but he is said to have Gaelic roots.

At any rate, it is believed the remnants of the Picts were absorbed into the newcomers brought by MacAlpin. This combination of people groups resulted in the residents of Scotland that we know today.

Since the Viking threat was not yet over, it was incumbent upon MacAlpin to shore up Scotland's northern defenses (the same northern defenses that were likely vulnerable to attack from the Vikings in the first place). He amassed a large army and created a strong bulwark against future Viking raids. Due to the Picts' and Scots' common struggle against the Viking threat, some historians have theorized that the Pict survivors might have gladly accepted MacAlpin's rule as a means of survival. Siding with MacAlpin held the promise of future protection from the marauding bands of Vikings who had devastated them in previous go-arounds.

Even so, it was not long before Pictish customs and language disappeared from the scene altogether. The descendants of this historic merger would not speak Pict but rather Scottish Gaelic. They would also conform to Gaelic ideology by embracing Scottish variations of the Christian faith. This, too, was perhaps a further means of presenting a united front against the invading Vikings since the Vikings were pagans at the time. The peoples of Scandinavia would not enter into the Christian fold until much later in the game, with most not converting until after 1000, although the process began in the 900s.

The Vikings also remained a formidable thorn in the Anglo-Saxons' side. The situation came to a head in the 870s when Danish Vikings began making inroads in northwestern Britain. It took a young king from Wessex named Alfred to stand in the gap. Alfred rallied a large army and met the Vikings in an open battle near Edington. His forces were victorious and managed to stop this latest Viking onslaught in its tracks.

Upon the Vikings' defeat, their demoralized leader, Guthrum, apparently knowing that his time was up, decided to convert to Christianity and encouraged his followers to do likewise. He did this to confirm the agreement he had made with Alfred, as he wished for peace. However, this baptism made it clear to all involved that the Anglo-Saxons had triumphed both on the battlefield and on an ideological and cultural level.

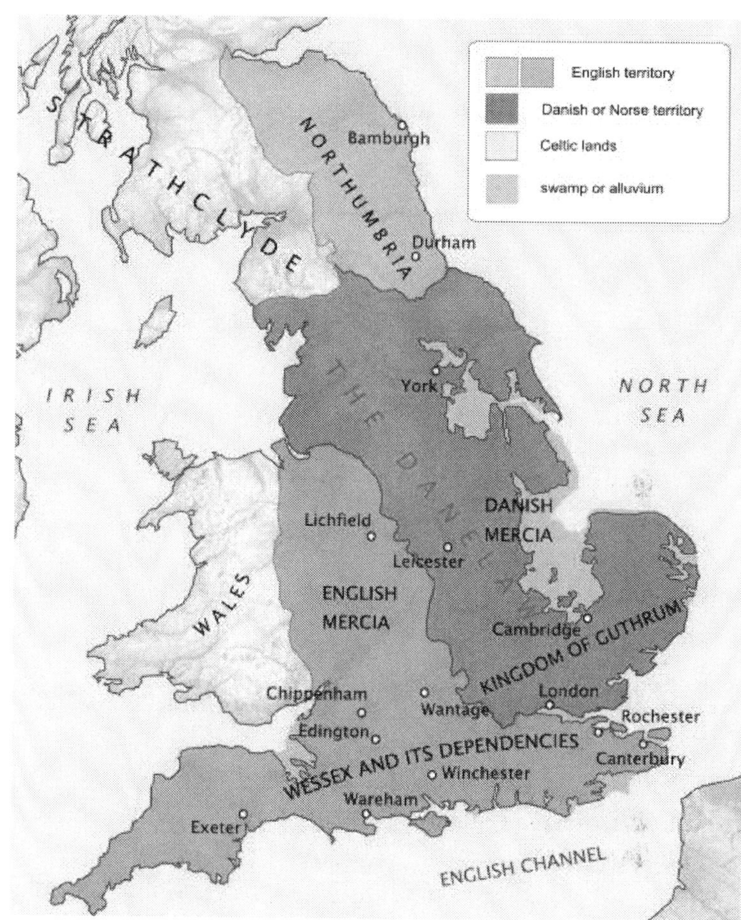

Britain in 878.[3]

Wessex became the main focal point of authority in Britain. And Alfred—later known as "Alfred the Great"—would not squander the gains he had made. Instead, he would further invest in them. With his main enemies at bay, King Alfred worked on bolstering his defenses. He wished to have not just a standing army but also a rotational system of local militias led by his immediate subordinates in the nobility class. These militias could be called upon at any time.

Alfred created a network of burhs, a series of strong fortifications spiraling out from the Wessex capital of Winchester. As a final yet incredibly important touch, Alfred revamped Wessex's naval capacity, creating an effective naval force to deter Viking incursions by sea. These modifications would prove to be useful when the Vikings launched renewed raids in the 880s and 890s.

With his northern flank secure from any further Viking incursions, by the time of his demise in 899, Alfred the Great had managed to expand his kingdom all the way to London in the south, West Mercia in the west, and Kent in the east—establishing a blueprint for what would eventually become England today. The consolidating power of Alfred served to reshape the region. As writer and historian Richard Dargie once put it, "Alfred's greatest victory lay in aligning the cause of Wessex with a wider burgeoning sense of 'Englishness.'"

Upon Alfred's passing, it was up to his son Edward to carry on the mantle. To make it official, Edward was hailed as the "King of Angles and Saxons" in 900, a title his father held later in life. King Edward was a notable champion of the realm, just like his father before him. Like Alfred the Great, he constructed mighty forts throughout the region. He was at war with the Vikings intermittently.

Edward (remembered as Edward the Elder) battled the Danes in Northumbria, always seeking to repulse them ever farther northward from the Humber, which separated Wessex from the Danelaw or Dane's Land. The culture and laws of the Danes had a tremendous impact on those around them. Many Norse words and customs would be melded with the surrounding cultures that were already in place.

But as remarkable as Edward was, in many ways, his sister, Æthelflæd, was even more remarkable. She came to prominence early on as a true fighter and defender of the realm.

As a young girl, Æthelflæd managed to foil her own attempted abduction. The Danes had conducted a raid and tried to take off with her while the princess's handlers looked on. She would have likely suffered a terrible fate if it was not for her formidable, fiery spirit to struggle. She put up such a fight against her assailants that they gave up and made a hasty retreat. Æthelflæd later married the king of Mercia (who had the very similar sounding name of Æthelred). She was absolutely adored by her subjects and would forever be known as the "Lady of the Mercians."

Edward's heir was his son Æthelstan. It is said that Æthelstan was an energetic, ambitious man with proven acumen on the field of battle. He came to the role of king ready to take Wessex from defensive to offensive campaigns. Soon, his forces were pouring into neighboring regions, expanding the borders of his kingdom until they essentially reached those associated with the borders of modern-day England. For this reason, Æthelstan is said to be the first king of England.

Under the steady hands of Æthelstan, the rest of Northumbria was brought into the domain of Wessex. He also pushed into the west into the lands of the Cornish past the Tamar River. The biggest threat to his reign emerged in 937 when a loose confederation of Scots, Britons, Cumbrians, Irish, and Scandinavians came together to take on the ever-expanding military machine of Wessex.

As powerful as the Wessex army had become, the combined might of these desperate foes nearly undid all of Wessex's gains. This struggle culminated in the Battle of Brunanburh, which is remembered as one of the bloodiest in British history. Nevertheless, in the end, Æthelstan and his Wessex-based Anglo-Saxons were victorious and drove their enemies out. Æthelstan would perish two years later but would die knowing that his kingdom was secure.

Along with the decisive victory, it has been said the integral system of administration that Æthelstan put in place had much to do with the lasting success of Wessex and its successor state of England. Æthelstan established a complex system of administrators who were all interconnected with each other and ready and willing to effectively carry out their duties.

From top to bottom, posts such as ealdorman, sheriff, and hundred-man ensured the kingdom was taken care of at every level. For instance, the hundred-man was in charge of a shire that consisted of roughly one hundred residents. Through this elaborate system, the lands of England were cut up into various sections and doled out. However, the people still remained connected to each other.

A rewards system was also put in place, in which those who loyally served the kingdom would be rewarded with land grants. This focus on gaining a landed estate would continue throughout English history. Further enshrinement of the universal legal code and systems of revenue accruement would also do much to keep the peace among citizens while ensuring the kingdom remained financially solvent. The system would hold firm, even under turbulent conditions, as was evidenced when Vikings temporarily seized York after Æthelstan's demise in 939.

However, this proved to be just a momentary relapse, as the stronger Wessex system pulled York back into its orbit by 954. As strong as the realm Alfred the Great had founded had become, it was faced with a grave new threat by the late 10th century. Renewed Viking raids—this time from Denmark—threatened to topple everything that Alfred the Great and his successors had built. This led to much of England coming under the rule of a Viking warlord known as Cnut the Great.

Norse armies, equipped with their huge broadswords and battleaxes, posed a ferocious threat to anyone who came across them. This struggle produced the Irish warrior Brian Boru, who fought several factions of Viking holdouts and became the high king of Ireland in 1002.

In England, a new star was rising in the form of Edward the Confessor. Edward, who was the son of Æthelred the Unready, had been invited to succeed the Norseman Harthacnut. He proved to be a powerful and unifying king.

Edward's reign was stable, but upon his death in 1066, new drama would ensue, this time from the shores of Normandy. Edward did not have a direct heir, and William, Duke of Normandy, decided he was entitled to rule over the English throne. He said he was the grandson of King Edward's uncle, Richard II of Normandy. This claim was not recognized in England, and upon Edward's death, a nobleman named Harold Godwinson was named as the successor. Some say that Edward gave the throne to William or that Harold promised to support William's claim. There is no written proof of either of these claims, although William stated they happened.

William was willing to make his claim by force if necessary. The bold duke gathered a large army and crossed the Channel to invade England. Harold was crowned king of England on January 6th, 1066, and William of Normandy launched his invasion that September.

Just prior to William waging war, he tried his hand at diplomacy. Upon hearing of Harold being crowned, he wrote Harold directly, bringing before him his claim to the throne. However, Harold replied that it was not his decision to become the new king, reminding William that he had been chosen by the nobility. Harold basically tried to wash his hands of the dispute by claiming he was chosen and now must live out his obligations. But William, of course, would not accept this. After months of preparation, William and his forces landed on September 28th, 1066, at Pevensey, England.

He constructed a fortress right where he landed. William would oversee further operations from this beachhead. His efforts would culminate in the Battle of Hastings, which took place on October 14th, 1066. This titanic battle between the forces of William of Normandy and King Harold II decided who would rule England.

The two armies confronted each other some seven miles from the southeastern English town of Hastings. The two armies were both large, but King Harold's army was primarily infantry, whereas William had a professional cavalry and a strong contingent of archers. Harold was low on skilled soldiers because his armies had already been bled dry during two previous threats that he had to face shortly after he was crowned.

Harold had to fend off both a Viking incursion and a threat from his own brother, coming out on top in the Battle of Stamford Bridge. Stamford Bridge was about two hundred miles north of Hastings, and Harold and his forces made the journey in four days, an astounding feat.

To offset the deficit between William's skilled warriors and Harold's less experienced infantry, Harold attempted to launch a surprise attack against William to catch his army off-guard. However, his attempt was discovered, and Harold found William's army ready for him. The fighting began on the morning of October 14th and lasted until night fell.

A depiction of the Battle of Hastings as seen on the Bayeux Tapestry, a 230-foot-long and 20-foot-tall embroidered cloth that details the Norman conquest.[4]

The battle began with a mighty salvo from William's bowmen, who sent volley after volley of arrows into the English defensive lines. William's assault was followed by his men with lances, who charged ahead to mow down English positions. This charge was mostly ineffective and prompted William to send in the cavalry.

William's number one tactic during this exchange was to have his forces pretend as if they were getting ready to retreat at critical moments during the conflict. They would pull back, tricking their enemy into pursuing them, only to turn around and drop the hammer on top of them. This tactic was apparently used several times during the conflict. The battle finally came to an end when Harold fell in battle. His absence on the battlefield led his army to be routed.

The body was identified by his own mistress—Edith Swanneck or Edith the Fair—who just happened to be present on that day of carnage. It is said that she identified Harold's butchered corpse by way of marks on the body known only to her.

In the meantime, William had to prove to his own men that he was still alive. A rumor had spread through the ranks that William had fallen, leaving the men unsteady and ready to retreat. William rode around with his helmet turned up, showing his face and pointing at himself while shouting that he was still alive.

Back in England's halls of power, the fight continued. Shortly after word was received of Harold's demise, a new king was crowned: Edward the Confessor's great-nephew, Edgar Ætheling.

Edgar was young and inexperienced. He was a mere plaything of the noble class. William faced only minor resistance as he made his way farther inland. Ultimately, the token resistance of the nobility and their puppet king Edgar, who was never officially crowned, would surrender. William would end up being crowned as England's new king on December 25th, 1066.

However, the coronation did not exactly go as planned, as a disturbance was sparked over a common misunderstanding. William's Norman troops apparently heard the gathering crowd at Westminster Abbey shouting, "God save the King!" and misinterpreted it as a threat rather than a call to William's longevity. Fearing that an attack was imminent, they began torching surrounding structures in an attempt to drive off the mob. Despite this mishap, William was handed the English crown as planned.

There were still some loose ends to tie up, and further conquest of the rest of England would continue over the next few years. The veritable military occupation of Norman forces would last for about twenty years until all resistance was crushed. Perhaps it is no surprise that the more untamed lands to the north proved the hardest to subdue. The Normans took over much of Wales but never invaded Scotland, although Norman influence made its way north regardless.

Although Anglo-Saxon culture was overshadowed by the Norman culture, it would still continue. The Normans would rule England for three hundred years.

Chapter 2: Medieval Madness

"There'll always be an England, while there's a country lane. Wherever there's a cottage small beside a field of grain. There'll always be an England. England shall be free ... If England means as much to you as England means to me."

-Vera Lynn

Although the Anglo-Saxons had been conquered by William, Duke of Normandy, the social infrastructure they had established was largely left in place. The Normans would largely replace the Anglo-Saxons as landlords, but they abided by the same familiar feudal system the Anglo-Saxons themselves had established, although some have argued the Anglo-Saxon brand of feudalism was more akin to outright slavery. The Normans, from whom we get the official term "feudal" (*feu* is French for land), for the most part, essentially just rebranded the practice.

Although it was most certainly a rude awakening for the Anglo-Saxon elite to lose ownership of their lands, for the poorer classes who labored on their estates, nothing much had changed except for the fact they were suddenly under new management. That is not to say there was not a general feeling of being occupied by a foreign power among the lower classes.

The fact that their taskmasters were native French speakers had the effect of making the native-born English feel at odds in their own country. The language of power was now a foreign tongue rather than the language of their birth. This sentiment was captured by a chronicler of that period, a monk named Orderic Vitalis. When writing about the Norman conquest, Orderic bluntly expressed, "Foreigners grew wealthy with the spoils of England while her own sons were either shamefully slain or driven as exiles to wander hopelessly through foreign kingdoms."

At any rate, in the Norman system of feudalism, the king was on top, and his nobles were below him. The most powerful nobles owned large tracts of land—they were the original "landlords." They, in turn, divvied up parts of their lands to lesser nobles. These lesser nobles granted lands to members of more respectable classes, such as knights and merchants, and in some instances, they rented portions of the land out.

The lowest class of society was landless and toiled on the estates of the rich landowners. They were almost entirely beholden to the will of their landlords. Like the Russian serfs, they were not free to leave the lands they worked and were destined to a life of backbreaking work for the nobility, who gave their workers meager shelter from the elements and a vague promise of protection should any outsider come and threaten them.

Under this system, the king was meant to be connected to all of his subjects in a solid chain from top to bottom. The king was also technically the default owner of all the lands in his realm. Although nobles could claim large estates and pass that land to their heirs, if a landowner found themselves in a situation in which land could not be passed on after their demise (for instance, if there was no heir apparent), that land would automatically become the king's possession. Daughters could receive land, but they sometimes needed a male retainer.

The system was much the same as what happens to modern-day properties with no one to claim them; if there is no claimant, those properties will eventually default to government ownership. In medieval England, it could be said that the king was the embodiment of the government, and if no one could actively claim a parcel of land, it would automatically revert to his direct control.

William the Conqueror proved to be a shrewd steward of properties and took this role very seriously. In 1086, he sent out a team of specialists to conduct a complex survey of the country to document who owned what and to estimate the value of their properties. This enabled William to effectively enact taxation that fairly represented the true status of the landholders in his domain. It even tallied up how many sheep and plows each landed estate had!

As intricate and effective as this survey was, it was deeply resented by the landed nobles, who felt they were being intruded upon and marched off to an unavoidable economic judgment. They even referred to the meticulously compiled survey as the Domesday Book in reference to the biblical Book of Revelation.

Despite the protests of the nobles, the end of the world was not near. But the end of William the Conqueror's reign was very well drawing nigh. The following year, in 1087, Norman King William perished. After William's passing, his son, William Rufus, was given control of England, while Normandy fell into the hands of William's other son, Robert.

The Crusades were kicking into high gear around this time. Shortly into Robert's reign over Normandy, he left to take part in the holy war brewing in the Middle East. He made sure to give William II charge over his dominion in his absence. On the surface, it probably seemed the greatest threat to stability would have been if Robert had perished while crusading. However, there was a greater threat. The younger William could have easily made Normandy a permanent vassal state, just as both England and Normandy had been under the control of his namesake and father, the late William the Conqueror.

But neither of these things happened. Robert survived the Crusades just fine. It was actually his brother, William, King of England, who perished first in 1100; Robert was returning from his crusade when he died. William did not die in some heated battle in a faraway land but rather in a freak hunting accident on his own estate. He was accidentally felled by an arrow. One of his brothers, Henry, was present at the time. Henry decided to seize the initiative rather than allow his crusading brother Robert to return and attempt to exert control. He rushed off to Winchester, took hold of the treasury, and was subsequently handed the crown just a few days thereafter.

Upon his return to Normandy, Robert, a veteran of the Crusades, was infuriated to hear of these underhanded happenings. He gathered his forces in Normandy and threatened to invade, just as his father had done all those years before. But since most of the nobles sided with Henry, there would be no repeat of the Battle of Hastings. Robert ultimately had to admit defeat. He agreed to remain in Normandy, and the threat of war seemed to be over.

However, Henry was convinced he could do more than bully his brother into submission. He decided to gather the bulk of his forces and invade Normandy itself. His invasion was a smashing success, and Robert was not only soundly defeated but also taken prisoner. As a result,

Normandy and England were once again reunited—this time under the sole rule of King Henry. This was Henry's greatest triumph, and for the rest of his reign, he became obsessed with the idea of being able to pass his vast territorial holdings to one heir.

These aims were squashed when Henry's son and heir apparent perished in a mishap on the high seas in 1120. Henry would reign for several more years and ultimately designate his daughter, Matilda, as his heir. Matilda was married to a powerful French noble named Geoffrey Plantagenet, who controlled a sizeable section of France called Anjou. Henry was always keen on expanding his kingdom and hoped this connection would help merge Anjou with the territory his daughter Matilda was set to inherit.

But as is often the case with the best-laid plans of mice and monarchs, things did not turn out as King Henry had wished. After his passing, his daughter Matilda ended up fighting for control against another claimant, Henry's nephew, Stephen of Blois. In the ensuing crisis, Matilda lost popular support, and the nobility ended up siding with Stephen. Even so, Matilda tried to hang on, leading to an all-out civil war that rocked England for over a decade.

An image of Henry II.[5]

The Anarchy, where England suffered a breakdown in law and order, was resolved in 1153 when Stephen and Matilda called for a truce and hammered out an agreement in which Stephen would be recognized as monarch on the condition that Matilda's son, Henry, would be allowed to wear the crown after Stephen's death. Surprisingly enough, the promise to give Matilda's son the crown was honored. Upon Stephen's demise, Henry II became the first king of England to enjoy an entirely peaceful transition of power in quite some time.

Henry was also blessed to come to prominence at a time of great progress in medieval England. Great strides had been made in many fields of industry. Around this time, horseshoes and collars were being developed to ease the burden and increase the productivity of horses. These developments, in turn, led to the development of horse-drawn plows, which proved to be far more proficient than the older variation of oxen-driven plows.

These advancements greatly increased the output of crops, giving England a great boost to its agricultural stability. Under Henry's reign, watermills were developed, allowing the grinding of grain by way of hydropower. Roads were also much more reliable at this time, and greater travel was achieved, enabling stronger networks of commerce between the various parts of Henry's kingdom.

Along with these general improvements, King Henry II also made improvements in the rule of law by shifting legal jurisdiction from regional "baronial courts," which were not known for fairness or impartiality, to his own royal courts. The king's courts used a jury system of twelve jurors to determine the outcome of cases, enabling a much fairer verdict than the lopsided ones that barons had been arbitrarily handing out.

Those in a real bind knew they could appeal their case to the king's court to get a fair hearing. The system certainly was not perfect, but as the current writer and historian Simon Schama put it, "Nonetheless, it was still an immeasurable advance on the feudal monopoly of justice common elsewhere in baronial Europe." Perhaps the most important development occurred toward the beginning of the 12th century when judges of all regions began to rely upon a uniform standard of law.

Such things, no doubt, seem like a given to most of us in the modern world today, but prior to this development, it was anything but. Before the development of what was ultimately termed "common law," one could find the rules and regulations varying wildly; it depended on who was interpreting the law. A lasting tradition of uniformity was established through common law, and this same sense of needing a universal legal code was ultimately gifted to Britain's later colonies, including those that would one day become the United States of America.

The city of London saw enormous growth during the 12th century. By the 1150s, London was becoming a bustling center for both commerce and political wrangling. The city was often divided into sections based on class, and depending on where you were, you could run into either corner markets hawking basic meats to the peasants or find delicatessens selling finer upscale items such as venison to the richer citizens who could afford it.

Henry II would be succeeded by the famous Richard the Lionheart, who spent more time away crusading in the Holy Land than actually ruling England. The heirless Richard was succeeded by his brother, John. Today, King John is often viewed as a corrupt monarch who took advantage of the feudal system. In those days, the nobility had their own local courts where they exacted fines against those who had transgressed local ordinances.

John was known to purposefully bounce local court cases up to the king's court, which he was personally in charge of, in an effort to bilk as many resources from the court proceedings as possible. John also increased the fees paid by inheritors of land to line his own pockets.

Under the feudal system, it was customary for one about to inherit the land that had been lorded over by their forebearers to pay a small fee to the king to make the inheritance official. John was known to greedily jack up these fees to bolster his own finances. This was viewed as both greedy and miserly in the extreme. King John was already rich, and yet here he was, repeatedly trying to suck his subjects dry. He also taxed local merchants at unheard-of exorbitant rates. It is safe to say that King John was not very popular with the masses.

The only saving grace of such a harsh taskmaster was the fact that the king and his armies had pledged to protect the lives and properties of his subjects from any outside threat. But John proved he could not fulfill this basic duty in 1204, as the king of France managed to seize hold of Normandy, thereby forcing countless members of the nobility to forfeit their estates.

In the end, these embittered nobles realized King John had milked them for what they were worth by taking full advantage of the feudal system but could not even hold up his part of the bargain by protecting them from outside invasions. If there was such a thing as poll numbers for British monarchs back in medieval times, King John's approval rate would have been terrible.

The pope took notice. Sensing how weak King John was, he decided to engage in some power playing of his own. John had previously resisted the pope's pick for the archbishop of Canterbury, but the pope was now ready to throw down the gauntlet in order for his demands to be met. He excommunicated King John, essentially giving his blessing to the king of France to launch an invasion of England.

The pope then took the extraordinary measure of ordering every church in England to shut its doors. A complete shutdown of churches in those days was a very serious matter. If folks could not go to church, they felt their very soul was in mortal danger. Due to the outside aggression from France and the internal pressures of shuttered churches, King John finally submitted to the pope's demands and allowed his pick for the archbishop of Canterbury to go forward in 1213.

King John had apparently made a mockery of feudalism, and from the nobility to the peasantry, his subjects were fed up. While King John was backed into a corner, a sizeable portion of the nobility presented him with an ultimatum for reform, which would ultimately become known as the Magna Carta. Often recognized as a forerunner for other major documents of political reform, such as the Constitution of the United States, the Magna Carta was drafted to ensure certain rights and freedoms would be respected by the king.

The Magna Carta from 1215. It is one of only four left in existence. You can see this document in the British Library.[6]

The document ensured, among other things, that English subjects (at least landed subjects) would have a fair and legal trial if prosecuted. Subjects were also protected against unwarranted abuse by the king's subordinates. Although this document would later be used as a model for even greater freedoms, it was not very effective at the time, as war still broke out. But it had been cobbled together by a frustrated nobility as a means to keep their troublesome king within the well-recognized limits of feudal society.

In that sense, it was created more to ensure the status quo than to achieve radical reforms, but it still paved the way for greater freedoms to come. Although it was a long evolutionary process, the establishment of the Magna Carta can be said to be the beginning of the end of feudalism in England.

Feudal life had previously been ruled by a sovereign monarch who was the underlying owner of all the land. Other people could be landlords but only with the approval of the king, which meant their land could essentially be taken from them at any time. With the Magna Carta, there were clear rules and regulations in place to limit the scope of the monarch's power. The eventual balance between Parliament and the monarchy would be achieved through fine-tuning the details of this revolutionary document.

From this point forward, England would have a series of kings who either granted concessions based on the Magna Carta or attempted to dial back the reforms of this pivotal document to better foster absolutist rule. But no matter what happened or who was in charge, for the rest of English history, the nobility of the land continuously sought to hold their leaders accountable.

Another great change in feudal society at this time was the noble class's refusal to wage the king's wars for free. In the past, the king reserved the absolute right to call the nobility to fight in his wars for a period of no less than forty days. The nobility demanded an end to this practice, and the English kings from here on out were forced to pay their troops, which led to many ramifications in the future.

Most notably, the eventual successor to the English Crown—Henry III—would have a horrible time finding enough money to fund his wars. He resorted to taxation, but his stringent measures led the nobility to revolt against him. During Henry III's reign, the First English Parliament convened in 1258 when the frustrated nobility, led by a powerful earl named Simon de Montfort, brought the leading lights of England together to essentially conspire against the king.

The coronation of Henry III.[7]

Simon, who spoke French, referred to the meeting with the Old French word *parlement,* which means "speaking" or "discussion." Just think of the phrase, "Parlez-vous français?" and you will get the idea of why Simon de Montfort called it a *parlement.* The establishment of Parliament led to the English monarch losing even more power, as the noble class took control of the treasury, got their hands on the tools of taxation, and began to dictate to the monarch about who should be his advisors.

Henry III and his son, Edward I, were able to defeat Simon de Montfort on the battlefield in 1265, but ironically enough, the English Parliament he had helped establish would not be defeated so easily. And the newfound rights and privileges of the nobility would remain intact. Henry's successor, Edward I, respected Parliament. He knew the nobility's power and typically tried to appease Parliament rather than antagonize it.

A portrait thought to be of Edward I.[8]

Edward worked with the nobility to establish a representative legislative body. In 1275, King Edward I ordered every region to assign two designated representatives to stand for them in Parliament. This was the beginning of "representation" in light of regional "taxation." American revolutionaries at the Boston Tea Party would cry out a similar phrase. By the time of Edward's rule, people realized that if they were being taxed by the Crown, they deserved some form of representation in Parliament.

Another blow to feudalism was the decline in vassals. The poor classes were beginning to no longer be chained to the land they worked on. They were gaining more freedom of mobility. Landlords increasingly recruited the leaders of the peasantry to serve as their eyes and ears on their property. Peasants were hired to collect rents and oversee properties, establishing traditional roles like jurors, reeves, and haywards. Some of these positions exist in altered forms today. The modern-day equivalent of a reeve, for example, would be a chief magistrate.

Placing local peasants in property management positions had several benefits. First of all, no one knew the peasantry better than a peasant. Therefore, recruiting from the peasant class ensured that a manager was equipped with adequate knowledge of the life and culture of those who rented out land and toiled on the estate.

Peasant managers also "softened" the image of the feudal system. Toiling away on the land of the elites did not seem as harsh if the main taskmaster the peasants interacted with was one of their own or someone from a similar background. It also promoted the idea that they could move up the social ladder.

But one of the most fundamental changes to medieval society was not reforms. It was not initiated by the peasantry or the landed elite. Rather, it was a horrible plague known as the Black Death.

This scourge struck England in the middle of the 14th century under the leadership of King Edward III. King Edward III would be affected by the plague early on, as his daughter Joan perished from the dreaded illness. Joan had been traveling through Bordeaux, France, to meet and marry her fiancé, Peter (Pedro) of Castile, in Spain. However, there would be no marriage. Her grieving father would write to his attendants, "No fellow human being could be surprised if we were inwardly desolated by the sting of this bitter grief for we are human too."

The plague that had afflicted Joan had been spreading throughout southern Europe for some time, and it reached England via its southern ports. Although Edward was certainly not a scientist who understood the spread of a pathogen, he at least recognized where the disease entered the country, as he immediately sent the archbishop of Canterbury to offer penitential prayers at Kent since the southern ports had become home to the plague.

The ports of the world were indeed passing along more than merchandise. The plague is believed to have originated somewhere in the Near East and was then imported to the Mediterranean by visiting merchant craft. It spread like wildfire throughout southern Europe until it was finally picked up by additional travelers and sent farther abroad to Britain, impacting Wales, England, and Scotland. The illness spread rapidly, and whole villages were soon decimated by the Black Death.

Many felt what they were experiencing was nothing short of the end of the world. And since just about everything in those days was viewed through the lens of religion, many could not help but think that God was somehow punishing them. Ironically enough, just prior to the plague, the world was taking part in an overall boon in prosperity and a population explosion. So many people crowded together in close quarters would aid in the plague's transmission, which would ultimately reduce the biggest population centers of Europe.

Rats have long been blamed for spreading the plague, but due to the rapid spread of the disease, it seems far more likely that humans were the hosts of infected fleas and lice. All it took was one bite from an infected flea to become infected.

People were also not as aware of the benefits of hygiene as we are today, which allowed the disease to spread more easily. The disease went largely unnoticed until the symptoms became more pronounced. The symptoms were terrible. Those afflicted with the Black Death broke out in boils from head to toe. Painful buboes, or swollen lymph nodes, were filled with puss. People also developed a hacking cough and terrible fever. Soon into this infection, the victim would find themselves losing almost all of their energy until they were finally consigned to just staying in bed. And soon after that, most would lose their entire will to live.

Those who could live out their last days in a sick bed cared for by a loved one were, of course, the lucky ones. English chronicler Thomas Burton would later write, "The pestilence grew so strong that men and women dropped dead in the streets." There was, in essence, a complete breakdown of society. As simplistic as medieval life might have been compared to our modern-day world, the effect the illness had on everyday life was devastating all the same.

For example, those in the cities were accustomed to buying bread from local bakeries. But with bakers and their employees dying by the dozen, they found their local baker's shelves bare.

Even the grisly fact that there were so many dead bodies lying around was a reminder of this breakdown. Normally, there would have been someone on hand to immediately remove the bodies of those who had perished, yet with so many sick and dying—and others unwilling to go near diseased corpses—there was suddenly no one to pick up the dead.

English chronicler William Dene wrote about this misery, saying, "Alas, this mortality devoured such a multitude of both sexes that no one could be found to carry the bodies of the dead to burial, but men and women carried the bodies of their own little ones to church on their shoulders and threw them into mass graves from which arose such a stench that it was barely possible for anyone to go past the churchyard." Perhaps it is an incredible understatement, but it must have been a truly terrible sight to behold.

The large number of deceased also put a considerable strain on the church since it was hard for priests to keep up with the growing death toll. Prior to the plague, a priest giving someone their last rites was considered very important. But the realities of such massive casualties made it impossible to carry this tradition on like normal.

Instead, the church began to make great concessions, encouraging those who could not have access to a priest to confess their sins to a lay person. Before, only a priest could hear one's confession, but due to the dire circumstances, with priests sick, dying, or unwilling to visit plague houses, it was deemed suitable for the average person to serve as a replacement.

This demonstrated that religious rules were not always set in stone. It could be said that this initial chipping away at the rigid religious structure may have laid down some of the groundwork for England's later reformation. At any rate, after the first onslaught of the plague had subsided, many were left questioning just about every aspect of medieval life.

There were deep thinkers who questioned religion and the nature of reality. Other, perhaps more practical thinkers questioned the unsanitary conditions of English cities. The latter was of the belief (and there was some truth in their estimations) that the cramped, dirty cities were becoming breeding grounds for illness and disease.

In their critique, they cited the filthy streets that often had both animal and human waste flowing down them every time it rained. And they cited the foggy, baleful air of London, fearing that some terrible "miasma" of illness was hanging over their heads. Although these critiques of city life were not completely scientific in their analysis, they were on the right track. If cities like London were not so unsanitary, the citizens might have fared a little better during this terrible episode.

King Edward III, to his credit, recognized as much and enacted street cleaning measures to be carried out in London. Much of it was too little, too late.

In the aftermath of the Black Death, there was a distinct shift in the public's thinking. The old social order of medieval times had been irrevocably shattered. For the peasants in the countryside who were not directly affected by the plague, they found themselves virtually abandoned by the nobles and lords who had sworn to protect them.

Those with money had fled to more remote, isolated estates in a bid to stay alive. With their taskmasters gone, the old social contract of peasants toiling on lands in exchange for the protection of the nobility had been broken. The peasants were left on their own. If they wished to protect what little they had from roving thieves, they would have to do it themselves. This created a greater degree of self-sufficiency and a streak of independence that would only continue to grow.

Chapter 3: Enter the Tudors

"In England there are sixty different religions, and only one sauce."

-Francesco Caracciolo

King Edward III inherited a large, sprawling kingdom. And throughout all of the trials and tribulations England had faced, he was determined to increase his prestige further.

Edward's funerary monument.[9]

Edward was a lover of knights and chivalry. During a court appearance in 1348, a lady of the court accidentally lost her garter. Edward let his chivalrous nature take over. While others laughed, he simply picked it up and wrapped it around his own leg, stating, "Let him be ashamed who sees wrong in it."

This legendary act of rescuing a mortified damsel from utter embarrassment led to the establishment of the Order of the Garter. The order consisted of twenty-four knights and acted in a similar fashion as King Arthur's Round Table.

King Edward III passed away in 1377. After the passing of this chivalrous and larger-than-life ruler, the English crown was handed to Edward's grandson, Richard II.

Richard's reign would soon run into trouble when an attempt to raise taxes led to an open rebellion among the peasant classes. The protest was led by Wat Tyler, and the poor people stood up as one and declared they were all "formed in Christ's likeness" and should be treated equally. One can easily hear echoes of this proclamation for equality hundreds of years later in America's Declaration of Independence.

The Declaration of Independence similarly proclaims, "We hold these truths to be self-evident, that all men are created equal, that they are endowed by their Creator with certain unalienable rights, that among these are Life, Liberty, and the Pursuit of Happiness." It also proclaims that "all men are created equal under God."

The Peasant's Revolt under Tyler was as rapid as it was shocking. It ran its course in just a few weeks, but during that time, the peasant masses managed to seize much of London. It was only after the ringleader, Wat Tyler, was killed that the situation changed. But his death wasn't the end of the protests; rather, it served as a signal to King Richard II that it was time for a compromise.

After Tyler was killed, the situation became untenable, with folks rioting in the streets. King Richard II no longer had the stomach for any more discontent. He let it be known that he would agree to many of the protesters' demands if they went home and allowed the reforms to take shape. It was a strong order, but many in the mob realized this was likely their best opportunity. A king's word was golden, and they had King Richard II making them promises.

As such, they decided to give it a chance and see what compromises could be made. Many reforms were passed, and many of the demands of the peasants were met. But even so, things did not go so well for King Richard, as he was forcefully removed from power in 1399.

After his removal, another succession crisis took place since Richard II had no immediate heir. The only real contender was Edward III's great-grandson, Edmund Mortimer, Earl of March. The other contender was Richard's cousin, Henry of Lancaster, who was the child of a nobleman who traced his lineage back to King Edward III's paternal grandmother.

Henry (also known as Henry Bolingbroke) was the one responsible for Richard's removal. Henry had been previously exiled by Richard II for plotting against the king during an uprising in 1388. In 1399, Henry rallied a substantial number of supporters. He returned to England and forced King Richard II off the throne.

Henry IV was officially crowned king in Westminster Abbey on October 13th, 1399. Upon gaining the crown, he would be dubbed Henry IV. Despite frequent domestic turmoil, King Henry IV made impressive waves on the international level. In December 1400, he even gained the distinction of being the only English king to play host to a visiting Byzantine emperor, Manuel II Palaiologos.

Henry IV perished in 1413, and his son, Henry V, took over. After a brief reign, Henry V passed away in 1422 and was succeeded by his infant son, Henry VI. This infant king would face more strife than his predecessors. For most of his reign, King Henry VI was knee-deep in the Hundred Years' War between England and France.

Any recollection of English history would be remiss without at least a brief mention of the Hundred Years' War and its role in shaping England. This war was one of the greatest conflagrations to affect Europe during the Late Middle Ages. It was a series of constant conflicts that spanned from 1337 to 1453.

Although the war had some rather complicated threads, all strands led back to a long-standing dispute between English and French claimants to the French throne. The two claimants—the English House of Plantagenet and the French House of Valois—went to war to assert their claims to the French throne and other territorial disputes. The war would carry on from one king to another, with both sides continuing to insist their claims be recognized. The fighting only ceased when the House of Valois emerged victorious, retaining its hold on France.

The seemingly endless fighting on behalf of royal claimants might seem rather absurd and pointless to us from a modern perspective. But nevertheless, the conflict had lasting effects on Europe. For one thing, the constant fighting ensured the armies of western Europe developed into highly efficient standing armies, and impressive new innovations, such as artillery, were perfected.

But back to our subject at hand: King Henry VI. Henry VI was not necessarily a bad king, but he was not very effective as a ruler, especially when it came to rapidly unfolding situations like internal unrest and external warfare. His inner circle felt he was not up for the job and began to plot against him. In light of Henry VI's abject weakness, several noble families became increasingly powerful; since they often provided troops, they also had their own standing armies. The leading lights of the nobility sought to take King Henry VI down. The conflict that ensued is known as the Wars of the Roses.

In 1461, Edward IV, the son of the duke of York, defeated the royal forces and locked Henry VI in the Tower of London. After nine years on the throne, an army led by the Lancastrian family defeated Edward, forcing him to flee and put Henry back on the throne. However, this change on the throne did not last long, as Edward would again raise troops and knock Henry VI off the throne in 1471. Henry VI was placed in the Tower of London and perished shortly thereafter.

The drama continued when Edward IV died in 1483. His brother, Richard of Gloucester, was the lord protector of Edward V, Edward IV's son and heir. However, the young Edward V and his brother mysteriously disappeared, with many believing Richard had ordered their deaths. Richard took the throne in 1483, only to be challenged just a couple of years later in 1485. This challenge was lodged by Henry Tudor.

Henry was willing to take the crown by force if necessary. He cobbled together an army and took the fight directly to Richard. Even though Tudor's army of five thousand was dwarfed by Richard's army of eight thousand, Henry's troops fought ferociously. Henry Tudor defeated Richard in battle and was crowned King Henry VII, ushering in the first king of the Tudor dynasty.

In many ways, King Henry VII was a man of the people and tried to craft policies that were beneficial for the growing body of farmers and merchants. Unlike his predecessors, who focused on war

A portrait of King Henry VII.[10]

and expansion, Henry VII looked inward at his realm and sought to improve England's commercial might. This led to England finally having a monarch who sought to avoid conflicts. Henry VII used all of his skills in diplomacy to avoid conflict with both Scotland and France. Rather than fighting violent wars, King Henry VII found himself in a trade war with the Hanseatic League.

The Hanseatic League was a conglomeration of merchant guilds based out of northern Europe; it was particularly situated in German-speaking lands. The Hanseatic League had a decisive impact on English trade, as it essentially closed England off from trading partners in the regions where the Hanseatic League held a monopoly. England was also facing a decline in trade with France and Italy. However, King Henry VII was able to cement a trade deal with the Netherlands that opened up the door for greater and more robust trade with the rest of Europe.

Another way King Henry VII helped to ensure stability was by stipulating that only he could have his own army. Such a thing seems like common sense today (why would you let the powerful people of society have their own soldiers?), but prior to King Henry VII's ascension to the throne, just about every noble family on the block had their own standing army.

A portrait of King Henry VIII.[11]

Rather than shoring up the nobility's support, Henry VII did his best to gain the backing of the merchant and guild classes, which were essentially the middle classes of England at the time. They, like him, sought prosperity over conflict and appreciated the king's efforts to avoid war while bolstering the economic output of England.

The only thing that King Henry VII was willing to spend an excessive amount of money on was the outfitting of a new fleet of foresight of knowing that England's success would depend on being able merchant craft. He did this with the to travel across the high seas to trade with other nations. Due to Henry VII's wise stewardship, by the time of his passing in 1509, England was financially solvent and poised for even greater economic success. His successor, Henry VIII, had a very solid foundation upon which to build.

Henry VIII was not as financially minded as his father. He had no problem at all with spending money. Not long into his reign, Henry VIII commissioned the expensive remodeling of Richmond Palace, making it one of the most luxurious in Europe. However, to his credit, King Henry VIII was, in many ways, a great showman who understood the importance of maintaining a popular public image. And part of his ostentatious showiness was an effort to gain public affection.

Aiding him in gaining the public's interest was the fact this young king decided to marry early on, wedding a beautiful and socially prominent woman by the name of Catherine of Aragon. Just as royal weddings today galvanize the public in Britain and beyond, the same could be said back in the days of King Henry VIII. And his marriage to Catherine of Aragon was certainly a public relations boon.

Although Henry VIII's father was an able steward, he was a quiet man who did not do much to excite the general public. Seeing the crowning of a young king and his marriage to the Spanish princess was very exciting for the public. The new king and queen presented themselves to their subjects in an elaborate coronation ceremony on June 23rd, 1509. All of this pomp and ceremony was like a breath of fresh air for an England that had grown somewhat weary of its previous king. Although Henry VII had been financially solvent, he was reclusive.

As refreshing as the coronation of Henry VIII might have been, there were some loose ends to tie up from the previous administration. His father had implemented a special task force named the Council Learned in the Law, which was in charge of securing payment of debt. If the title "Council Learned in the Law" does not sound arrogant and presumptuous enough ("learned in the law: is just another way to say "know it all"), the most effective councilors on this task force had rubbed the public the wrong way.

In particular, two of the most brutal enforcers—Richard Empson and Edmund Dudley—had provoked the people's ire. These two were extreme in their measures of extracting what they wanted from their targets and, at times, even overstepped the bounds of the fairly broad legal authority they had been given. The council carried over into King Henry VIII's reign, but it was incredibly unpopular.

Both Empson and Dudley had already faced prosecution for allegedly overstepping their authority by the time of King Henry VIII's coronation. So, it was up to him to decide what to do with his father's most overzealous ministers. Should he pardon them or let them hang? Ultimately, the two were executed on charges of treason. It is not known if Henry fully endorsed their demise, but he certainly did not stop it.

Some historians have made the cynical observation that King Henry VIII might have learned a "valuable lesson" from this ordeal, as he learned how easy it was to assuage public discontent by punishing one small element of the kingdom's governance. If the public was upset with the direction things were going, instead of blaming the king, their blame could be directed at a small group of ministers instead.

Besides these two scapegoats, Henry kept most of his father's ministers, and they were able to competently steer the royal ship, regardless of Henry VIII's own aptitude for leadership. His most trusted advisor would soon emerge in the form of one Thomas Wolsey. Wolsey began his career as a priest and served as a chaplain in Canterbury before ministering directly to the royal court.

Upon taking the throne, Henry VIII recognized Wolsey's talent and made him the almoner, which meant Wolsey was in charge of all the alms being collected for the neediest members of the realm. After taking note of his effectiveness, Henry VIII decided to promote Wolsey directly into his inner circle in 1511. Thomas Wolsey proved himself a very efficient minister, and in 1515, he was made lord chancellor. Henry was so fond of Wolsey that he even pulled some strings to have the pope arrange for Wolsey to become his personal legate in England.

With powerful ministers like Thomas Wolsey in place, King Henry VIII largely let his governmental machinery run itself while he pursued his own interests in life. His greatest interest was to produce a male heir to the throne. He and his wife Catherine tried for several years, but the pair seemed unable to do so. Catherine did give birth to a healthy daughter named Mary, but all of the other children she birthed failed to survive.

Still seeking a son, Henry's roving, impatient eyes began to look elsewhere. Henry had already been unfaithful to his wife, having indulged in a wide variety of mistresses, but even he had to follow some semblance of protocol. And no matter how many sons he might produce out of wedlock, none of them would ever be accepted as a legitimate heir. This meant that if Henry wanted a legitimate son, he had to be born within the bounds of marriage. Henry realized he would have to somehow put away his wife Catherine and marry someone new in the hopes that his new bride could (hopefully) give birth to a son.

Henry's troubling desire to have a legitimate male heir would have him bending age-old rules and traditions. Interestingly enough, Henry rationalized his decision to put Catherine to the side by pointing to the Bible. He picked out some verses from the Book of Leviticus, which read, in part, "If a man shall take his brother's wife, it is an impunity: he hath uncovered his brother's nakedness: they shall be childless."

This verse resonated with Henry VIII since Catherine had been wed to Henry's unfortunate older brother, who perished in his teens shortly after his (apparently unconsummated) marriage. Henry reasoned that he had wrongly taken his brother's wife, violating a biblical prohibition, and was therefore being punished by being made to "be childless." It was a rather ingenious bit of religious-based rationalization on Henry's part, and it is possible that he actually believed it to be a valid reason.

With this convenient rationale in hand, Henry began entreating Pope Clement VII to issue an annulment to his marriage to Catherine of Aragon. Henry was not asking for a divorce; instead, he wished to make it as if his twenty-year marriage to Catherine did not exist and was never valid in the first place. If the annulment was granted, Henry was ready to put Catherine in a convent so that she would no longer have to live with the "shame" of having been in an improper relationship.

The execution of these arrangements fell on the shoulders of King Henry's favorite minister, Thomas Wolsey, who just so happened to be England's papal legate. Wolsey would not have been too sad to see Catherine go since he had long had an antagonistic relationship with the queen. She was an outspoken critic of some of Wolsey's policies and his excessive spending habits.

In addition to getting rid of Catherine's unwanted critiques, Wolsey saw an opportunity to arrange a marriage between King Henry and a French princess, thereby uniting England in a bond of friendship with a previously troublesome and unpredictable neighbor. Little did Wolsey know that Henry already had his heart set on a veteran of his court: Anne Boleyn.

Nevertheless, Wolsey dutifully did his part and began the process of petitioning the pope for an official annulment. There would be much unforeseen difficulty in achieving this feat. The pope was typically fairly compliant with England's wishes since Pope Clement viewed the English king as a loyal ally. Yet, the pope had his hands tied since he was also beholden to the Holy Roman emperor, Charles V, who was directly related to Catherine of Aragon (she was his aunt).

Stuck between a rock and a hard place, the pope had to figure out which monarch would do the worst damage if he offended them. Considering the size and power of the Holy Roman Empire, which comprised much of central Europe, in addition to Spain (Charles V was also king of Spain at the time), Pope Clement logically determined the repercussions of offending Charles V would have been much more severe. As such, he began the process of letting King Henry VIII know that there would be no annulment. He wanted to let the king down gently in a diplomatic and polite fashion.

Back in England, Catherine had figured out what her husband was up to and was beyond frustrated. One can, of course, understand her wrath. But in those days, women had few recourses against their husband's whims even under normal circumstances, let alone when their husband was the king of England. Thus, there was not a whole lot that she could do about it. She certainly could not punish her husband for his actions. But she could direct her scorn on someone else. Thomas Wolsey was the perfect target.

Since Wolsey was an instrument of the king, she took her wrath out on him. Although Wolsey was only following the king's orders, Catherine suspected that he had a personal motivation in carrying out these orders in light of her previous disapproval of him. In 1527, the pope, still unwilling to offer up a firm answer, decided to buy more time by advising papal legate Wolsey to convene a court in England to look into the matter further.

Wolsey was made the head of this court, thereby lending great hope that the annulment would go forward as planned. But little did anyone realize the long game that Pope Clement—a member of a famous family of political strategists, the Medicis—was playing.

However, King Henry was not placated by the show of cooperation that the pope displayed. Giving voice to his suspicions, he sent out threatening feelers to the Vatican, hinting that if things did not go as he intended, he might have to break from the Catholic Church entirely. Such suggestions were not taken lightly, considering the fact that Europe was in the full grip of the Protestant Reformation at the time. The greatest irony in all of this was that King Henry VIII was not at all in line with the Protestants.

King Henry had once been dubbed a "defender of the faith" by the pope. He was a staunch supporter of the Catholic doctrine. The sole reason for his proposed break with the Catholic Church was not due so much to a difference in religious beliefs but rather anger with the pope for not allowing him to have his way as it pertained to his marriage. Incredibly enough, it would be the self-interest of one king that ultimately led to England's first fissure with the Roman Catholic Church.

It was at this point that Wolsey began to become deeply troubled by the course that events seemed to be taking. His fears of a real rupture between England and the Catholic Church were expressed in a heartfelt letter to the pope in 1528. In contemplation of a real rift between Henry and the church, Wolsey agonized, "I close my eyes before such horror."

Several more lines of saddened reflection later, he ended this plea for cooperation, saying, "I throw myself at the Holy Father's feet." Wolsey was in a tough position, but he understood King Henry would be the hardest mountain to move as it pertained to keeping the peace. He knew that Henry VIII's mind was made up and that there was absolutely nothing he could do to make him reconsider.

So, Wolsey looked to the pope, believing him to be a more pliant individual with whom to reason. However, Pope Clement was in some rather dire straits. The previous year, Holy Roman Emperor Charles V's forces had marched on Rome, forcing the pope to seek refuge in his fortress of Castel Sant'Angelo.

Charles V was not directly responsible for this event. The situation was, in large part, one that had spiraled out of control. In the lead-up to this debacle, the armies of France and the Holy Roman Empire had been skirmishing in northern Italy for quite some time while the pope attempted to strategically place himself on the winning side. The papacy did come out on top when their ally, the Holy Roman Empire, defeated France. But in the immediate aftermath, HRE troops remained stationed in northern Italy. This prolonged occupation led to severe resentment among the locals on the ground. And the longer the troops were there, the more this resentment grew.

The imperial troops were also agitated by their prolonged stay and lack of appropriate provisions. Given enough time, this powder keg was bound to blow. Charles V did not even have to issue a command for war to erupt between his troops and local forces, culminating in the sack of Rome.

Although he did not authorize it, Holy Roman Emperor Charles V was savvy (or perhaps devious) enough to take advantage of the situation. Although aligned with the church, Charles V had already had his differences with the current pope, the biggest of which was a late-breaking development that the pope was in talks with France and apparently ready to switch sides! Now that this untrustworthy pontiff was literally backed into a corner, Charles V found himself in a position of unparalleled strength and leverage over the Vatican, and he was not going to let go too easily.

Needless to say, given the fact the pope was at the complete mercy of Holy Roman Emperor Charles V, he was not in a good position to anger him. He certainly could not sanction England's king to cast aside Charles V's aunt, Catherine of Aragon. Despite his inability to grant the annulment, the pope saw a strong potential ally in England, one that could save the papacy from the Holy Roman Empire. So, the pope continued to dither and delay, unwilling to make a final decision and ceaselessly playing these two sides against each other.

In the meantime, a court of inquiry convened in England, which was led by Wolsey, and attempted to find a possible alternative to Henry's annulment. Reconciliation between Henry and Catherine was mentioned, but it was, of course, immediately shot down. Henry did not need reconciliation—he needed a son. And he was certain no amount of marriage counseling could bring him that.

As the participants of the proceedings continued to try and find alternatives, it has been said that Catherine was asked to take a vow of chastity and join the convent as a nun to free Henry to remarry. However, strong-willed Catherine refused to do any such thing. She stated she would only join a convent if her husband joined a monastery and became a monk!

King Henry VIII took his case to the British public by making a series of passionate, emotional statements. In front of gatherings, he stated how much he loved his wife but that he had to follow the rules if it was ordained by the special court that his marriage to Catherine must be annulled. Henry was obviously attempting to win the people to his side so that when the announcement was made, he could appear as an innocent bystander meekly abiding by the divine ruling rather than one orchestrating the whole thing behind the scenes.

In 1529, another great twist in this ever-complicated story occurred, as a false report reached England saying that Pope Clement had died. If true, this would have meant a new pope would need to be selected. Almost immediately, King Henry VIII encouraged his trusted advisor and fixer, Thomas Wolsey, to throw his hat into the papal election. Wolsey was the papal legate in England, so he was already a powerful member of the clergy, but winning the seat of the papacy would have seemed like too great a leap for him. But if his king encouraged it, he was willing to make an attempt.

Ultimately, Wolsey did not have to do so because King Henry VIII would soon learn that Pope Clement did not die but was merely very sick. Clement recovered from his illness and continued to stand as an impediment to King Henry's desire for an annulment.

Around this time, Emperor Charles V defeated his nemesis, the French king, and restored the pope to Rome. With the pope under his thumb, Charles V became a direct benefactor. Clement would have found it impossible to cross him. So, in the end, the pope let Henry know he would not approve of the annulment after all.

Henry was infuriated. Almost immediately, he took his wrath out on the pope's closest representative—papal legate Thomas Wolsey. Wolsey was summoned to the king's court, where he knew he would likely be sentenced to execution. However, Wolsey apparently could not handle the stress. Incredibly enough, he perished of his own accord en route to the proceedings. If King Henry felt bad for what had happened to his old friend, it did not seem to show.

Instead, Henry charged full steam ahead with his plans. He began to push for a break with Rome and to have the king of England become the official head of the church. This directive was later made official in 1534 with the Act of Supremacy, which was approved by Parliament.

After putting Catherine away, Henry raced off to wed Anne Boleyn, whom he married in 1533. Things would not go so well for this new Tudor marriage. Even though Anne would bear Henry another daughter, the future Queen Elizabeth, her failure to give birth to a son resulted in her own execution in 1536.

Henry VIII was more than ready to move on and found a new wife, Jane Seymour, whom he wed less than two weeks later, on May 30th, 1536.

Jane would succeed where others had failed, giving birth to a male heir, Edward, on October 12th, 1537. However, Jane would not live to receive Henry's praise. She perished about two weeks after due to complications that occurred during the birth. Henry was said to be deeply grieved by the loss of Jane Seymour, but he chose to marry once again, this time to Anne of Cleves, on January 6th, 1540.

For whatever reason, this marriage did not seem to work out from the start. In July, the marriage was declared unconsummated and annulled. Henry was generous enough to give Anne a settlement and made sure her needs were taken care of. In truth, it could be that Henry simply decided he liked someone else better. Shortly after Anne was put aside, he married a woman named Catherine Howard, who had been in the direct employ of Anne's household.

But alas, this marriage would not last long and would end under even worse conditions since poor Catherine Howard was beheaded on charges of treason in 1542. This leads us to King Henry VIII's sixth and final wife: Catherine Parr. Henry wed Parr on July 12th, 1543, and the two remained married until Henry VIII's death in 1547.

Despite Henry VIII's volatile streak, Catherine Parr is said to have had a soothing effect and was able to reason with him where others could not. In fact, Catherine Parr managed to patch up the damaged relationship Henry had with his daughters, Mary and Elizabeth, both of whom he had deemed illegitimate, making them unable to wear the crown. Catherine Parr convinced Henry to reinstate his daughters in the line of succession. This was made official by the Third Succession Act, which was passed in 1543.

This was smart thinking since his only son, Edward, would pass just a few years after taking the throne. King Edward VI perished on July 6th, 1553. Thanks to the Third Succession Act, Henry VIII's eldest daughter Mary, could be crowned queen, avoiding a potential civil war over the succession.

Henry VIII was ready to move heaven and earth to make sure he had a son on the throne. And yet, ultimately, his son's reign would be exceedingly brief, while his daughters would rule much longer. Despite all of the drama, intrigue, and six wives, his eldest child from his first marriage to Catherine of Aragon would sit on the throne.

Our story of the Tudors is not yet over, but before we dive into their stories, we will first take a look at one of the most earth-shattering events to happen in England: the English Reformation.

Chapter 4: England's Reformation Takes Shape

"The British do not expect happiness. I had the impression, all the time that I lived there, that they do not want to be happy; they want to be right."

-Quentin Crisp

The English Reformation was different than the one that had taken place in mainland Europe. Mainland Europe's Reformation, centered in the German-speaking lands, resulted from a doctrinal dispute with the Catholic Church. These disputes were centered around theology. There were arguments over everything, from the existence of purgatory to baptismal practices and how to take communion. But the biggest debate of all was over the sale of indulgences.

The Catholic Church had developed the belief that the pope had the authority to excommunicate parishioners if he felt it was necessary and lessen their time in purgatory. Catholics pointed to the words of Jesus when he declared to Peter (whom Catholics view as the first pope) that "whatever he binds on earth will be bound in heaven." Catholics took a literal interpretation of this, viewing the pope to be imbued with a binding authority. If he so decreed it, one's time in purgatory could be lessened.

As this belief developed, loved ones of the deceased petitioned the pope to lessen the deceased's time in purgatory. In time, this petition came to include an ample donation to the church. There is nothing too unusual about donating to churches; Catholic and Protestant churches alike still widely accept donations of all kinds. Churches would not be able to function and carry out good works, such as aiding the poor or building schools, if they did not receive contributions.

And it was very much the same during the Reformation. The pope was always commissioning building projects and needed money to finance them. This money often came through the sale of indulgences, which can be thought of as charitable donations with a catch (that catch being the papal promise of lessened time in purgatory in exchange for a donation).

The thing Martin Luther really seemed to take umbrage with was the sheer aggressiveness of the indulgence sellers. He was particularly disgusted by the way papal representatives went around poor villages in Europe hawking indulgences. There was even a famous catchphrase developed by a Catholic priest and contemporary of Luther named Johann Tetzel that went something along the lines of "As soon as a coin in the coffer rings, the soul from purgatory springs!" Corruption was rampant in the church as well; although donations were spent on building projects, much of it also went into church officials' pockets. It all became a bit too much for Martin Luther to stomach, and he would ultimately question the pope's supposed unbinding ability to lessen the time one might spend in purgatory.

Although there were those in England who disagreed with church doctrine, the main reason for England's breakaway from the church was not due to doctrinal disputes but rather the self-centered whims of England's monarch, Henry VIII. Despite his annoyance with the pope for not granting him an annulment, King Henry VIII was a dedicated Catholic. As such, his desire to break away from the church had nothing to do with religious doctrine and everything to do with deciding who would have authority over church matters.

Henry basically wanted to create his own mini replica of the Vatican in England so that he could preside over all of its happenings. Thus, the Church of England was designed to be a copy of the Catholic Church. Even so, some were itching to deviate from the path laid down by the Roman Catholic Church, and these proto-Protestants would soon come to the surface.

Major waves had been made by English Protestant William Tyndale back in 1526 when he successfully created an English translation of the Bible for everyday people to read. Prior to this, folks in England would have had to learn Latin just to read the scripture for themselves. Even more consequential was the fact that Tyndale translated his version directly from Hebrew and Greek sources, circumventing the Latin text altogether.

This created some subtle changes in the text, which outraged the Catholic Church. Tyndale was ultimately condemned, and Bishop Tunstall of London began a campaign of destroying Tyndale Bibles. And books were not the only things to be destroyed. Whoever was found with these condemned translations was likely to be prosecuted as well.

King Henry VIII's number one Catholic representative, the papal legate Thomas Wolsey, played an integral role when it came to punishing dissenters. Some of the most vicious campaigns against Protestants took place during the early 1530s, during which time Protestant dissenters were regularly burned at the stake for their religious views. Even while all of this was happening, King Henry VIII, frustrated with the pope's lack of cooperation with his marital affairs, decided to formally break away from the church.

Following Parliament's issuance of the Act of Supremacy in 1534, King Henry VIII was placed as the official head of England's church. Although Henry had denounced Martin Luther, who kicked off the Protestant Reformation, he ended up taking some cues from him in regard to the proto-nationalist notions that Luther had evoked. Luther, whether through pragmatic strategy or sincere belief, had always been able to pique the interest of heads of state by insisting they should have the final say over their nations rather than the pope in faraway Rome.

Henry could not help but agree, seeing that his annulment would never be officially sanctioned by the Catholic Church. Doctrinally, the Church of England was meant to be a clone of the Roman Catholic Church, but the severing of ties with papal authority would only encourage the strains of Protestant dissent to grow. During this time, many of England's previous stances were reversed. For example, Henry VIII sanctioned the translation of the Ten Commandments into English, a feat that would have previously been considered anathema.

The reversal would become even greater by 1538 when King Henry VIII began to call for a full English translation of the Bible itself. He would come to regret this decision, as once the lay public began to read the scripture for themselves, they could draw their own interpretation. Without official control over scripture and how it was presented to the masses, this would inevitably lead to different viewpoints. King Henry also feared that different interpretations would foment dissent against his authority.

In many ways, King Henry must have realized that he had shot himself in the foot. He had broken with the pope to ensure he had the final say in religious affairs but instead opened up Pandora's box. This Pandora's box unleashed a multitude of viewpoints and greatly increased the potential for dissent against his authority. Realizing as much, the incredibly frustrated King Henry VIII issued the Act for the Advancement of True Religion in 1543.

This act placed rules and regulations on who would be able to study scripture. Henry only wanted seasoned veteran preachers dedicated to the traditional views of the church reading the Bible, lest others develop contrary ideas of their own.

After Henry's passing, his son, Edward, came to the throne. Since Edward VI was still a child at the time, a regency council was put in place to stand for him until he came of age. The interesting thing about the king's counselors was that many of them were sympathizers of the Protestant cause. They and their associates had gleaned substantial benefits from seizing lands that had belonged to Catholic clergy. They realized that to maintain a monopoly over these benefits, they would have to make sure that England's new king continued to steer the nation away from Catholicism.

At this point in England's history, Protestants were still a minority. The Protestant movement was rapidly growing, but most people in England were faithful Catholics at this time. To have a council of Protestant-minded ministers tugging a young, impressionable king toward the Protestant cause meant that some deception likely took place. Thanks to Edward's ministers of state, the Act of Uniformity was passed by Parliament in 1549, which replaced the traditional Latin-based Mass with a uniform piece of liturgy called the *Book of Common Prayer*.

It was now the law of the land that prayers would be spoken in English rather than Latin. The new book provoked public outcry and even led to massive revolts in the cities of Devon and Cornwall, which would later be termed the Western Rebellion. King Edward died on July 6th, 1553, leaving much of his kingdom greatly divided over the Reformation. Upon his demise, the throne went to his half-sister, Princess Mary.

A portrait of Queen Mary I.[12]

To the delight of the Catholic faithful, Mary wished to return England back to the church. Protestant factions knew the writing was on the wall, as Mary was a staunch Catholic. They had attempted to prevent Mary's coronation. In fact, they tried to insert a prominent Protestant named Lady Jane Grey on the throne. Grey's claim to royalty was due to the fact that she was a great-granddaughter of Henry VII. On July 19th, 1553, Mary and her entourage swept into London and drove Grey and her supporters out.

Despite the fact that Mary would ultimately go down in history as a tyrant, at the time, she was supported by the majority of the public. Many felt some sense of relief when Lady Jane Grey, whom they viewed as an imposter being foisted upon them by the Protestant nobility, was removed and the rightful heir to the throne secured. Lady Jane Grey was ultimately arrested and put on trial for "high treason." She was found guilty as charged and executed on February 12th, 1554. She was seventeen years old.

It was not long before Mary turned her wrath on the Protestants of England, issuing bans on Protestant gatherings and arresting Protestant leaders. While she was locking Protestants up, Mary made an effort to release Catholic theologians who had been imprisoned during previous crackdowns. Understandably enough, the Catholic segment of England was happy with these developments, while the Protestant faction was miserable.

Making the Protestants of England even more upset was the news that Mary intended to wed the Catholic king of Spain, Philip II. Philip was not only the leader of one of the most powerful Catholic nations but also the son of Holy Roman Emperor Charles V, meaning he was the ruler of Spain and the scion of one of the most powerful men in Europe. The notion that England would be wed to such a formidable foreign power was viewed with incredible alarm. Even non-Protestants were on edge due to fears of what kind of foreign entanglement this union might bring for England.

Parliament spelled it out quite bluntly when a petition went out from the House of Commons that insisted Queen Mary should not wed a foreigner. Perhaps inheriting a bit of her father's stubborn streak, the queen refused to listen. Even after an armed insurrection broke out, she stood her ground. Her armies decimated the dissenters, and on July 25th, 1554, she married Philip II of Spain as planned.

This was welcome news to the pope. The Roman pontiff seemed to think England had sufficiently repented of its Protestant ways and issued a proclamation saying all had been forgiven and that England was welcomed back into the Catholic fold.

In England, life was good if you were a Catholic, but for those who still held onto some semblance of Protestant beliefs, they were in for some pretty brutal persecutions. In 1555, Queen Mary instituted heresy laws designed to punish and root out religious dissidents. This step led to the hunt of Protestants, who were then forced into unfair trials, with many being executed for their unwillingness to conform to the Catholic doctrine. Over three hundred Protestants were burned at the stake during this period, and many more were imprisoned. Due to this oppression, Queen Mary would forever become known as "Bloody Mary."

This nightmare would only come to an end when Mary passed on November 17th, 1558, succumbing to stomach cancer. After Mary's demise, Queen Elizabeth came to the throne. Elizabeth sided with the

Protestants and paved the way for England to complete its Reformation that had technically begun under Henry VIII.

A portrait of Queen Elizabeth I.[13]

Before we continue our story of the Tudors, it is worth taking a look at a historical figure that exemplifies the strife between Catholics and Protestants. Elizabeth I did not take the throne without some difficulties. Some called for Mary, Queen of Scots, to be the monarch of England. As the name implies, Mary was the monarch of Scotland, but she had a legitimate claim to the English throne, as she was the granddaughter of Margaret Tudor, the daughter of Henry VII. Mary, Queen of Scots, practiced Catholicism, and some were eager to bring England fully back into the Catholic fold.

However, history had other plans for Mary. Elizabeth was able to secure her rights to the throne, and Mary faced an uprising from her closest advisors. She was forced to abdicate, leaving the throne to her one-year-old son, James. Mary fled to England, hoping her cousin would take her in.

Elizabeth did take Mary in, but not the way she had anticipated. Mary, Queen of Scots, was imprisoned, although she still lived as her station afforded. She was not confined to some dreary cell in the Tower of London.

Alas, Mary's story does not end happily. After over eighteen years in captivity, Mary was sentenced to death due to her involvement in a plot to assassinate Elizabeth.

It is clear that England was ready for a Protestant queen since Mary's attempts to overthrow or assassinate Elizabeth never came to fruition. King Henry VIII had begun the process by cutting ties with Rome, while Edward, under the guidance of Protestant ministers, had furthered it along by reforming integral parts of church practice. Mary stood as the lone Tudor unwilling to move forward with church reforms, but her efforts failed. By the time of Elizabeth, there seemed to be no turning back the clock, and under her steady hand, the English Reformation would be complete.

Chapter 5: England and the Irish Question

"It's a mark of self-confidence: the English have not spent a great deal of time defining themselves because they haven't needed to."

-Jeremy Paxman

The question of what the ultimate fate of Ireland would be had loomed large in the minds of English rulers for centuries. In the last two years of Queen Mary's life, she established the first Irish plantations in the counties of Offaly and Laois. These plantations were essentially large tracts of land that were seized from the local Irish and then had English settlers transplanted onto them.

For all intents and purposes, this plantation strategy was the start of outright colonization of parts of the Irish homeland. English subjects were crowded in England and looking to expand. And considering this was before the Americas became the go-to place for colonists, the abundant lands of Ireland seemed like a natural enough destination. The Irish resented this encroachment. They disliked the seizure of land and found the insertion of what was fast becoming an increasingly alien culture intolerable.

Before the English Reformation, the Irish and English were often at odds with each other. But after the English Reformation, they were even further separated. The Irish remained staunchly Catholic, while the English began to accept Protestantism wholeheartedly. King Henry VIII entreated Irish bishops to change their ways, but the Irish Catholic Church steadfastly refused.

By the time of Elizabeth, who came to the throne in 1558, there was an added religious element to the animosity between the Catholic Irish and the Protestant English, the latter of whom were newcomers to Ireland. The Irish were so alienated by the English that they often sided with foreign powers, as was the case in 1580 when rebellious Irish factions attempted to join forces with French and Spanish troops. This threat was defeated by England, but the potential for Ireland to become a backdoor to England's enemies remained.

This was demonstrated a few years later when the Spanish Armada sailed up the coasts of Ireland, hoping to hook up with Irish Catholic rebels. Due to logistical failures, bad weather, and the superior firepower of English ships, the Spanish fleet was ultimately repulsed. Nevertheless, the Irish would remain suspect in the eyes of many, including the famous Elizabethan poet Edward Spencer.

Spencer wrote the following rather unflattering words about the Irish: "Out of every corner of the woods and glens they came creeping forth upon their hands, for their legs could not bear them; they looked like anatomies of death, they spoke like ghosts crying out of their graves; they did eat of the dead carrions, happy were they could find them." Not exactly a resounding endorsement.

The Tudor dynasty ended up fighting four different wars against Ireland to get the Irish to submit to royal prerogatives. Even though the Irish held on to Catholicism, the campaigns waged by the English ruined much of the Irish way of life. The impact was felt the most keenly in Northern Ireland, especially in the region of Ulster.

The effect of English colonization can still be felt today, as most of the best real estate in Ulster is under the control of English Protestants, while the poorest, worst lands are the domains of Irish Catholics. The Anglicization of this region is painfully felt in the place names that have developed. In Ulster, we find a town that was once proudly called "Derry" transformed into "Londonderry."

It is almost laughable in some ways, but, of course, there were many then, as there are now, who do not find this situation at all funny. But as it pertains to Ireland in the late 1500s, one of the biggest dissenters of the day was also perhaps one of the most unlikely: Grace O'Malley, the "Pirate Queen."

Grace O'Malley was the daughter of an Irish chieftain by the name of Owen Dubhdara O'Malley. Owen Dubhdara O'Malley was the leader of a self-governing principality in the patchwork of domains that made up Northern Ireland at the time. This situation began to change under King Henry VIII, who sought to divvy up some of the unincorporated lands of Ireland. Henry VIII instituted a policy of "surrender and regrant," in which he encouraged chieftains like Dubhdara to "surrender" themselves to the authority of the English monarchy. In turn, their lands would be officially "regranted" to them.

However, this meant the Irish chieftains would have to wash their hands of Irish law altogether and essentially be made an English earl who was subservient to the English monarch. Some chieftains were okay with this bargain and did as they were told, but there were others who refused. The animosity between those who complied and those who did not became downright intolerable, further dividing the social structure of Ireland.

Grace O'Malley's father was among those who refused to comply with the English call to submission. Grace grew up fast and strong. Although it was not common for women to take on leadership roles in those days, her strength of character helped propel her to a position of leadership among her people. During the frequent infighting among the various Irish clans, her husband, Dónal, was slain.

But Grace O'Malley proved her valor. She led a successful defense of the family castle, vanquishing her enemies. Shortly thereafter, Grace turned away from landed estates to the high seas. She acquired three galleys and recruited as many kinsfolk as possible to become her deckhands. This was the point when Grace O'Malley first became involved in piracy.

Grace certainly defied the social norms of her day. After her first husband's death, she unabashedly embarked upon a series of romances before remarrying a man named Richard Bourke in 1566. For other women, this would have damaged their reputation, but for Grace O'Malley, the Pirate Queen, it only added to her notoriety. One of the most infamous accounts of Grace on the high seas, which seems to fully encapsulate her "devil-may-care" attitude, occurred sometime in 1567 when her ship was intercepted by a Turkish pirate.

The Turks boarded the craft and were determined to take treasure and make the crew slaves. Grace was in bed when the Turks boarded the ship, having just birthed her son Theobald Bourke, also known as Tibbott-ne-Long. Any mother who has given birth can testify to how important rest and recovery are in the post-birthing process. But rest was not in the cards for Grace O'Malley.

As soon as she heard the ruckus taking place above deck, she rushed out of her cabin. With a gun in each hand, she leveled them at the Turks. She then made a statement that would go down in infamy: "Take this load from unconsecrated hands!"

O'Malley was referencing the old Catholic belief that women were "unconsecrated" or "unclean" after childbirth. It is unclear if Grace was making a mockery of the church, her assailants, her own situation, or perhaps all three, but she most certainly made an impression on her opponents.

They were actually so shocked by the sudden appearance of this infuriated Irish lady that they froze right in place. They just stood there while O'Malley fulfilled her pledge, unloading both barrels on the intruders. She killed multiple targets, and the rest ended up fleeing in terror.

At any rate, as it pertains to the so-called "Irish Question," you better believe that Grace O'Malley had plenty to say. And she would ultimately take her case directly to Queen Elizabeth herself. The year was 1593, and both Grace O'Malley, the Pirate Queen of Ireland, and Queen Elizabeth of England were well past their prime. Nevertheless, these two elder stateswomen sat down and had a frank, heart-to-heart discussion.

There were many matters to talk about. O'Malley's region of Ireland was being run by a tyrannical English governor named Richard Bingham. Various rebellions had broken out due to unrest, and O'Malley's son had been arrested for his part in the insurrection and was expected to hang. O'Malley spoke to the queen openly and honestly about her struggles, and the two eventually came to terms.

Queen Elizabeth agreed to fire Bingham as long as O'Malley pledged to cease and desist any further support of revolts in Ireland. Queen Elizabeth had compassion for O'Malley's rebel son and immediately issued an order to have him released from prison. For a time, Ireland was at peace. But fast forward to the year 1641, long after both O'Malley and Elizabeth were gone, and one would see that all hell was about to break loose.

That year, an all-out revolt erupted in Ireland, which saw the Irish attacking the Protestant English and Scottish settlers. In this major outbreak of violence, it is said that at least three thousand were slain. Most of the killings occurred in and around the region of Ulster. Making matters worse was the fact the current English monarch, Charles I, was married to a woman named Henrietta Maria, who was Catholic. This fact and other subsequent actions taken by the king would make others distrustful of him, especially those in his primarily Protestant Parliament.

There were rumors the king actually supported the uprisings in Ireland (or was at least sympathetic to them), and the Irish rebels were quick to monopolize this fact. The flames of discord were eventually fanned to such an extent that England erupted into a civil war. King Charles had to rush off to Nottingham, where he amassed troops loyal to his cause to prepare a march on Parliament.

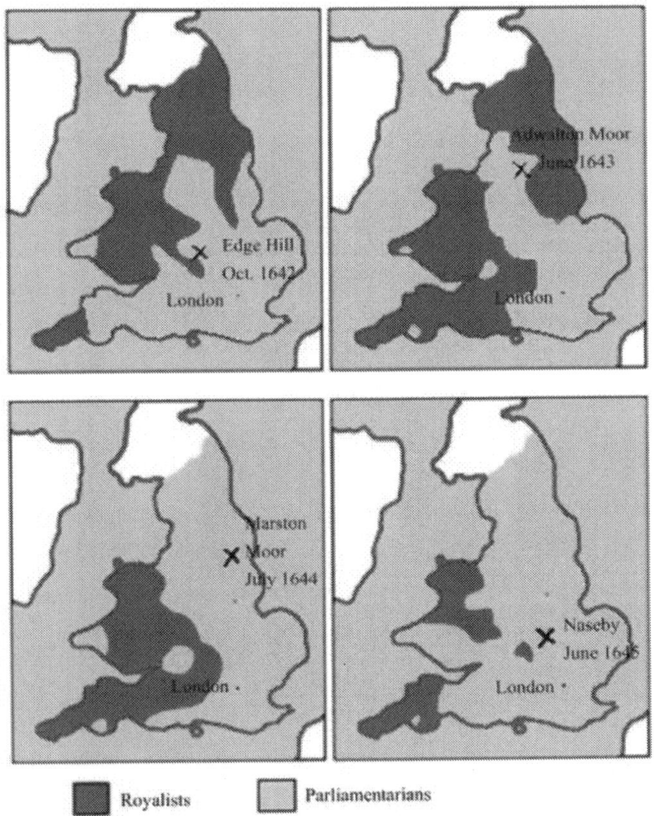

Four maps that show the progression of the English Civil War. The top left shows the situation in 1642, while the bottom rights shows the territory held by the two sides in 1645.[14]

The royalists made their stronghold in the northwestern parts of England, while the parliamentary forces secured the southeast. The royalist army quickly lost steam since bankrupt Charles found it difficult to pay them. Since King Charles's troops jumped ship in the droves, the royalist army was ultimately defeated in 1645, and Charles was forced to flee. He came back in 1648 to try and win the throne again but failed. Charles was executed in 1649; he was the only English monarch to be executed.

In the aftermath, the Parliamentarians had to figure out who would run England. A popular military commander named Oliver Cromwell ended up filling the gap, taking control in 1653 under the guise of "Lord Protector of England." Cromwell's reign was brief but eventful. Under his tenure, Jamaica was taken from Spain and made an English colony, and the Westminster Confession of Faith was declared as the prevailing doctrine of the Church of England. Cromwell was also involved in increasing the number of plantations in Ireland until he died in 1658.

Under Cromwell, land surveys in Ireland were conducted, and many of these territories were handed directly to Cromwell's loyal troops as a reward for their services. This led to many more plantations being established. Cromwell was just a mere flash in the pan, and two years after his death, the son of the deposed King Charles, Charles II, was welcomed onto the empty royal throne with open arms.

A portrait of King Charles II.[15]

The ramifications of the plantation system that had been foisted on Ireland would gravely impact the Irish. The effects of this system can still be felt to this day.

Chapter 6: Britannia Rules the World: The Empire

"The maxim of the British people is 'Business as usual.'"

-Sir Winston Churchill

It can be difficult to define the precise moment Britain became an empire. King Henry VIII first used the term, although he only oversaw England, Wales, and Ireland. During his high-profile struggle with the pope for an annulment, he issued the Statute in Restraint of Appeals in 1533, in which he solemnly stated, "This realm of England is an Empire."

Henry's wording was gauged more for effect than reality since he was attempting to portray himself as a sovereign emperor whose authority could not be overruled by the pope. At the time, one could hardly call England an empire since it had no real overseas colonies of which to speak. Instead of inserting themselves overseas, the English focused their energies on establishing plantations in Ireland.

This was, in many ways, a dress rehearsal for what would be done overseas. The first British colonies in the Americas came about in the early 1600s with some toeholds in the Caribbean. Its most important early settlement was Jamestown in what would one day become Virginia, a southeastern state in the United States.

The role Queen Elizabeth I played in the explorations of new lands and waters cannot be overstated. Elizabeth made England compete with Spain, opening the doors for further exploration by granting patents to explore new lands. She sent bold adventurers like Walter Raleigh to claim lands for England. Raleigh established a settlement on an island off North Carolina called Roanoke. This settlement would not last, but it set a precedent for more attempts.

After Queen Elizabeth I's passing in 1603, many of the initiatives she had begun would continue. The early settlements in the Americas would be followed by more extensive colonies that were built throughout the rest of the 17th century. As we mentioned in the previous chapter, this included the seizure of Jamaica from Spain in 1655.

England was so successful with its newfound colonies that Scotland tried to get in on it. In 1695, the Scottish launched the Darien scheme in which Scottish settlers landed on the Isthmus of Panama and established a fledgling colony. The colony struggled for a couple of years before it fell apart due to agitation from neighboring Spanish settlements and frequent outbreaks of sickness and disease.

Despite the fact the colony was a failure, it helped persuade Scotland and England to forge closer ties. England was horrified at the idea of Scotland exercising independent foreign policy in the Americas. At the same time, a greatly chastened Scotland had become more open to the idea of a merger so Scotland could partake of the benefits of England's growing empire. This led the two parties to agree to the Acts of Union of 1707. The United Kingdom of Great Britain was born.

Britain steadily expanded up the eastern seaboard of the United States, securing what would ultimately become the Thirteen Colonies. It was also making inroads into what would become Canada. However, the lands of Canada were already being actively settled by the French. It was almost inevitable these two nations would eventually butt heads.

Colonial competition between the two came to blows in the early 1700s, opening up a conflict in North America called Queen Anne's War, which began in 1702. It would not be until 1713 that the fighting would cease, thanks to the Peace of Utrecht. This treaty set clear boundaries between the British and the French in Canada. Britain acquired new lands in Newfoundland and Nova Scotia, allowing it to have a vast swath of territory that began in the uppermost reaches of Canada and ended just north of Florida, which at that time was still part of the Spanish Empire.

The Peace of Utrecht would keep the peace for the next few decades until the eruption of the French and Indian War. This war was part of a larger global conflict called the Seven Years' War. This war began in Europe after the hostilities unleashed from the tumultuous War of the

Austrian Secession, which had Austria and Prussia at odds with each other and other European powers being forced to take sides.

Without getting too bogged down in the details of this complicated affair, just know that Britain and France ended up on opposing sides in the conflict. So, Britain and France began fighting each other in mainland Europe, and their battles quickly spilled over into their North American colonies as well. The American theater of this conflict is commonly known as the French and Indian War due to the fact that France had strong alliances with Native American tribes.

The French and their Native American allies fought against the British, who had some Native American tribes on their side as well. The British were ultimately able to defeat the French both on land and at sea, the latter of which played a crucial role due to the merciless bombardment unleashed by the British on French cities. France was forced to surrender in 1763, and the subsequent Treaty of Paris essentially handed over almost all French Canadian territories to the British. The British had a sprawling empire in just the Americas, but little did they know that they were about to lose a key part of it.

Just a little over a decade later, General George Washington, who had fought valiantly for the British during the French and Indian War, led American troops in a rebellion against the British. Ironically enough, the deep ramifications of the French and Indian War kicked off the American Revolution.

Although Britain was the victor of the French and Indian War, it was drained financially from all of the money it had expended to execute the war on multiple fronts. British authorities issued high taxes on the American colonies to recoup their losses. This exorbitant taxation created immense hostility in the Thirteen Colonies since locals had grown weary of suffering huge tax increases without even having a say in the matter. They had no formal representation in Parliament. This frustrating situation led to the popular outcry of "No taxation without representation!"

This frustration led to major protests, such as the Boston Tea Party in 1773, when Americans dressed up as Native Americans, made their way onto a ship loaded with tea, and proceeded to dump all of the tea into the harbor. They demonstrated their disgust at the high taxes on tea by dumping the goods rather than being forced to pay the taxes on them.

Typically, when the story of the American Revolution is told, the situation is presented in fairly cut-and-dry terms, presenting the Americans as well-defined dissidents and the British as well-defined oppressors. But, in truth, there were those in Britain who agreed with the colonists and wished to help them. Outspoken Parliament member John Wilkes is one of the most well-known examples. Wilkes may not have agreed with outright rebellion, but he was in lockstep with the notion that the colonists deserved better representation in Parliament.

If such voices encouraging reform had been heeded, there might not have been an American Revolution at all. But history did not play out that way. The voices calling for calm and constructive dialogue were eventually drowned out on both sides, and an all-out war erupted. The revolutionary struggle lasted from 1775 to 1783. In the end, Britain managed to hang on to Canada and its other overseas colonies, but it lost its Thirteen Colonies. A massive chunk had just been removed from the British Empire.

Nevertheless, Britain would soon gain ground on the other side of the world. Britain had already been involved in India through teams of traders and explorers, such as the British East India Company. Initially, relations between the British and the Indian population were fairly cordial. The British were just one of many competing powers wishing to do commerce and conduct business. It was not until the British began to seize Indian lands for themselves that this situation began to change.

In 1757, British troops took on the Mughal Empire, which controlled much of the Indian subcontinent, and seized the region of Bengal. The British gradually increased their territory from here on out. It inaugurated its very first governor-general of Bengal, Warren Hastings, in 1773, who rapidly consolidated British authority over its Indian territories.

Britain's next major milestone was when its old nemesis, France, was defeated in the Napoleonic Wars in 1815. With France out of the picture, Britain could really focus on empire-building in India and beyond. It is said that from 1815 to 1914 (sometimes called the "imperial century"), Britain added some ten million square miles and some four hundred million souls to its dominion.

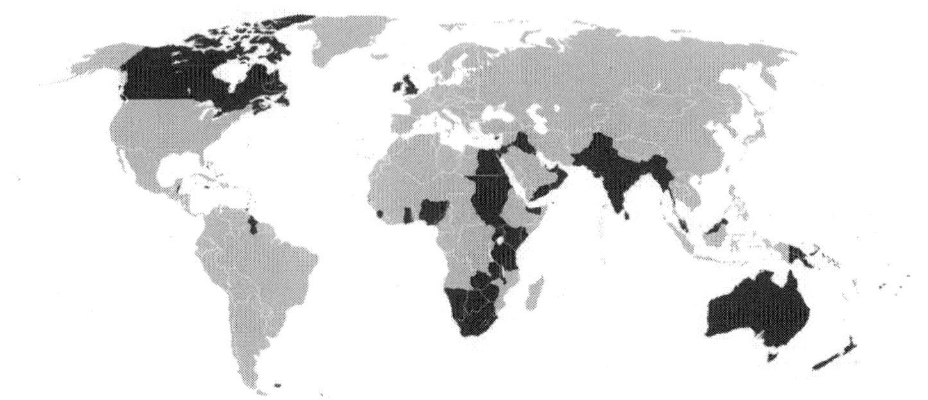

The British Empire in 1921.[16]

Many criticize the British for "lording" over others, but the British did quite a bit of good along the way as well. They improved infrastructure in their colonies, encouraged education, and improved some aspects of civil society, which are rather benevolent acts for an occupying power. However, the British also took away lands from those who lived there, exploiting the land for raw materials and other goods. In some colonies, the people faced discrimination, poverty, and disease, and their former way of life was uprooted. For most, the jury is still out on whether it was good or bad that Britannia once ruled the world.

Chapter 7: Britannia and the World at War

"I think it's something to do with being British. We don't take ourselves as seriously as other countries do."

-Joan Collins

It is interesting to note that the years 1815 to 1914 are often referred to as Britain's "imperial century," a century that is sandwiched between the end and the beginning of tremendous warfare. At the start of Britain's imperial century in 1815, Napoleonic France had just been defeated. This left the British Empire largely without a major antagonist for about one hundred years. Yet, in the final year of Britain's imperial century—1914—Britain would be dragged into a global war once again.

In 1914, the First World War erupted. As terrible as World War One was, it was sparked by an isolated incident. Archduke Franz Ferdinand was visiting Sarajevo in Bosnia when he was gunned down by a Serbian nationalist named Gavrilo Princip. It was a tragic episode, but it could have been handled without the world going to war. Yet, when it was learned that Princip had ties to a Serbian nationalist group, Austria-Hungary began making draconian demands.

Tensions between Austria-Hungary and Serbia were nothing new, and since Austria knew it had Serbia backed into a corner, it asked outrageous demands. When these demands were not met, Austria declared war on Serbia. This set off a chain reaction, as allied nations began declaring war on each other. Serbia's ally Russia declared war on Austria. Austria's ally

Germany declared war on Russia. England and France were drawn into the fight, declaring war on Germany. Germany was aided by the Ottoman Empire, establishing the solid block of Central Powers that would take on the Allied forces of Serbia, Britain, France, Russia, and eventually the United States.

Germany, as centrally located as it is, had long feared being surrounded on all sides during a conflict. To prevent this, the German military implemented the Schlieffen Plan. This plan involved quickly mobilizing troops westward toward France in the hopes that France could be neutralized early in the war so that Germany's attention could be better focused on the Russian threat. The Schlieffen Plan called for going around the most heavily fortified parts of France by crossing through Holland, Belgium, and Luxembourg instead.

No one in the German high command really seemed to care these countries were neutral. For the German high command, steamrolling through these countries to get to the backdoor of France was just a means to an end. Initially, the Germans had the advantage and seemed poised to deal a knockout blow to the French, but the British Expeditionary Forces, who had just arrived on the scene, quite literally saved the day.

Aided by the British, the French lines held, and both sides dug in. The intense trench warfare resulted in a standoff, which would characterize the Western Front for most of the war. Each side tried to make inroads against the other, but for the most part, gains would be minimal, and losses would be great.

This was the case during a British-led offensive in 1915 that had the British and French slamming into German positions near the towns of Champagne and Artois. The Allies tried their best to break through the German positions, but in the end, they were pushed back by machine gun fire with nothing to show for their efforts but a great loss of life.

In the meantime, the Germans decided to take the fight to the British homeland itself. They did this by floating air-filled Zeppelins (a type of airship) over the skies of London. Once in place, these Zeppelins dropped incendiary explosives on the city.

Although the Zeppelins did not drop bombs accurately on their targets, they did a lot of damage and killed several people. Interestingly enough, the leader of Germany, Kaiser Wilhelm II, was initially against using Zeppelins in this manner, citing his fear that they might obliterate much of "London's cultural heritage." The Kaiser was eventually overruled by his generals, though.

For the people of Britain, it must have been truly a terrible sight to witness these behemoths suddenly appear on the horizon. But Britain was not completely defenseless against these airborne monsters. Once the proper combination of searchlights and powerful artillery were in place, it was quite easy for them to knock these airships out of the sky. All they had to do was light up the target and let loose with their artillery. Just one hit and the Zeppelin would crumble. The Royal Air Force also got in on the action, and British fighter craft were soon making short work of the German Zeppelins.

Although the main focus of the war was on the Western Front, an incredibly consequential theater of conflict for both Britain and the world was being engaged in Asia Minor or, as we call it today, Turkey.

During World War One, Turkey was the seat of the Ottoman Empire, which at that time still controlled much of the Middle East and North Africa. Since the Ottoman Empire aligned itself with the other Central Powers (Austria-Hungary and Germany), it was automatically the enemy of Britain. Intense fighting took place when British troops landed on the Gallipoli Peninsula in mainland Turkey and participated in the subsequent Battle of Gallipoli.

The battle was a miserable failure for the British. Due to poor planning and logistical problems, British troops ended up stuck on the peninsula for several months, fighting a bloody stalemate against ferocious Turkish troops before the Allies retreated. Although the Ottoman Empire and the other Central Powers were defeated in the end, the Ottoman troops put up an effective front in the Battle of Gallipoli.

The next time the Ottoman Turks would face off against the British in a major way would be in what has been dubbed the Battle of Armageddon. Taking place in the ancient Israeli fields of Tel Megiddo, the lines were once again drawn between the Turks and the British. This battle was actually a series of battles, which are numbered from the First Battle of Gaza to the Third Battle of Gaza. During the Third Battle of Gaza, the British managed to make an offensive drive into the Turkish positions at Beersheba.

To the delight of Britain's crusader past, the British fought all the way to Jerusalem itself. These developments led to the famous scene of British General Edmund Allenby making his way into Jerusalem in December 1917. This event would have huge ramifications for the entire world. The

Ottomans would ultimately be defeated, and the region of Israel/Palestine, which had been under the Ottoman administration for hundreds of years, would be placed under a British mandate.

The British would control the region for the next few decades. After World War Two, in 1948, the United Nations recognized the state of Israel.

At any rate, in World War I, the Allies would be victorious on all fronts, and the Central Powers of Austria-Hungary, Germany, and the Ottoman Empire would be defeated. Austria-Hungary and the Ottoman Empire were broken up.

The end of the war created new nation-states or saw the emergence of independent states in the Balkans, the Middle East, and North Africa. Some territories would end up under the control of other powers. For example, Japan, which fought with the Allies during World War One, received much of Germany's extra-territorial holdings in Asia.

Germany faced the most severe financial and military restrictions. The Treaty of Versailles, which signaled the end of the war, impacted Germany by demanding severe reparations and significantly curtailing its military. Many Germans resented this. By the time Adolf Hitler rose to power in the 1930s, they were openly applauding his pledge to rip up the treaty, stop paying reparations, build up the German military, and retake lost territory.

Although there is a multitude of factors involved in the lead-up to World War II, the harsh terms of the Treaty of Versailles certainly played a large role. Britain took center stage during much of Germany's saber-rattling in the 1930s. The British attempted to appease and prevent aggressive German behavior from sparking another world war. The British public largely had no appetite for war, and British Prime Minister Neville Chamberlain's efforts to keep Britain from becoming embroiled in a war with Germany over faraway territorial disputes were viewed as pragmatic.

But when Hitler overplayed his hand and invaded Poland in 1939, even Neville Chamberlain's pragmatic patience ran out. At this point, Britain and France declared war on Germany. Germany declared war right back.

At first, the Allies did very little besides issue a blockade and feverishly rearm their militaries. By 1940, Britain had turned its attention toward Norway and Sweden, which was where Germany imported its iron ore. Plans were made to seize these ore deposits by force. The Germans beat the Allies to it and launched an invasion of Norway that spring. The Allies attempted to send a relief force to Norway, but the Germans seized control of the country so rapidly that the Allied efforts were deemed futile. As a result, the British pulled back. The next thing anyone knew, German tanks were racing into France that summer.

In a virtual repeat of the Schieffelin Plan, Hitler was determined to drive through the Low Countries of Belgium, Holland, and Luxembourg so that France could be quickly knocked out of the war. Unfortunately for France, this time around, the offensive worked. France was overwhelmed in the face of the blitzkrieg unleashed upon it and forced to surrender.

Those British still fighting this apparently lost cause in France were forced to engage in a rearguard fighting action as they retreated back to the beachhead of the small port of Dunkirk. Here, the British valiantly fought off the Germans so that their troops could be evacuated. Many were ferried across the English Channel in privately owned ships.

It was an impromptu escape from mainland Europe, but it worked and prevented a good chunk of the British army from being destroyed. The newly installed British Prime Minister Winston Churchill latched onto this moment and declared it a demonstration of "courage and determination at Britain's darkest hour."

Churchill went on to speak before his fellow legislators and declared, "We shall defend our island, whatever the cast may be, we shall fight on the beaches, we shall fight on the landing grounds, we shall fight in the fields and in the streets, we shall fight on the hills; we shall never surrender."

Shortly thereafter, the Royal Air Force engaged in what has become known as the Battle of Britain. In this struggle, British fighter planes squared off against German fighter planes as both struggled to gain dominance over Britain's skies. After three months of engaging each other, the British managed to come out on top. This was important since Germany intended to knock out Britain's air force and then launch an outright invasion.

The German invasion, codenamed Operation Sea Lion, was unable to take place because of the Royal Air Force's fierce resistance. But even though these plans were thwarted, German planes continued to conduct nightly bombing raids that would later be referred to as the Blitz. Despite the odds, Britain was able to hang on, and thanks to two misguided attacks launched by the Axis Powers of Germany and Japan, two of the world's most powerful militaries would soon be fighting on its side.

First, Germany invaded the Soviet Union, sending Russia into the Allied camp. And then, Japan attacked the United States, bringing America's might and industry on the side of Britain as well. By 1943, Russia was driving Germany back from eastern Europe. The third member of the Axis Powers, Italy, surrendered that year. In 1944, US and British troops landed in western Europe.

In May 1945, Germany surrendered, and in September of that same year, Japan surrendered as well. Britain had seen the war through to its end and helped lead it to a successful conclusion. But the British Empire of old was on life support and would soon be dismantled entirely.

SECTION TWO: Scotland, Wales, and Northern Ireland

Chapter 8: Scotland: A Tale of Three Williams and a Glorious Revolution

"There's an accent shift, on average, every 25 miles in England."

-David Crystal

Scotland stands as a majestic and enchanting land. None other than the famed bard William Shakespeare captured the essence of Scotland best. To be sure, Shakespeare himself was English through and through, but his masterpiece play *Macbeth* gives us a great window into what the Scotland of old must have been like.

In order to understand Shakespeare's tale, one must know a little bit about the backdrop that inspired him. From his perch in the 1600s, William Shakespeare cast his mind back centuries into Scotland's past when Scottish warlords battled for dominance. Norse incursions were common during this period, adding yet another layer of complexity to the landscape.

Shakespeare's *Macbeth* took place in the 11th century in the wild northern reaches of Scotland's interior. The main character, Macbeth, was a real Scottish king who reigned from 1040 to 1057. In the play, Macbeth gets wrapped up in typical royal intrigue and finds himself compelled to resort to murder to stay in power.

The real Macbeth was King Macbeth mac Findlaech. Macbeth's grandfather was King Malcolm of Scotland; after Malcolm's passing, his grandson, Duncan, became king. Duncan would become entangled with Norse warriors who infiltrated Britain and ended up embroiled in hostilities with England.

Even though Shakespeare murders Duncan in his play, the real Duncan actually perished on the battlefield. Another myth was Shakespeare's portrayal of Macbeth as a neurotic, impulsive ruler who could be quickly disposed of. The real-life Macbeth was quite decisive and remained in power for seventeen years. In the end, Macbeth was taken out by Duncan's son, Malcolm III Canmore.

Fast forward one hundred years from Macbeth's death, and another famous William emerges (this time, one from Scotland): William Wallace. William Wallace came to prominence at a time when Scotland was being severely oppressed by the English Crown. Scotland had just faced a succession crisis after its king died without an immediate heir, leading to the establishment of the Guardians of the Kingdom of Scotland.

Initially, the Guardians shepherded the dead king's granddaughter. The hope was that Margaret, the "Maid of Norway," would one day lead Scotland. But this slim hope was lost when she perished in 1290. Scotland was in some really dire straits, as various factions began to throw their weight around in their bid to lead.

In this tense atmosphere, King Edward I of England was invited to help broker a successor. In the end, John Balliol was chosen. However, Balliol would ultimately be viewed as nothing more than a puppet of the English king who helped bring him to power. He earned the nickname "Toom Tabard," which means "Empty Coat."

The Scottish public began to groan under this oppressive proxy of England, and William Wallace was one of them. Wallace was particularly disgusted with the occupying English forces who had taken up root ever since Toom Tabard had been installed on the throne. Thus, Wallace began to strike out against the occupiers. It is not clear how much of these early tales are accurate, but it is said that he engaged in a few hit-and-run attacks on troops stationed in the region.

However, his real vendetta began immediately after he was accosted by English troops as he was leaving a local church. Wallace was apparently minding his own business when a foul-mouthed soldier began hassling him in a very personal manner. In the close-knit community of which

Wallace was a part, personal details were typically well known. Wallace had just wed a lady named Marion Braidflute, and this lout apparently knew all about it.

The troublemaking soldier took one look at Wallace, whose belt was adorned with a fine dagger on his side, and howled, "What should a Scot do with so fair a knife—as the priest said who last f***** your wife!" The words were obviously meant to provoke William Wallace, but since he had only a handful of friends with him compared to the large number of English troops who stood in the street, he knew he would be no match.

As such, Wallace attempted to ignore the vile jibes thrown at him. The troops would not stop, and Wallace finally snapped. Erupting in pure fury, he unleashed his blade, taking out several of the hecklers. Thanks to the narrow, winding streets, he was able to cut his way to freedom, leaving his enemies slipping and sliding in the puddles of blood congealing under their feet.

It is ironic that a narrow passage saved him during this melee since years later, at his most famous moment as a Scottish rebel leader, the narrowness of a bridge doomed his antagonists. The tactic used in the Battle of Stirling Bridge was simple but stunningly effective. Wallace and his men were on one side of the bridge, while the larger English army sent to subdue them was on the other side.

Wallace goaded the English into crossing the bridge. The English were then immediately bottlenecked, forced to march in no more than two columns. As the English emerged two by two on the other side, it was quite easy for Wallace and his rebels to waylay them. The English were decimated in "pairs." Two would emerge from the bridge, only to get hacked to pieces by the full force of Wallace's rebels. Almost the entire English entourage was decimated before the remnant that survived finally realized their mistake and fled in retreat.

Regardless of his great triumph at Stirling Bridge, William Wallace, the great Scottish freedom fighter, was eventually defeated and captured. On August 23rd, 1305, he was executed in just about as horrific a manner as anyone could imagine. Stripped of his clothes, he was literally dragged through the streets naked before he was forced up to the hangman's gallows. The noose was placed around his neck, and he was dropped, hanging from a rope. However, just before he was about to expire, the executioner cut the rope.

Unbelievably, the semi-conscious Wallace then had his genitals cut off. This was most certainly painful enough to bring Wallace to a fully conscious state. And as he screamed in horror, William Wallace's belly was sliced apart and his bowels extracted. His entrails were set on fire and burned in front of his own eyes. Wallace lived through all of this and only perished when his heart was literally torn from his chest.

Even after he was dead, the abuse continued. He was decapitated, and his body was chopped into four pieces. Each limb was severed, with a hunk of gory flesh still attached. William Wallace's fate presents us with a tale too terrible for even the darkest of Shakespearean dramas to imagine.

A statue of William Wallace.[17]

A few decades after the end of Shakespeare's life, there was more than enough drama going on in Scotland. The Glorious Revolution, which took place in 1688, revolved around the dual monarch King James, who was known as King James II of England and Ireland, as well as King James VII of Scotland.

In what was essentially a simultaneous external invasion and internal coup, William III of Orange invaded Britain, while ministers ousted the king of England in favor of his daughter and William's wife, Mary II. All of this drama centered around the fact that James was Catholic. Although he was somewhat popular when he first sat on the throne, his policies quickly grated on the nerves of the Protestant majority of England.

For this reason, many began looking toward his Protestant daughter Mary as a potential alternative. Mary was the release valve for the anxieties of many since they believed Mary would soon sit on the throne rather than her Catholic father. Mary was also married to William of Orange, a Protestant cousin who administered the Dutch Republic. However, these plans were disturbed when King James unexpectedly sired a son named James Francis Edward.

This was unexpected since James's wife was in her forties at the time. Little James Francis Edward was born to King James and his wife, Mary of Modena, on June 10th, 1688. Due to the laws of succession, a male heir automatically superseded a female heir, placing baby James as the immediate heir apparent. The birth of this new heir set in motion the plot to get rid of King James.

Young James disturbed King James's opponents because they knew the boy would likely be raised in the Catholic faith. As infighting continued to grow, James's opponents actually "invited" William of Orange to come to England to stage an intervention. On November 5th, 1688, William of Orange landed in force.

Just before William's landing, a supporter of King James in Scotland, one Viscount Dundee John Graham of Claverhouse, otherwise known as "Bloody Clavers," was prepared to support his Scottish royal brethren by gathering an army of some thirteen thousand warriors. As the situation grew increasingly tense, he prepared to send them south to serve as a vanguard for King James.

For those in the king's immediate circle, the situation looked increasingly untenable. Even this large militia would be of little help, considering they were facing the forces of the Duke of Orange. Fearing the worst, the queen and the young heir were quietly evacuated on December 9th. Apparently not taking much stock in Bloody Clavers's support, King James himself went into exile on December 23rd, 1688.

Perhaps the reason this revolution is considered so "glorious" is that it was essentially bloodless. No one was willing to fight for King James in the end. That April, Protestant Mary was made queen by the Protestant-leaning Parliament members. And not only that but William was also made king in an arrangement that gave England joint monarchs.

The coronation of William and Mary.[18]

That spring, the Parliament went a step further to ensure its Protestant dominance would continue. In February 1689, the Act of Settlement was put forth, which banned any Catholics from sitting on the throne. Today, we would no doubt flinch at such discriminatory practices, but the Protestant Parliamentarians certainly had their reasons.

Britain had lived through several centuries of turmoil due to the conflict between Protestants and Catholics, and the Protestant majority simply wanted to ensure the matter was finally "settled" and that there would not be a sudden return to a Catholic monarchy, which might upset the status quo. We can see what happened when the status quo was upset when Henry VIII's staunchly Catholic daughter Mary took the throne and attempted to reverse just about every Protestant-based law in the books.

With the Act of Settlement, the Protestants considered the matter settled and insisted that in the future, only Protestant kings and queens would rule England. Despite the religious overtones, this was a major milestone in the transformation of England into a constitutional monarchy. The Parliament had an active say in not only how the monarch ran the country but also over who could even be king or queen in the first place.

As it pertains to the Glorious Revolution, we have not quite reached the end of the story. In the fateful summer of 1689, Viscount Dundee sent his troops, who came to be known as Jacobites (Latin for James), down the slopes of Killiecrankie in the vicinity of Blair Atholl. He did so with the intention of leading a belated counterrevolution of his own, referred to as the Jacobite uprising.

Viscount Dundee led the charge, and upon making contact with the opposition, he was pounded in the head with a musket shot and perished shortly after that. After Dundee's death, the struggle would continue until May 1690, but nothing would be able to undo what the Glorious Revolution had begun. The end result served to confirm the status quo in regard to Protestants and Catholics in Scotland.

Chapter 9: A Brief Guide to Welsh History

"To be born in Wales, not with a silver spoon in your mouth, but, with music in your blood and with poetry in your soul, is a privilege indeed."

-Brian Harris

Wales has a long history of settlement that can be traced back to the earliest epochs of prehistory. The region first entered into the historical record around 48 CE when Romans came to the region to make it part of the Roman Empire. Wales would remain under Roman dominion all the way until 383. By the time the Romans had left, Wales had greatly changed. Most were Christian and set about to create a patchwork of independent kingdoms.

The Welsh chieftains would periodically come to blows with their neighbors, the Anglo-Saxons, but the Anglo-Saxons did not have the wherewithal to defeat the Welsh outright. They did continuously encroach upon the borderlands they shared with Wales, though. In the meantime, the Welsh continued to fight amongst each other, with various warlords vying for power.

Wales was not truly united under one ruler until Gruffydd ap Llywelyn came to power in 1055. Anyone who takes a momentary glance at Scottish history will notice the curious phenomenon of rulers with "ap" as their middle name. Although "ap" is most likely going to make the modern-day person think of a software application on their smartphone, back in Wales, "ap" was merely a Welsh word for "son of."

It was a Welsh tradition to recognize fathers by utilizing their first name as one's last name. For instance, if your name was John and your father was Bob, you would be dubbed John, son of Bob, or John "ap" Bob. And the "son of" lineage would carry on down the family line from there. As it pertains to Gruffydd ap Llywelyn, he was the son of a previous powerful Welsh ruler named Llywelyn ap Seisyll.

Gruffydd rose to prominence by killing or gaining compliance from any potential rivals. He became the first Welsh king to lead over a truly united kingdom (not to be confused with *the* United Kingdom). Not only that, but Gruffydd ap Llywelyn was also able to expand out of Wales and seize parts that the Anglo-Saxons had previously held. The Welsh would never again be on the offensive like they were under this dynamic Welsh king. He ultimately perished in 1063, leaving a power vacuum in his wake.

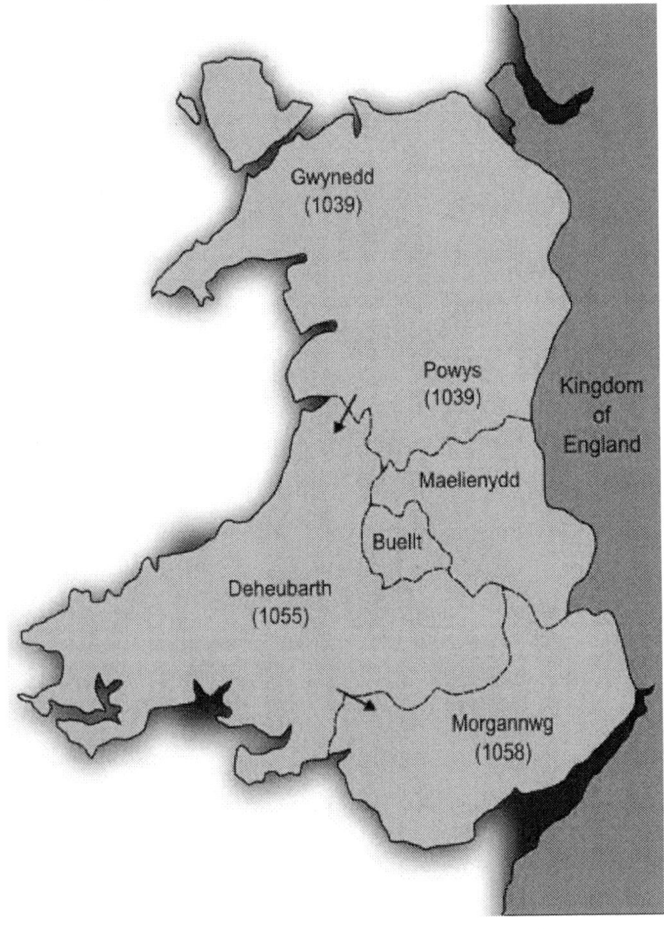

Map of Gruffydd ap Llywelyn's conquests.[19]

By the time of the Norman invasion in 1066, the situation in Wales was unstable, and the Normans rampaged through the Welsh region of Deheubarth. William the Conqueror eventually led his troops into Dyfed and set up many fortresses. The Welsh were finally able to regroup and push back, and in 1094, many of the previously lost lands were regained. The death knell for the Normans in Wales occurred over a hundred years later in 1136 when the Norman forces were crushed at the Battle of Crug Mawr.

Led by the valiant Welsh leader Owain Gwynedd, this engagement settled the matter for good, at least as far as the Normans were concerned. But it would not be the end of attempts to colonize Wales. King Edward I of England would ultimately subdue Wales. In the summer of 1277, the armies of King Edward were sent into Wales for a final confrontation.

By this time, the Welsh were just a shadow of what they had been. They had been greatly reduced in number, and the sitting Welsh ruler—Llywelyn ap Gruffudd—was forced to hole up with what few troops he had and prepare for a long siege in his fortress at Gwynedd. At this point, even the fiery Llywelyn could not help but see the writing on the wall and sued for peace, which led to the Treaty of Aberconwy. The treaty reduced the Welsh ruler's kingdom to nothing more than Gwynedd itself.

However, the treaty would not last, and Edward launched another invasion in the spring of 1283. This spelled the end of Welsh independence and led to Edward taking the title of prince of Wales. The title is still held by the royal family to this day. The title goes to the next in line for the throne; with Queen Elizabeth's passing, the title now belongs to her grandson, Prince William.

From this point forward, Wales would essentially be a territory of the Crown but would not be officially a part of the kingdom until the issuance of the Laws in Wales Acts, which were a series of laws passed from 1535 to 1542.

Despite their subjugation at the hands of the English, the Welsh had long been passionate about their independence. They desired to hold on to their lands, but even when that was taken from them, they continued to celebrate their culture and way of life. Much of Welsh literature plays into this, with literary figures held up as heroic figures who may one day reclaim the glory of the Welsh past. Probably no other Welsh literary character fulfills this role better than King Arthur.

Some might be surprised to hear Arthur is associated with Wales, as in later years, the legendary King Arthur and his Round Table were thoroughly Anglicized. But the tales of King Arthur are indeed Welsh in origin. The first mention of Arthur can be traced back to a Welsh cleric whose name comes down to us as Nennius. From the writings of Nennius, the *Historia Brittonum* (*The History of the Britons*) was put together in the 9th century.

This work describes Arthur as a great leader who fought in twelve major battles, the greatest of which was the legendary Battle of Badon, where Arthur allegedly decimated 960 enemy troops with his own hands. Such things are hard to entertain from a historical perspective, but it is from these legendary tales that the notion of a great and powerful king named Arthur first entered the medieval consciousness.

Along with Arthur came the Welsh figure of Merlin. As anyone who has read Arthurian mythology will know, Merlin was King Arthur's mentor and guide. He was also a magician and visionary mystic who not only had things to say during Arthur's lifetime but also allegedly spouted prophecies for the future of Wales. After the Welsh were overrun by the English, some of these prophetic folktales came to prominence as the last hope of an oppressed people.

In the *Historia Brittonum*, we get a glimpse of Merlin's origin story. Before his story became Anglicized, the Welsh name for Merlin was actually Myrddin, which roughly translates as "mad man." Myrddin is said to have been a mystic who lived by himself in the rugged Welsh highlands of Snowdonia. Here, he had a vision of the future of Wales, which was represented by two dragons. He saw a red dragon locked in combat with a white dragon. It was a terrific struggle, but ultimately, the red dragon was triumphant and forced the white dragon to flee.

Merlin (Myrddin) understood the red dragon to be Wales and the white dragon to be England. According to Merlin's prophecy, Wales would triumph over England one day. After England conquered Wales, any talk of this prophecy was strictly forbidden. English authorities feared these tales would inspire future revolts and rebellions from their Welsh subjects.

Many of the Arthurian legends were coopted by the English, both in order to make the tales more palpable for a wider English audience and to muffle and mute the revolutionary and nationalistic overtones of the narrative. King Edward I, who had much to do with the final subjugation of Wales, even went as far as to create an elaborate hoax, claiming that King Arthur's tomb had been found in Glastonbury. This was done to prove that the great Welsh king was dead and accounted for rather than living in exile in the magical land of Avalon, waiting to one day return as the original Welsh mythology foretold.

English kings did not want the Welsh to think their hero was about to swoop down from Avalon and lead them to freedom. They sought to bury the story by claiming they had the buried bones of Arthur in their possession. Although England made great efforts to bury the Welsh language, culture, and traditions, the Welsh refused to give in. Calls for independence can be heard throughout Wales today. In January 2021, a survey was taken to see if the Welsh would be interested in holding a referendum on Welsh independence. Although 47 percent voted no, 31 percent voted yes, which was a major increase from past surveys.

Chapter 10: The Time of Troubles in Northern Ireland

"There are two traditions in Northern Ireland. There are two main religious denominations. But there is only one true moral denomination. And it wants peace."

-David Trimble

Northern Ireland has always been a point of contention in the British Isles, but it was not until the 1920 Government of Ireland Act that the boundaries of Northern Ireland were drawn. This act effectively divided Ireland into two self-governing regions: the Republic of Ireland and Northern Ireland. The Republic of Ireland would still be part of Britain, breaking away from the British Commonwealth in 1948. Today, Northern Ireland is still part of the United Kingdom. Under the Government of Ireland Act, Northern Ireland consisted of six counties and would be governed from the city of Belfast.

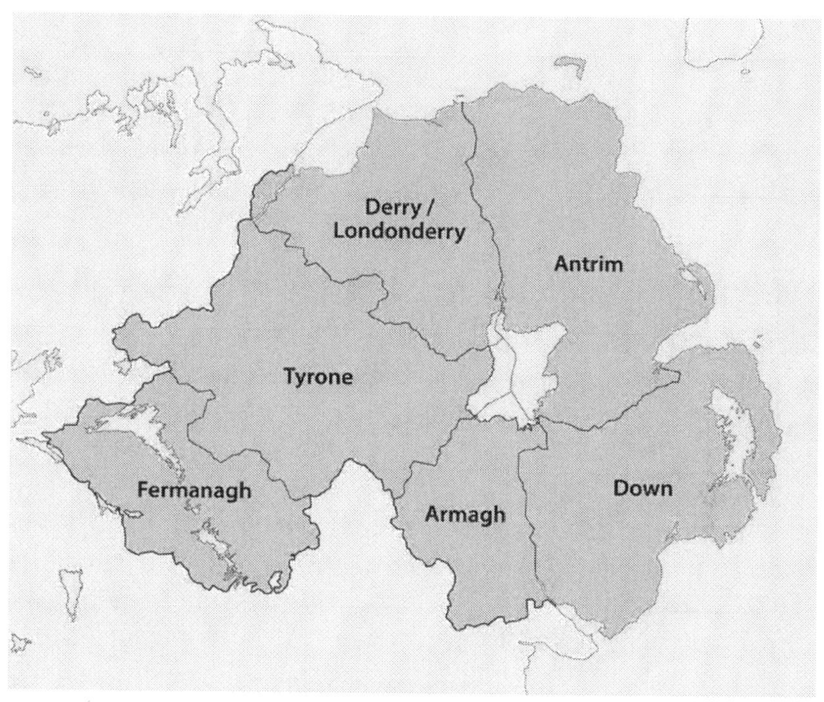

The six counties of Northern Ireland.[20]

Northern Ireland, as a separate entity, was officially established on May 3rd, 1921. However, not everyone agreed with this arrangement, and Protestant unionists and Catholic separatists duked it out in the streets. This massive unrest would become known as "the Troubles."

The main flashpoint was the province of Ulster, which was predominantly Protestant. All of the government positions in Ulster were controlled by Protestants, and Catholics were consistently blocked from taking up positions of authority. In some instances, they were even prevented from voting. And it was not only in Ulster that these problems were occurring; there was an instance in Belfast in 1920 when Irish Catholics and Irish Protestants erupted in terrible violence at a Belfast shipyard. The following year saw the infamous Belfast's Bloody Sunday, in which at least twenty lost their lives.

Belfast's Bloody Sunday occurred on July 10th, 1921, on the heels of a brokered ceasefire between the Irish Republican Army (IRA) and British authorities. Just hours prior to the start of the ceasefire, the British authorities decided to raid IRA compounds in West Belfast. While British police were doing this, they were suddenly attacked by IRA fighters. In the immediate exchange, one British cop was killed, and several others were injured.

The outbreak of fighting sparked several simultaneous outbursts of violence all throughout Northern Ireland. Before it was all said and done, at least twenty people would be dead, and hundreds of properties would be vandalized. In the aftermath of this bloodshed, the Anglo-Irish Treaty was signed on December 6th, 1921. This treaty established the Irish Free State.

The Irish Free State encompassed twenty-six of the thirty-two Irish counties, with Northern Ireland making up the six that were not part of the free state. The terms of the treaty declared that Northern Ireland could eventually be incorporated into the Irish Free State if it so desired, or it could choose to opt out permanently by petitioning the British monarch. This led to a meeting of the Parliament of Northern Ireland on December 7th, 1922, where a direct address was made to King George V.

The declaration stated, "Most Gracious Sovereign, We, your Majesty's most dutiful and loyal subjects, the Senators and Commons of Northern Ireland in Parliament assembled, having learnt of the passing of the Irish Free State Constitution Act 1922, being the Act of Parliament for the ratification of the Articles of Agreement for a Treaty between Great Britain and Ireland, do by this humble address, pray your Majesty that the powers of the Parliament and Government of the Irish Free State shall no longer extend to Northern Ireland."

Thereafter, it was incumbent upon the Irish Boundary Commission to set up the proposed border between the Irish Free State and Northern Ireland. This was easier said than done since there were endless squabbles about where the border would be. The infighting was so terrible that this task was not accomplished until 1925. The fighting would continue sporadically for much of the rest of the 20th century, with some of the worst instances of bloodshed happening in the 1960s and 1970s.

Known as the Troubles, the fighting would not cease entirely until the 1990s. During this period of intense violence, it is estimated that some 3,254 people lost their lives, not to mention the tens of thousands who were horrifically injured. Street fighting erupted on nearly every corner, and random bombings became all too common.

Despite the bloodshed, the Irish Catholics of Northern Ireland insisted they were merely fighting for a fair shake. Northern Ireland was mostly Catholic and argued it wanted equal representation in the Protestant-led government. In addition, there were groups that wanted to form a united

Ireland and called for separation from Britain. Some groups, like the IRA (Provisional Irish Republican Army), used terrorism to spread their message.

From 1967 to 1972, the Northern Ireland Civil Rights Association fought to put a stop to alleged discrimination and disenfranchisement of Catholics. But rather than achieving civil reform, this Irish civil rights movement sparked intense backlash, and terrible violence once again erupted, this time led by paramilitary groups.

The situation became so bad that in 1972, the autonomous regional government of Northern Ireland was shut down and suspended. Peace was eventually restored, but it was a slow process. First of all, efforts had to be made to convince the paramilitary groups to stand down.

After intense negotiation, ceasefires were declared by almost all of the paramilitary fighters, and their weapons were seized. Next, the police were significantly reformed, and British troops were pulled from the hot spots. It has been a long, drawn-out process, but today, Northern Ireland is largely at peace.

However, due to recent developments, there are those who fear there could be a modern-day resurgence in violence. In recent years, there has been a noticeable uptick among young people interested in the hardline stances of the IRA past. There is an increase in nationalism and sentiments of isolationism.

Recently, the ultra-nationalist Irish political group known as Sinn Féin, whose name means "We Ourselves," has gained traction in Northern Ireland. Sinn Féin holds out the promise of allowing the Irish to be, well, Irish, or at least their interpretation of what it means to be Irish. And while there is certainly nothing wrong with a nation wishing to celebrate its culture and heritage, it is indeed troubling to many to see Sinn Féin come to prominence since they had such strong ties with the IRA during the darker periods of Northern Ireland's turbulent past.

Sinn Féin managed to stun the world by winning a huge share of votes in the 2022 election, marking the first time such a hardline nationalist group in Ireland has come to such prominence. As of this writing, Sinn Féin, led by Irish firebrand Mary Lou McDonald, now holds seven seats in the United Kingdom's House of Commons. Is Ireland headed back to the dark days of the Troubles? Or will this new embrace of Sinn Féin and Irish populism somehow lead to something better? Only time will tell how this might affect Britain.

Conclusion: In Consideration of Britain

Britain entered history as a wild and untamed island on the fringes of "civilized" Roman society. Roman greats, such as Julius Caesar, attempted to tame the isle and took on its Celtic inhabitants, resulting in climatic battles. In the end, the best the Romans could do was subdue a large chunk of England and seal it off with a wall, courtesy of Roman Emperor Hadrian.

As Europe entered the Dark Ages, Britain was swarmed by Germanic tribes, who became to be known as the Anglo-Saxons. They coopted and contributed to the Roman framework that was already in place. In time, many of these newcomers became Christians and adopted Roman legal practices as they set about establishing kingdoms of their own.

The Anglo-Saxons faced very little opposition and set about establishing the boundaries of what would become modern-day England. In the 9th century, the Viking hordes began to swoop down on Britain, creating conflicts with the locals. The Anglo-Saxons would alternately fight, intermarry, and otherwise struggle with these Scandinavian newcomers.

As troubling as the Vikings could be, the Normans proved to be the greatest threat to Anglo-Saxon life. French-speaking tribes who hailed from Normandy, France, just across the English Channel, would come to control much of England. Led by William the Conqueror in 1066, the Normans lorded over England for centuries until they were finally superseded by other forms of English nobility.

In the 1500s, the Tudor family took on prominence, with Henry VIII establishing his firm grip on English society. He even broke ties with the Catholic Church and put himself at the head of what would become the official Church of England. This began England's trend toward Protestantism and brought about a greater sense of nationalistic fervor.

The Glorious Revolution of 1688 served to ensure the precepts of the Magna Carta were followed to an even greater extent, further hammering out just how a king or queen of England should rule in Britain's constitutional monarchy. With these internal problems sorted out for a time, Britain would go on to rule the waves. Far-flung colonies would be established in both the Western and Eastern Hemispheres. The sun would not set on the British Empire for quite some time.

It was not until the end of World War Two that cracks began to emerge in the polished veneer of British imperialism. Imperial outposts in both the Middle East and Southeast Asia began to break away shortly after the war came to a close. India was torn loose in 1947, leading to much bloodshed and violence in the aftermath of its independence and subsequent partitioning, which rendered the modern-day state of Pakistan out of the northwest corner of the Indian subcontinent.

More global territorial changes were on the way, as the old dominions of Britain's previus empire began to crumble. All throughout the 1950s and 1960s, several African colonies vied for independence from Britain. As the decades wore on, the British Empire became smaller and smaller. Even so, when push came to shove, Britain proved it was still willing to fight for some of the leftover crumbs of extraterritorial domains that were still under its authority.

This was evidenced in the Falklands War, which took place in 1982. The Falkland Islands are a small group of otherwise obscure islets off the coast of Argentina. The Argentines wanted to claim the islands as their own, but once provoked by the threat of outright invasion, Britain laid down the hammer. British troops were deployed, and the islands were secured. The war still remains controversial, but Britain achieved its objectives, and the Falkland Islands remain part of the greatly diminished extraterritorial holdings of Britain.

Hong Kong was not quite so fortunate. According to an old agreement, Britain was forced to relinquish its Chinese territory back to mainland China. The handover still remains controversial since Hong Kong was one of the few former colonies of Britain that had a majority of the population wishing to remain under Britain's control. The people of Hong Kong had grown up with the democratic freedoms and capitalist economic policies of the West, and most had a hard time adjusting to being under the rule of communist China.

Britain would go through a variety of changes in the subsequent decades. In 2003, Britain partnered with the United States in the War on Terror, joining US forces in both Iraq and Afghanistan. British troops pulled out of Iraq in 2011, and ten years later, they were forced to pull out of Afghanistan.

The word "forced" must be used since the abrupt withdrawal of US troops under President Joe Biden largely seemed to catch Britain by surprise. Nevertheless, British operations in Afghanistan came to a close just in time for the British military to put its laser focus on the eruption of war in Ukraine in 2022—a conflict that is arguably more consequential than the war in Afghanistan had become.

Great Britain has since taken on a leading role in trying to find a solution to the ongoing crisis in Ukraine. As of this writing, no one is quite sure how all of these things might end. But one thing is for certain: the mighty island of Britain will most certainly play a part in it.

Part 2: Britons

A Captivating Guide to the Ancient People Living in Britain Before the Anglo-Saxon Invasions

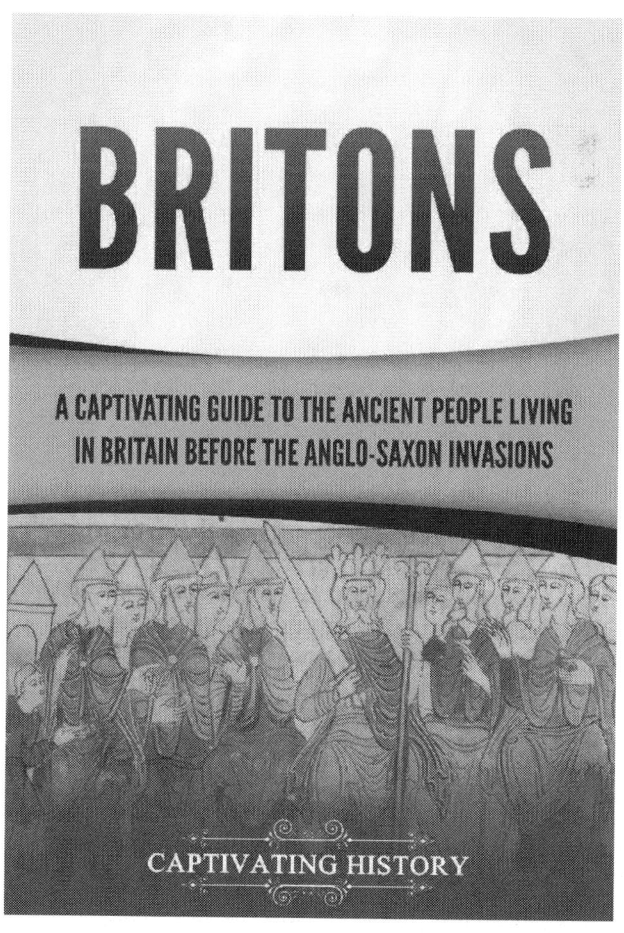

Introduction

There are few tales that are as rich and compelling as that of the ancient Britons. These were the tribes that inhabited what we now know as Britain before the Roman conquest. The Britons are known for creating the famous Stonehenge and the legendary exploits of King Arthur. It is a realm where we find myths and history blend together, sometimes so seamlessly that it is hard to find a grain of truth. This book aims to find those grains of truth, guiding you through the maze of Britain's ancient past.

As we begin, we must acknowledge the difficulty of this task. The ancient Britons did not leave extensive written records of their own, so we must rely on archaeological findings, Roman accounts, and later medieval chronicles to weed out the truth. These sources all have their own biases and limitations, and they challenge us to reconstruct a world that existed over two millennia ago. However, it is this challenge where the beauty lies. We're inspired to explore, to question, and to imagine. We will go on an adventure into the past, finding glimpses of a culture that has profoundly shaped Britain.

This book, while grounded in the latest historical research and archaeological discoveries, strives to breathe life into the words on the page, the stories of the people who lived, loved, and struggled in ancient Britain. We'll explore the daily routines of a Celtic village and the changes that came with the Roman villas. We'll look at the chants of the Druid priests and the clashing of swords between rival tribes.

The story of the ancient Britons, like many of the cultures of our human past, is a story of resilience and transformation. It is a long tale of how a group of tribes, each with their own customs and beliefs, were more similar than they were different. It is a story of adaptation, revealing how these strong people struggled against Roman conquest and cultural assimilation. Under the great shadow of the Roman Empire, the Britons developed a society that blended the ancient with the new. It's not just about the heroes and the leaders whose names appear in textbooks and on television; it's also about the everyday people whose lives contributed to the richness of Britain's past.

The craggy hills, dense forests, and winding rivers of ancient Britain were not just the backdrop to these historical events either. The landscape of Britain played a crucial role in shaping the lives and eventual destinies of those that lived there long ago. The geography of Britain, full of natural fortifications and resources, influenced settlement patterns, tribal territories, and the eventual outcomes of various conflicts. The Britons' lives were deeply intertwined with the physical realm that surrounded them.

We'll reflect on their remarkable cultural achievements as we move through the centuries. Their art, language, and literature, often overshadowed by the contributions of the Romans, show their rich and unique heritage, even though other civilizations viewed it as primitive.

As the dawn of the Anglo-Saxon era came, the Britons laid the foundations for what would become modern Britain. In *Britons,* we take a journey of discovery, puzzling together the mysteries held in history and bringing light to the lives of an almost forgotten people. Let us explore the rich and intricate tale of ancient Britain.

Chapter 1 – Prehistoric Beginnings

First Inhabitants

The history of humans is often shrouded in mystery, and the early chapters of Britain's past are particularly intriguing. Spanning almost a million years, the story of this island is one of survival, adaptation, and resilience. Over this vast period, Britain has gone through many changes, shifting from warm Mediterranean-like conditions to harsh, ice-covered epochs. Such dramatic swings in climate sculpted not just the terrain but also the lives of those who dared to call it home.

Amidst this constantly changing environment, the earliest humans etched their existence into the land. Evidence of their presence, unearthed by the dedicated work of the Ancient Human Occupation of Britain (AHOB) project, reveals a narrative of persistence against the odds. Tools, animal and plant fossils, and other artifacts scattered like breadcrumbs across the landscape recount tales of at least ten separate waves of human occupation. Each wave signifies a pattern of retreat and return, a constant battle with the relentless forces of nature. As ice ages loomed and withdrew, these early humans followed suit, their survival intrinsically linked to the whims of their environment.

Archaeologists have discovered stone tools in Happisburgh, Norfolk, and Pakefield, Suffolk, dating back between 950,000 and 700,000 years ago. These tools were crafted by the hands of *Homo* antecessors and provide valuable insights into the challenges faced by our ancestors as they adapted to changing climates in order to survive. The tools reveal that the early humans were able to thrive in a variety of conditions, from harsh and cold environments similar to southern Scandinavia to a more forgiving Mediterranean-like climate. Our species' ability to adapt to diverse environments is a testament to our ingenuity and resilience.

Homo heidelbergensis

A pivotal chapter unfolded around 500,000 years ago with the advent of *Homo heidelbergensis*. This period is etched in the annals of prehistory through tangible remnants unearthed in Boxgrove, West Sussex. Here, the silent witnesses of a bygone era–a leg bone and teeth–offer a glimpse into the life of these early humans. The fossilized remains tell a story of skill, collaboration, and ingenuity.

Homo heidelbergensis exhibited remarkable adeptness in butchery. They were not merely scavengers of the wilderness but also masterful butchers of large fauna. Their ability to skillfully process the carcasses of large animals like horses, deer, and wooly rhinos hints at their physical prowess and a sophisticated understanding of anatomy.

Their legacy is also immortalized in the stone tools and hand axes they left behind. These were not rudimentary implements; they were crafted with precision and care. The creation of tools indicates a society where cooperation was not just beneficial but also essential. *Homo heidelbergensis* worked together, planned hunts, and shared skills. They laid down the early foundations of communal living and societal structure. In the harsh world of prehistoric Britain, they were not merely surviving; they were also thriving and crafting a legacy in stone and bone that endures to this day.

Neanderthals

As dawn broke over ancient Britain around 400,000 years ago, the land whispered tales of new transient visitors: the Neanderthals. This ancient kin, distant yet familiar to modern humans, roamed the vast prairies of this island, following the herds along with the seasons.

The Neanderthals mastered the harsh and fluctuating climes of Britain. Their presence was fleeting yet profound, spanning until about fifty thousand years ago. They were skilled hunters, traveling the plains and bringing down large game, like mammoths.

Modern Humans

Around forty thousand years ago, a new character emerged: modern humans. With a spark of innovation and adaptability, these latest arrivals began a story that continues to this day. A jaw fragment in the depths of Kent's Cavern, Devon, is the earliest evidence we have of their presence, but it would take some time for them to become prevalent in Britain. It was not until some twelve thousand years ago that their story in Britain shifted from seasonal visits to a continuous stay.

These early modern humans, unlike their predecessors, wove communities and connections across Britain's landscapes. They were not solitary people. They were social beings who thrived in larger groups, their lives interwoven with extensive networks. They crafted a myriad of tools, each incredibly ingenious. They developed a new method for creating blades that were thinner and more efficient compared to the flaked tools of their predecessors. These thin blades were made from flint and were used to cut, scrape, and butcher animals.

Flaked stone burins were essentially a type of chisel that could carve and engrave wood, bone, and antler. Burins were used to create more tools and for art. A small stone tool with a rounded edge was created to process hides. The end scrapers, as they are called, removed the fat and flesh to prepare the skins for use as clothing and shelter. Small pointed blades called Gravette points could be attached to spear shafts for hunting. These early people also made items, like needles, harpoons, fish hooks, and awls, from bones and antlers.

The legacy of the early modern humans who once inhabited Britain extends beyond their mere survival. The artistic relics they left behind reflect a people who perceived the world as more than just a place of habitation. For them, it was a land of wonder, open to interpretation and expression. In the artistic vestiges of the early modern humans, we discern the emergence of a unique consciousness that distinguishes them from all those who had walked Britain's landscapes before them.

Neolithic Revolution

Around six thousand years ago, Britain's landscape underwent a remarkable transformation with the advent of farming. This pivotal moment heralded the Neolithic era, a time that reshaped the physical landscape with the emergence of fields and crops and the cultural nature of the island. Gone were the days when survival hinged solely on a hunter's skill or a gatherer's knowledge. A new rhythm of life began to take root, one bound to the seasons and the cycles of growth and harvest.

This shift to agriculture brought with it a cascade of changes. Pottery, which had once been simple and utilitarian, began to bear intricate designs, symbolic of a society evolving its self-expression. Tools, previously forged for the immediacy of hunting, were fashioned for a farmer to use. Even the rituals surrounding death transformed, reflecting a newfound connection with the earth.

The genetic mapping of Britain's ancient inhabitants reveals a story of migration and cultural fusion. Analysis of human remains from the Mesolithic and Neolithic periods uncovers a noteworthy shift in ancestry, coinciding with the emergence of farming practices. This genetic change points to the influx of people from mainland Europe who intermarried with Britain's existing hunter-gatherer communities.

Farming, a way of life nurtured in the Near East and later blossomed along the Aegean coast, didn't just travel as an idea; it was carried in the hearts and minds of the farmers who journeyed across western Europe.

Neolithic innovations were embraced in much of northern Europe, flourishing in regions like northern France, Belgium, and Germany, while Britain lingered in its Mesolithic past. It wasn't until a millennium later that Britain witnessed a seismic shift from hunter-gatherer traditions to Neolithic ways. This delay in embracing agriculture remains clouded in mystery. Did the gradual exposure to continental ideas inspire Britain's natives to cultivate the land? Or did a wave of Neolithic farmers, carrying the seeds of these new ideas, wash upon Britain's shores? The answers still lie hidden in the silent stories of ancient soil and stone.

Impact on Mesolithic Population

As the Neolithic era took over Britain, it cast a new light on the island's Mesolithic inhabitants. These communities were small in number but well established. Their subsistence was anchored in hunting and gathering, practices that had been honed over millennia. The arrival of Neolithic farmers marked not just the start of a new era but also the intermingling of two worlds.

Whether a gradual change within the existing communities, the arrival of new peoples to the island, or a combination of the two, how the people fed themselves changed. The hunter-gatherers began to leave a more subdued imprint on the physical landscape. Their smaller numbers, when compared with the larger, more settled communities of farmers, meant their numbers gradually disappeared among those of the farming communities.

Stonehenge and Other Megaliths

On the plains of Wiltshire, England, stands Stonehenge, a famous monument that still baffles archaeologists and historians alike. This monumental stone circle, crafted with meticulous precision, remains one of the most compelling mysteries of the ancient world. Constructed over centuries, from 3000 to 1500 BCE, Stonehenge is a marvel of engineering that is hard to replicate even with modern machinery.

The enigmatic origins and purpose of Stonehenge have long been a fascinating subject of inquiry. The site's ancient megalithic structures, located in the Salisbury Plain of southern England, have puzzled archaeologists for centuries. Despite extensive research, many questions remain unanswered, and the true purpose of Stonehenge remains shrouded in mystery.

Stonehenge by Stephen and Alicia.[21]

Stonehenge was once thought to be a temple of the Druids, but that has since been crossed off the list of possibilities. The structure predates the Druids by approximately two thousand years, placing it in an era that lacks historical documents. Despite this, Stonehenge continues to hold a substantial place in modern Druidic tradition, attracting pilgrims who seek a connection with ancient practices and wisdom.

One of the most enduring theories about Stonehenge's purpose revolves around its celestial alignment. The monument's orientation aligns with the rising sun during the summer solstice. This suggests it might have served as an astronomical observatory. Ancient astronomers might have tracked the movements of celestial bodies, using Stonehenge as a type of solar calendar to mark the passing of seasons. The correlation between the solstice sunrise and Stonehenge's alignment with the cosmos suggests a profound comprehension of natural cycles and their significance in agriculture and ritualistic practices. This knowledge was undoubtedly instrumental in ensuring that communities were in tune with the environment and able to regulate their activities accordingly.

More recent archaeological excavations at Stonehenge have unearthed intriguing new insights. The discovery of human bones, many showing signs of cremation before burial, suggests that Stonehenge was a site of astronomical significance and a final resting place for some. Stonehenge could have been a kind of ceremonial complex, possibly serving as a temple for the dead. It might have been a place where the living could connect with their ancestors.

The presence of a secondary monument, dubbed "Blue Stonehenge," located just over a mile from Stonehenge and comprising twenty-five Welsh bluestones similar to those found at Stonehenge, further supports this theory. Current theories talk about high-ranking individuals engaging in elaborate ceremonies honoring the dead. The relationship between these two sites suggests a complex social and spiritual landscape rather than individual sites. Perhaps they weren't connected at all but belonged to families, tribes, or clans. It's hard to interpret how these sites would have related to each other.

As no written records from the time survive, the true purpose of Stonehenge remains a matter of speculation and mystery. This absence of definitive answers only adds to its allure and significance. It remains a symbol of humanity's enduring desire to understand and connect with the universe. We view it as a monument to our ancestors' quest for meaning in the stars and the earth beneath their feet. We may never know what meaning they placed on this structure.

Other Megalithic Sites in Britain

Britain is home to a remarkable collection of over nine hundred stone circles. The megalithic sites date primarily from the Neolithic period (around 4000 to 2000 BCE) and offer a glimpse into a world where nature and ritual played a central role in daily life. While some of these structures have succumbed to time, the legacy they leave behind continues to awe and inspire.

The Avebury Stone Circle in Wiltshire stands out as the largest stone circle in the world. This monumental structure predates even the more famous Stonehenge and arguably surpasses it in both size and mystique. Close to Avebury lies Silbury Hill, an impressive artificial mound that serves as a prehistoric marvel of Europe. These monumental constructions hint at the sophisticated understanding and intelligence in engineering of the ancient peoples.

Further north, in Keswick, rests the Castlerigg Stone Ring, one of Britain's earliest stone circles. This site offers a panoramic view of the surrounding landscapes, hinting perhaps at a purpose beyond our current understanding. In Cornwall, one finds Carwynnen Quoit, an ancient dolmen (a large flat stone laid on top of upright ones, thought to be a tomb) also known as "the Giant's House." This structure, along with others like the Cheesewring and various stone rings like Duloe, Lanyon Quoit, Trethevy Quoit, Boscawen Un, and the Hurlers, speaks to a rich tradition of megalithic construction in the region.

Not all megalithic sites are made of stone rings or dolmens. The Cerne Abbas Giant in Dorset is a striking hill figure etched into the chalk hillside. It's thought to symbolize perhaps a deity or a mythical hero. In Oxfordshire, the Rollright Stone Ring complex, including the King's Men circle, the King Stone, and the Whispering Knights, forms a unique arrangement whose purpose and origins continue to elude and fascinate historians and archaeologists alike.

Chapter 2 – Dawn of the Celtic Age

The arrival of the Celts in Britain occurred over several centuries. The migration took place primarily between the Late Bronze Age and the Early Iron Age. The arrival of the Celtic culture was not marked by a single, decisive Celtic invasion, as earlier theories suggested, but rather by a series of movements and exchanges that gradually introduced Celtic elements to Britain and Ireland.

Originating from central Europe, the Celts were a diverse group of Indo-European tribes. Their expansion across Europe was multifaceted, encompassing both migrations and cultural diffusions. The oldest evidence of their presence is referred to as the Hallstatt culture, which dates back to around 700 BCE. This culture is known for its advanced ironworking and trade (particularly with the Greeks) and played a crucial role in shaping the European Iron Age. The La Tène culture followed, emerging around the Middle Rhine area. This culture became notable for its unique art style characterized by abstract geometric designs and stylized representations.

It used to be thought that the transmission of the La Tène culture into Britain and Ireland was through invasions and conflict. New evidence suggests now that it had more to do with trade and cultural exchange. Archaeological evidence in Britain supports this theory, as the Celtic culture appears in diverse regional societies, each with its own identity rather than a uniform "Celtic" culture. This challenges the conventional narrative of a homogenous Celtic society established through military conquest. Thus, the presence of La Tène-style artifacts in Britain is now understood in the context of trade networks and cultural exchanges.

Genetic studies have also meaningfully contributed to reshaping our understanding of this era. A key study from the University of York reveals substantial migrations into Britain during the Middle to Late Bronze Age, likely from regions in modern-day France. This migration blended populations, particularly in southern Britain, between 1000 and 875 BCE. This period of intense interaction between locals and newcomers likely facilitated the introduction of early Celtic languages and customs into Britain, a shift from the earlier belief that these elements only arrived during the Iron Age. This evidence suggests a "Celtic from the Centre" scenario, contrasting with the earlier "Celtic from the East" hypothesis.

The interaction between the Celts and the indigenous populations of Britain was not merely a one-way process. The exchange was mutual, with elements of the local British cultures also influencing the incoming Celtic groups. This resulted in a unique blend of cultural attributes visible in the archaeological record, which includes distinctive styles of pottery, metalwork, and settlement patterns.

The impact of the Celts' arrival in Britain extended beyond the tangible remnants of material culture. It had profound implications for the social and political structures of the time. The introduction of new ideas and practices led to the evolution of societal norms and governance. Tribal structures, which were possibly inspired by Celtic models brought through immigration, began to emerge, laying the groundwork for the complex network of chiefdoms and kingdoms that would characterize later British history.

Celtic Tribal Structure

At the heart of Celtic life in Britain was the agrarian economy, with farming and animal husbandry forming the bedrock of daily existence. Their agricultural practices were advanced for the time. The presence of artifacts like the iron plow changed agriculture as people knew it and gave them access to the heavier, denser soils that were nearly impossible to till previously.

Animal husbandry also played a critical role in their subsistence practices. The wealth of a chieftain was often gauged by the size of his cattle herd, underscoring the agrarian nature of their wealth and social status. Sheep played a vital role in the Celtic textile industry, while cattle were a primary source of meat and dairy products.

Tribes of Britain

Our knowledge of the tribes of Britain, yet again, comes from the writings of the Greeks and Romans. Therefore, they only date to the period of Roman Britain rather than the Iron Age. There is also little knowledge as to whether these names are how the tribes referred to themselves or were simply the names given to them by the Romans. A perfect example of this is the Durotriges. Roughly translated, this name means "hillfort-dweller." Though this could be their given name, most scholars find that highly unlikely.

The Atrebates people came to Britain from northern Gaul around the 1st century BCE. Their territory centered on what would be the Roman site of Calleva Atrebatum. This would be the areas of modern Hampshire, West Sussex, and Berkshire.

The tribes of Roman Britannia number around twenty: Atrebates, Belgae, Cantiaci, Catuvellauni, Dobunni, Dumnonii, Durotriges, Regni, Trinovantes, Iceni, Carvetii, Cornovii, Corieltauvi, Parisi, Brigantes, Deceangli, Demetae, Gangani, Ordovices, and Silures.

Further, Caledonia (the name the Romans used to refer to Scotland) was known to have at least eighteen tribes, which included the Caereni, Carnonacae, Creones, Damnonii, Decantae, Epidii, Lopocares, Lugi, Novantae, Selgovae, Smertae, Setantii, Taexali, Textoverdi, Venicones, Vacomagi, Otadini, and Carnovii.

Household and Kinship Structures

Celtic society was organized around households that straddled a balance between self-sufficiency and communal dependency. Households were the central unit of society. They were designed to be as autonomous as possible, but they remained deeply embedded within the wider kin group. This kin group acted as a safety net, providing support in times of need, whether for resources or in legal matters. Such a structure fostered a sense of communal responsibility and mutual aid within a tribe, which cemented social bonds and ensured the collective welfare of its members.

The household's role in Celtic society extended beyond economic activities. It was a center for social interaction. Traditions, stories, and skills were passed down for generations. The practice of fostering children, often within the kin group, strengthened familial bonds and ensured the spread of knowledge and skills in the tribe. This system of child-rearing contributed to a cohesive social structure, where relationships extended beyond immediate biological ties, fostering a broader sense of community and belonging.

The Role of Slavery

Slavery, a common practice within Celtic society, was intricately linked to their system of inheritance. Slavery was not based on racial distinctions. Instead, Celtic slavery was often a consequence of warfare and raids, with slaves then being integrated into various social ranks within the household. Interestingly, these slaves could form strong bonds with their owners and could, over time, gain their freedom and even land.

The possibility of social mobility for slaves, including the potential for land ownership, indicates a more fluid social structure than typically associated with slave-owning societies.

Tribal Governance and Kingship

The governance structure within Celtic tribes was not all the same; it varied across different regions. Leadership roles ranged from inherited kingships to elected rulers and councils. The concept of kingship in Celtic society was both sacred and symbolic. Kings were seen as representatives of their communities. Their rule was believed to impact the prosperity of their people and their relationship with the divine. The Proto-Celtic term *toutā* refers to the "people ruled by a king," indicating a well-defined sense of nationhood within each tribe.

Celtic governance demonstrated a balance between tradition and flexibility. As kingship was often hereditary, the existence of elected positions and councils reflected a dynamic political system responsive to the needs of a tribe. The Celtic model of leadership was not rigidly hierarchical; it allowed for the participation of various members of the society, including Druids and warriors, in decision-making processes. This blend of sacred kingship and practical governance ensured that leadership was both spiritually legitimate and practically effective.

Social Hierarchy

The Celtic society was stratified into several classes, with the commoners forming the base. Most commoners were farmers, living in settlements often outside the main tribal centers, where they could focus on their agricultural and pastoral duties. Above the commoners were the warrior aristocracy, the military backbone of the tribe. Above them was the ruling class of kings or chieftains.

This hierarchy was not rigid; it allowed for mobility and interaction among different classes, especially in matters of war and trade.

Warrior Aristocracy and Military Prowess

Warriors in Celtic society were not just part of the ruling elite; they were also a crucial part of their cultural identity. Celtic warriors were renowned for their bravery and skill in battle. Their military prowess was a means of defense or conquest and a source of social prestige and honor. Their elaborate weapons and armor, often beautifully decorated, were symbols of status and were as much a part of their cultural expression as they were tools of war.

Religion and the Role of Druids

The spiritual life of the Celts was intricately woven into their social fabric, with Druids playing a pivotal role. Druids were more than just religious figures; they were also educators, healers, advisors, and arbitrators. Their impact extended beyond the spiritual realm into the political and social spheres. In fact, they often held more authority than the king himself.

Druids were the keepers of knowledge. They were responsible for educating the youth and preserving legal and historical traditions. Druids were crucial in maintaining the cultural continuity of the Celts, ensuring that traditions, laws, and beliefs were passed down through generations.

Their rigorous training, often lasting two decades, involved the memorization of extensive poetry, legal rulings, and astronomical lore. This education enabled them to preside over religious ceremonies, offer counsel to chieftains, and mediate in disputes. Druids were responsible for the oral transmission of Celtic traditions, ensuring the preservation of their culture in the absence of a written script.

Their practices were deeply connected to nature. Druids often conducted ceremonies in sacred groves and near holy wells. These natural sites were not just chosen for their beauty; they were also believed to be portals to the Otherworld, a parallel realm inhabited by gods, spirits, and ancestors. The Druids' connection with these sites highlights their role as intermediaries between the human and divine realms.

Druids were central to the religious life of the Celts. Their education involved religious knowledge, but they also had to gain a deep understanding of the natural and psychological world. They are seen as the first philosopher-scientists of their time, possessing a knowledge that set them apart from the masses. This intellectual prowess was coupled with their mystical reputation, as they were believed to possess magical abilities useful in warfare and other aspects of life. The Druids' decline began with the spread of Christianity, which led to the gradual erosion of their status and power.

Sacred Sites

Sacred sites were central to Celtic religious practices. Rivers, groves, and especially springs were revered as gateways to the Otherworld. The Celts believed these natural settings had a special connection to the gods and were thus ideal for making votive offerings and conducting rituals. For instance, the site at Chamalières, a natural spring in central France, served as a crucial sacred site where thousands of wooden figures and a lead tablet with an incantation from the 1st century CE were discovered, indicating its prolonged religious significance.

Stone circles, such as the iconic Stonehenge, were also meaningful in Celtic religion. The megalithic structures are believed to have served as religious sites and astronomical observatories, marking important celestial events that were crucial to their ritual calendar.

Rituals and Offerings

Celtic rituals were complex and varied. They were often tied to the lunar phases and astronomical cycles. These rituals could be conducted in times of communal stress or according to a specific schedule. Offerings and sacrifices were a key part of their rituals, ranging from foodstuffs and precious goods to weapons and armor, especially those captured from enemies. The Celts practiced ritual destruction or burial of these objects, as seen in the discovery of hoards like the one at Hallaton in England, where over five thousand coins were buried at different spots alongside ritual animal sacrifices. This practice underlines the Celts' belief in the need to appease their gods to ensure the well-being of their communities.

The Distinctive Nature of British Celtic Mythology

British Celtic mythology shares common elements with the broader Celtic mythological tradition; however, it is characterized by its own unique deities, heroes, and narratives. The tales often reflect Britain's landscapes, from the rolling hills of Wales to the rugged coasts of Cornwall.

Deities Unique to the British Celts

The pantheon of British Celtic gods includes figures such as Brigantia, a goddess associated with the Brigantes tribe in northern Britain. She embodied aspects of war and sovereignty. Then, there was Belenos, who was especially worshiped in northern Britain. He was known as a god of healing and light.

These deities and others were revered not only for their supernatural powers but also as personifications of natural forces and tribal identities.

Legendary Heroes and Folktales

British Celtic mythology is rich with legendary figures and heroic sagas. One of the most famous is King Arthur, a figure who, though later embellished in medieval romance, has his roots in early Celtic lore. The Arthurian legends, with their themes of chivalry, magic, and adventure, encapsulate the values and ideals of the Celtic Britons. Also notable is Merlin, a wizard and prophet whose character combines elements of historical figures with mythical attributes.

The Otherworld in British Celtic Belief

The concept of the Otherworld holds a special place in British Celtic mythology. It is often depicted as an enchanted realm, sometimes an island or a hidden kingdom, where supernatural beings dwell. The Isle of Avalon, a mystical place where King Arthur is said to have been taken to heal after his final battle, is one such example.

Festivals: Celebrating the Cycles of Nature

The Celtic calendar was closely linked with agricultural cycles and seasonal changes. Major festivals like Imbolc, Beltane, Lughnasadh, and Samhain were celebrated with great fervor, each marking a significant phase in the natural cycle. These festivals involved rituals, feasting, and celebrations that reflected the Celts' deep reverence for nature and its rhythms.

With the advent of Christianity, many aspects of Celtic mythology were assimilated into Christian practices, ensuring their survival despite being transformed. Today, Celtic mythology continues to inspire modern literature, art, and neo-pagan practices, highlighting its enduring appeal and relevance. The Celtic tales of gods, heroes, and the mystical

Otherworld continue to captivate imaginations, as they offer insights into the worldview of an ancient people deeply connected to the natural and supernatural worlds.

The Early Britons

The people known as the Britons date back to the Early Iron Age. The term "Britons" in the context of Celtic studies refers to native speakers of the Brittonic languages in the ancient and medieval periods. This spans from the pre-Roman Iron Age to the Middle Ages.

The earliest known reference to the inhabitants of the island of Britain comes from a Greek geographer named Pytheas. Pytheas explored Britain between 330 and 320 BCE. The Greeks called the people of the island the Pretanoí or Bretanoí. The Latin name given to the Britons by the Romans was Britanni.

What we know of these people is limited. Archaeological evidence provides some insights, as do the writings of other peoples. By the time of the Roman conquest, the Britons had no known written language of their own. As such, our understanding of their culture and ways comes from outside sources looking in. Most of these sources are biased since they viewed the Britons as inferior or were members of a culture that eventually colonized the island.

With the sparse archaeological remains due to soil conditions, it is hard to estimate the Briton population during this time, and the estimates are widely varied. Although the estimates of four million are highly questioned, it is generally agreed that the population grew substantially during the Iron Age and surpassed over a million people. Estimates in regard to density and arable land indicate that this would have made resources tight, which could have led to the tensions the Romans witnessed between the tribes.

Iron Age Briton Settlements

There are a number of well-preserved Iron Age settlements in Britain that give us an idea of how the Britons lived. One of the best-preserved sites is located on a crannog or manmade island in southwest England. After the island was built, a platform of timber and clay was constructed for the base of the settlement.

From the number of wooden houses and barns excavated, archaeologists estimate that the village would have supported around two hundred people at any one time. These people lived in roundhouses made from woven sticks that were large enough to hold an extended family, each with its own barn or shed. At its peak, Glastonbury Lake Village held fifteen functioning homes, all surrounded by a wooden palisade. Whereas today we call it a lake village, during its time of use between 250 and 50 BCE, the area would have been more of a swamp instead of deep standing water.

Chysauster is another well-preserved settlement that dates back to at least 400 BCE. This area is an excellent place to study the settlements of the Britons, as the previous Bronze Age scattered roundhouses can be seen shifting into the village patterns of the Iron Age. At Chysauster, the Iron Age village was composed of ten courtyard roundhouses that would have housed around fifty to seventy people. Unlike Glastonbury, these houses had walls of stone topped with roofs of heavy thatch. These courtyard houses refer to the layout of the village rather than the construction of the house itself. The dwellings were laid out in rows, with each house having its own adjacent garden plot.

A central hearth within the roundhouse would have provided the Britons with cooking heat and warmth. Their diet was very similar to modern times, with bread and grains taking the forefront. They also ate a type of porridge, some meat, and honey. They greatly depended on dairy products. Small garden plots outside the home provided vegetables.

Early Briton Clothing

Archaeological evidence provides support for the Britons weaving fine textiles in the home and creating brightly colored dyes. The fabrics were often woven from wool, but there is some evidence of the use of flax for linen. Though these could be brightly colored, it was mostly restricted to natural hues like browns, reds, greens, and blues. Wealthier people might have had access to silk for their clothing. Silks were readily imported from the Mediterranean for tribal flags and banners.

Along with these textiles, there are remains of glass beads and pins. The people would have enjoyed bright colors and accessories like beaded necklaces and bracelets, as well as artistic metal pins to hold pieces of cloth together.

These ancient people also used leather. Leather and animal pelts frequently came from seals, otters, badgers, and foxes rather than cattle. Cattle were more prized for their milk than meat.

Briton men are described as wearing colorful tunics with sleeves that narrow as they reach the wrist. Beyond the glass and metal decorations, accounts from the Romans and the Greeks state that the neckline and cuffs were often embroidered. If the men wore breeches, these could be wide-legged or narrow and fitted below the knee.

Women wore a simple sleeved undertunic with a more elaborate tunic over that, which often pinned at the shoulders. This was often held down with a simple belt at the waist. As with the men, the women's clothing was often decorated with embroidery and fringe.

Chapter 3 – The Roman Conquest

Julius Caesar's invasion of Britain in 55 and 54 BCE, a landmark event in the annals of Roman military history, was driven by a confluence of personal, economic, and strategic motivations. He was not the first to conquer British soil (as we will address later), but his invasion is nonetheless memorable.

Personal Ambition and Prestige

In history, Julius Caesar stands as a man of towering ambition and political expertise. He sought to enhance his stature as a military commander and a statesman. By the time of his invasion of Britain, he had already established a formidable reputation due to his conquests in Gaul. Venturing into Britain presented Caesar with an opportunity to distinguish himself further. Success in Britain promised not only military glory but also political leverage in the cutthroat arena of Roman politics. Such a conquest would place him in a league of his own, overshadowing his contemporaries in terms of military achievements.

Economic incentives also drastically impacted Caesar's decision to invade Britain. The region was reputed to be rich in resources, particularly metals like tin and gold, which were crucial commodities in the ancient world. The prospect of accessing these resources and establishing new trade routes would have been a substantial lure for Caesar, as they promised both personal enrichment and increased wealth for the Roman state.

Strategic Military Considerations

The island was known to harbor enemies of Rome, as it provided refuge and support to the Gallic tribes who were at war with Caesar. Caesar aimed to disrupt these alliances by subduing Britain and strengthening Rome's position in Gaul. The military campaign in Britain was thus not merely an expeditionary venture but also a calculated move in the larger chessboard of Roman imperial strategy aimed at consolidating Rome's dominance in the western European region.

Julius Caesar's expeditions to Britain in 55 and 54 BCE were marked by a series of challenges, tactical maneuvers, and engagements with the native Britons. While not resulting in the immediate conquest of Britain, these campaigns were significant in the broader context of Roman imperialism and Caesar's personal military legacy.

The First Expedition (55 BCE)

In 55 BCE, Caesar embarked on his first expedition to Britain. This venture, which was undertaken late in the campaigning season, was more a reconnaissance rather than a full-scale invasion. The initial landing was met with formidable resistance from the Britons, who displayed remarkable prowess in chariot warfare. This mode of combat was fairly unfamiliar to the Romans and initially caused disarray in their ranks. In Roman culture, chariots were usually only used in racing.

Caesar's forces comprised around twelve thousand men from the Seventh and Tenth Legions. They faced the daunting task of disembarking on hostile shores under the gaze of Briton warriors. The legionaries managed to establish a beachhead after intense fighting, but the lack of Roman cavalry limited their ability to pursue and decisively defeat the Britons.

Compounding the military challenges were logistical issues. A severe storm damaged many of Caesar's ships, complicating his supply situation and leaving his forces vulnerable. Regardless of these setbacks, Caesar managed to extract concessions from local tribes, including hostages. However, the expedition was far from a resounding success. The Romans were unable to establish a permanent foothold, and the campaign served more as a demonstration of Roman power than a conquest.

The Second Expedition (54 BCE)

Caesar launched a second expedition in 54 BCE. This time, he had five legions and had greatly improved the preparations, particularly in terms of naval capabilities. Even with these enhancements, the campaign was again fraught with challenges. Adverse weather continued to be a major impediment, affecting the Roman fleet and supply lines.

The Roman forces were able to penetrate farther into the British interior and cross the Thames while engaging with various tribes. However, similar to the first expedition, the Romans faced fierce resistance from the Britons, who capitalized on their knowledge of the terrain and used guerrilla tactics.

One of the notable aspects of this expedition was Caesar's encounters with various British chieftains, which revealed the complex political landscape of Iron Age Britain. These interactions ranged from hostile confrontations to negotiated settlements, as different tribes sought to navigate the new reality of the Roman presence in their lands.

Despite making some headway, the second expedition did not result in a lasting Roman presence in Britain. The campaigns were limited by logistical difficulties and the resilience of the Briton defenders. Caesar eventually withdrew his forces back to Gaul, having secured a nominal submission from some of the tribes but without achieving a decisive military victory.

Military Significance and Legacy

Caesar's expeditions to Britain were significant for several reasons. Militarily, they tested the adaptability and resilience of Roman forces in a challenging and unfamiliar environment. The expeditions also demonstrated the limitations of Roman military power when faced with determined resistance and logistical constraints.

Politically, these campaigns allowed Caesar to present himself as a commander who had ventured into uncharted territories, thus enhancing his prestige in Rome. The mere act of crossing into Britain, a land of legend and mystery to the Romans, was in itself a noteworthy achievement.

These expeditions laid the groundwork for future Roman conquests in Britain, which would occur almost a century later under Emperor Claudius. These early forays by Caesar set the stage for the eventual Romanization of the island, which would have profound and lasting impacts on its history and culture.

Caesar's Accounts of the Britons

It's through Caesar's accounts of the Britons that we gain the most insights into the Britons and their culture before the Roman invasion. His accounts are detailed in his *Commentarii de Bello Gallico* and are some of the earliest surviving eyewitness descriptions of the people, culture, and geography of the island. Actually, Caesar's accounts are the beginning of the written history of Britain even though they were written by the enemy.

According to Caesar, the inland regions of the island were inhabited by native Britons. The coastal areas, however, had been conquered and populated by people who had crossed from what is now Belgium for war reasons and then decided to settle there.

Even Caesar noticed the cultural influences of the continental Celtic peoples. He described the Britons as having large numbers and that they lived in many buildings that were constructed in the same fashion as the Gauls. He claimed they did not eat hare, chicken, or goose but raised the animals anyway; he stated they did so for their own amusement. Their taboo against eating these animals was religious or spiritually driven.

He observed them using simple gold coins or bars of iron that were a certain weight for money. It makes sense that iron became a form of money since iron deposits on the island were not plentiful.

Much like the accounts of the Scottish Picts, Caesar noted that the Britons prepared for war by painting themselves with woad, a local plant that produced a dark blue color. He believed they did this as an intimidation tactic for battle. They also wore their hair long but shaved the rest of their bodies except for their upper lip. He noted they used chariots very effectively on the battlefield. The chariots allowed them to be speedy in battle while also creating chaos with the noise of the horses. The remaining men fought on foot, and the chariots provided a means of escape.

As with most of the writings of the time, some of what is stated must be taken lightly. Caesar claims the Britons might have practiced a form of polyandry. Ten or twelve men would live together and share wives. This was especially true of brothers. Any children born were considered to belong to the men or to the man to whom the woman was first married. This, however, could have been a gross misunderstanding of their type of extended family unit, as it would have been strange to a Roman, whose family unit was the nuclear family.

The Establishment of Roman Rule

The Roman conquest of Britain was actually started by Emperor Claudius in 43 CE. It marked a substantial expansion of the Roman Empire and a pivotal moment in the history of Britain, as this period of conquest and resistance highlights the military strategy, political maneuvering, and the initial stages of cultural transformation in ancient Britain.

Initial Invasion and Conquest under Claudius

Claudius's decision to invade Britain was driven by multiple factors. Foremost among these was his pursuit of political prestige. Claudius was keen on cementing his legacy, and he saw an opportunity for an outstanding military conquest in Britain. Additionally, strategic considerations played a role. The death of a prominent Briton king (the king of the powerful Catuvellauni tribe), Cunobelinus, changed the dynamics of southeastern Britain. His sons, Caratacus and Togodumnus, inherited the title of king of the Catuvellauni, and they were hostile toward Rome, unlike their father. They seemed to believe that Rome was a direct threat to their sovereignty, which was only exacerbated by the fragmented nature of the kingdom they had inherited. The sons played a role in the expulsion of Verica, a Roman client king of the Atrebates tribe. Verica fled to Rome to seek assistance, which created the pretext for the invasion. This political upheaval in Britain, as well as Briton raids in Gaul, presented Rome with a strong reason to intervene.

Upon launching the invasion, which was under the command of Aulus Plautius, the Roman forces landed in Kent and faced the formidable task of subduing the native tribes. The Roman advance was characterized by direct military engagements and strategic maneuvering. The army progressed to the Thames and overcame defensive obstacles set up by the Britons. These included some heavily fortified positions along the river. The Roman victory at the Thames and the subsequent capture of the tribal capital of the Catuvellauni, Camulodunum (modern-day Colchester), marked major milestones in the campaign. The success of these early operations can be attributed to the military might of the Roman legions, their engineering skills, and their strategic prowess.

Resistance and Roman Military Strategy

In spite of the initial successes, the Roman campaign faced significant resistance from the Britons. The native tribes, under leaders such as Caratacus, employed guerrilla tactics, leveraging their superior knowledge of the local terrain and the mobility of their chariots. The Romans were accustomed to more conventional forms of warfare.

In response to this resistance, the Roman military strategy evolved. The Romans established a network of small, strategically located forts to secure their conquests and to serve as bases for further expansion. This network played a crucial role in maintaining control over the newly conquered territories and in providing a springboard for future operations. The Roman approach to conquest was methodical, involving not just military force but also the establishment of administrative and logistical infrastructure to sustain a long-term presence in Britain.

The Roman strategy also included the integration of native elites into the Roman system, often through the establishment of client kingdoms. This approach facilitated a degree of local governance while ensuring loyalty to Rome. The strategic placement of these client states and the use of diplomacy alongside military might were key elements in the Roman approach to subjugation and governance.

Cultural Integration and Romanization

The Romans established a relatively strong foothold in Britain in 43 CE and continued to expand and consolidate their power through the mid-2nd century. It is thought that Britain was fully integrated into the Roman Empire by the late 2nd century.

The Roman occupation brought about major changes in the daily lives of the Britons. Roman culture, technology, and architecture began to permeate British society. One of the most visible signs of this integration was the development of urban centers. The Romans established towns and cities across Britain. You can even see today that many of these urban centers were based on traditional Roman urban planning principles. These urban centers, such as Londinium (London), Eboracum (York), and Aquae Sulis (Bath), became hubs of administrative, economic, and social activity. They featured Roman architectural elements, such as forums, amphitheaters, baths, and temples, introducing the Britons to Roman civic life and amenities.

Boudica's Rebellion

Boudica's rebellion is known as one of the most meaningful uprisings against Roman rule in Britain. It lasted between 60 and 61 CE. The rebellion was swift and fierce. It was a response to Roman oppression and the mistreatment of the Iceni tribe, as well as other tribes, in Roman-occupied Britain.

Background and Causes of the Revolt

The Iceni tribe, which was led by King Prasutagus, had been a client state of the Roman Empire and enjoyed a certain degree of autonomy. When Prasutagus died, he left his kingdom to his daughters and Roman Emperor Nero, aiming to ensure peace and the continued autonomy of the Iceni. However, Roman law did not recognize female inheritance. The Romans seized this opportunity to annex the kingdom. The disrespect shown to the Iceni royal family and the seizure of the kingdom's property was seen as a flagrant violation of the existing agreement between Prasutagus and Rome.

The immediate trigger for the rebellion was the brutal treatment of Boudica, Prasutagus's widow, and their daughters. The Roman administrators flogged Boudica and sexually assaulted her daughters. This act of humiliation was the last straw. The people had already been suffering under heavy taxation and financial exploitation. Most notably, Roman financier Seneca called in large loans made to the Britons, which ignited a firestorm of resentment against Roman rule.

Course of the Rebellion

The revolt began with an attack on Camulodunum (modern Colchester), the first Roman colony in Britain. The town had been established on lands taken from the Trinovantes in 49 CE and grown into a substantial settlement over the years. Boudica's forces, consisting of the Iceni and other allied tribes, descended on Camulodunum with ferocious intensity. The town was largely undefended and fell quickly to the attackers. Boudica's forces sacked the settlement and destroyed the temple of the deified Claudius, a potent symbol of Roman authority.

Following the fall of Camulodunum, Boudica's army moved south to Londinium (modern London), which was a flourishing commercial center at the time. Word had spread quickly, so the Romans anticipated this attack. The Roman provincial governor Gaius Suetonius Paulinus, who was engaged in a campaign in Wales, decided to abandon Londinium. His forces were insufficient to defend the city against Boudica's vastly larger army. As a result, Londinium suffered the same fate as Camulodunum, with its inhabitants either fleeing or being slaughtered, and the city burned to the ground. After Londinium, Boudica's forces continued to Verulamium (modern St. Albans), which was also razed.

Boudica's forces reportedly killed tens of thousands of people, both Roman settlers and Britons who had aligned with Rome. Modern-day historians aren't sure of the exact numbers, but they all agree that it was a large number. The revolt was characterized by its military successes and its sheer brutality, which showed the depth of resentment and anger against Roman rule.

The Roman response to Boudica's rebellion was swift. Gaius Suetonius Paulinus led the Romans after returning from his attacks on the Druidic island known to the Romans as Mona (today known as Anglesey), located off the northwestern coast of Wales. His strategic wisdom played a pivotal role in the Roman response.

Suetonius's Counter Strategy

Understanding the gravity of the situation, Suetonius took a calculated risk. He abandoned certain Roman settlements, deeming them indefensible against Boudica's massive force. Instead, he focused on gathering a sizeable Roman force capable of facing the rebels in a decisive engagement. This decision, while resulting in the temporary loss and destruction of key Roman settlements, allowed him to preserve his military strength for a critical confrontation.

The Final Battle

The climax of Boudica's revolt was a battle often referred to as the Battle of Watling Street, the exact location of which remains unknown. Despite being heavily outnumbered, the Romans had several advantages. Suetonius chose the battleground carefully, selecting a position that neutralized the superiority in numbers of Boudica's forces. The Romans were well disciplined, heavily armored, and battle-hardened. They faced a rebel army that, while large and fierce, was less organized and poorly equipped for a pitched battle.

The battle saw the Romans using their tactical expertise to great effect. They employed tight infantry formations and used their superior discipline and training to withstand and then repel the onslaught of Britons. The Romans leveraged their well-practiced military techniques and were able to inflict heavy casualties on the Britons. Hampered by their supply wagons at the rear, Boudica's army found themselves unable to retreat effectively, leading to a crushing defeat.

Boudica's fate remains shrouded in mystery. Tacitus writes that she was a coward who took her own life by ingesting poison. Her suicide was supposed to have been motivated by her need to avoid the humiliation of capture. Dio Cassius claims that Boudica fell ill and died with no other details. He claims that she received a grand burial that befitted her status as a leader and a symbol of the resistance.

The Aftermath and Significance

The defeat of Boudica's forces marked the end of Britain's most significant challenge to Roman rule. Suetonius implemented harsh measures to consolidate Roman control, although his successors later tempered these to avoid further antagonizing the native population.

Boudica's revolt highlighted the limits of Roman power, exposing vulnerabilities in their administration and approach to governing occupied territories. The rebellion also underscored the deep-seated resentment among the native population against Roman rule. Britons rebelled against oppressive taxation, cultural imposition, and disrespect for local customs and nobility. Atrocities were committed by both sides during the rebellion.

Even though Boudica's uprising ultimately failed, it became a symbol of resistance against oppression and has been immortalized in British history and folklore. It serves as a testament to the Britons' fierce independence and willingness to challenge one of history's greatest empires. The story of Boudica is often grossly romanticized, but it continues to stand as an example of the struggle for freedom and dignity in the face of overwhelming odds.

In the broader context of Roman Britain, the revolt had lasting impacts. It led to a reassessment of Roman governance strategies and marked a transition to a more conciliatory approach toward the native tribes. This change in policy helped stabilize Roman rule in Britain, which continued for several centuries until the eventual withdrawal of Roman forces in 410 CE.

Insights Provided by the Writings of Tacitus

Tacitus was a Roman orator and public official, not to mention the son-in-law of the famous Gnaeus Julius Agricola. Most of the insights he provided on the Britons come from his work *Agricola.* Though most of his accounts are about military campaigns in Britain, there are observations made about the Britons themselves. Although the insights may not be entirely true, they do provide us with insights into how the

Romans viewed the Britons.

For instance, he refers to them as barbarian people, but this was due to the Roman thought that they were superior than all other civilizations. He compares the Britons to the Gauls of the Continent, not just in looks but in society and beliefs as well. Tacitus found their language, celebrations, sacred rites, and superstitions to be rather similar. He believed the Britons were reckless but courageous, much like the Gauls had been before becoming "lazy" during years of peace.

When it comes to war, which is mostly what Tacitus witnessed, he believed their strength was in their infantry, unlike Caesar, who spoke more about their use of chariots. Tacitus also claims that by the time of the Roman occupation, the Briton kings were gone and that only chieftains remained. There was so much infighting that the Briton leaders didn't pose much of a threat to the Roman military.

Tacitus also wrote of the Iceni rebellion under Boudica. He claimed that the Britons saw her as a queen and that they did not make a distinction by gender when it came to their rulers. Whether this is conjecture or something he witnessed more than once, we don't know. He states that Boudica was able to inspire the entire nation to take arms; it is possible he said this to make the Roman victory look better. The actions of the Britons were fierce and labeled as barbaric, with their cruelty knowing no bounds. Tacitus even states that the Britons never laid down their arms out of fear of retribution and their guilty conscience. You can easily see how difficult it is to weed out truth from biased fiction based on Roman accounts.

The rest of Tacitus's writings are focused on the campaigns of his father-in-law in Britain to subjugate the tribes. Despite history proving that all the tribes of Britain were never subjugated, Tacitus claims Agricola was successful in his efforts.

Chapter 4 – The Romanization of Britain

The Romans transformed Britain between 43 and 410 CE. They worked hard to integrate their culture, law, and infrastructure throughout much of Britain. It wasn't just a process of cultural imposition but a very complex process of interaction between new Roman concepts and the already present native traditions. As we've already addressed, the initial process of conquest and subjugation was not well received.

Roman culture, with its iconic architecture, religious practices, and lifestyle, was introduced and frequently merged with local customs to ease the transition. It is easy to see the process unfold in the archaeological record. Roman towns, villas, temples, and roads developed over wide areas. The construction of these urban centers only sped up the process by creating centers of Roman control that stretched their authority over the countryside. These urban centers served as hubs for the Roman administration and economic and social activities.

The Roman economy was different from that of the Britons. As such, they brought noteworthy changes to the local Briton economy. Roman agricultural techniques boosted crop volumes, creating a tradable surplus. The Romans exploited Britain's natural resources and incorporated the influx back into the broader Roman economy. Trade and movement over the island became easier with the construction of Roman roads. Trade increased because of Rome's connections and the construction of new ports. Britain was quickly tied into the economic sphere of the Roman

Empire.

The Roman conquest brought on the introduction of Roman law and administration. Society changed fundamentally in the areas that were heavily occupied and developed. Roman law was comprehensive and codified compared to what we know of ancient Briton law. They quickly replaced the tribal laws. Rome believed that the transformation of the legal system was central to their conquest of the Briton people. Establishing a uniform legal framework in this new province was the first step to maintaining control over the populace. Roman law controlled a considerable amount of daily life, including property rights, commerce, marriage, and inheritance.

Administrative power was removed from the tribal chiefs and kings (unless they were deemed faithful to Rome). They established a new provincial government system, with a Roman governor in control who was supported by a network of local administrators. These local administrators were often native Britons who had readily adopted the new Roman customs and were loyal to the Roman state. It was a smart move by the Romans. This administrative network not only facilitated control of the province but also provided a way for the local elite to participate in the new Roman system and maintain some of their power.

Latin became the language of the administration and the elite. The local languages continued to be used by the majority of the population, but the Romans set these people aside as "different" and "other" compared to the new elite. Archaeologically, you can see this shift in language status in the surviving inscriptions and the onomastic (naming) record. They reflect a blend of both Roman and local names and practices.

As we'll see in later chapters, it was not a complete subjugation. Roman and native traditions blended together. Roman customs, practices, and lifestyles gradually permeated Briton society. This occurred the most among the urban populations and the elite. Archaeological remains show a clear shift in the food remains with the blending of Roman cuisine with Briton cuisine and vice versa. Clothing preferences shifted, and so did their chosen recreational activities.

The Romans introduced their gods and religious practices. These often merged with local Celtic deities, a common tactic in colonization efforts. Temples and shrines dedicated to Roman gods were built, and Roman religious festivals became a part of the local calendar. The religious changes are one of the easiest ways to see how far the effects of

Romanization reached. Although the areas near the Roman urban centers adopted the new ideas, the rural areas were vastly different. In these areas, the Britons maintained their traditional Celtic religions without much conflict.

With all these changes, society and social structure were turned on its head. The Romans presented a new social hierarchy. Romanized Britons now lived a step higher on the societal ladder than those who remained true to their heritage. Those Britons who chose to adopt Roman customs, language, and lifestyle were rewarded with higher social status. It was a quick way to continue the spread of cultural change and subjugation without conflict. The elite adopted Roman lifestyles, built luxurious villas, and often spoke Latin. They enjoyed privileges such as Roman citizenship, which afforded them legal rights that other Britons did not have. Lower classes often attempted to emulate the lifestyles of their social superiors.

Resistance

Beyond the epic battles of resistance led by Boudica, the Romanization of Britain was not a uniform process. Varying degrees of acceptance and resistance occurred all over the island. Some of the elites readily adopted the Roman customs and lifestyles to maintain their status quo or out of fear. It was a simple means to maintain their status and authority while under Roman rule. However, others wanted to preserve their way of life and struggled under Roman authority. This struggle lasted for centuries and led to a renaissance of Briton culture after the Romans abandoned the province.

Hadrian's Wall

The Roman approach to control and management is evident today in the landscape. With the construction of monumental structures like Hadrian's Wall, we can still see their efforts to subjugate the people, even if it meant cutting them off from those who remained loyal. These walls were so much more than a physical barrier. They symbolized power and control and also facilitated and regulated trade and movement.

Hadrian's Wall began to be constructed in 122 CE during the reign of Emperor Hadrian. This wall, the line of which is still visible today, is perhaps the most iconic Roman construction in Britain. This stone wall stretches about seventy-three miles across northern Britain, from the River Tyne near the North Sea to the Solway Firth on the Irish Sea. The wall posed a formidable barrier made of stone and turf. The northern tribes were deemed hostile enough toward Rome that they decided a wall with fortifications was a worthy expense.

Hadrian's Wall in Northumberland.[22]

The wall was lined with forts, milecastles, and turrets, and it served multiple functions. First and foremost, it was a defensive line against the more hostile tribes. It also served as a customs post for those who chose to maintain trade with the southern lands. This wall marked the northern boundary of Roman Britain. It's not that Roman impact and people were not above the line of the wall, but this was considered the limit of direct Roman rule. It was the beginning of the less integrated territories into the Roman system.

Archaeological research at Birdoswald Fort on the wall has shown that it was not just a fort. An entire community lived there. Geophysical technology allows archaeologists to get images of structures underground without excavations, and archaeologists have found two large settlements outside the main gates of the fort. These settlements were just as large as the fort itself. Some buildings have been found on the north side of the wall as well. If the people were truly afraid of the wild and untamed people of the north, then why would they build there?

The burials located here at this fort also support the presence of a large community. The burials were not only men either as you would suspect of a Roman military fort; women and children were buried there as well. Birdoswald was not abandoned after the Roman withdrawal, as it shows evidence of continued use. The newer building in the center of the fort is reminiscent of a hall. This suggests that perhaps a local lord saw the strategic value of the fort and claimed it for himself.

One of the most famous of Hadrian's forts was Vindolanda. This fort is still being extensively excavated and shows nine different fort constructions on top of each other. Unlike Birdoswald, Vindolanda showed much more conflict. The settlement that was located outside of the fort walls was abandoned after around 300 CE while the fort was rebuilt. The Vindolanda tablets, a handwritten account on thin, wooden tablets, provide us with a great deal of the information we have on life on the northern frontier of Britain. They provide information on military matters and include personal messages about families and slaves. For example, one inscription is a letter from a soldier to his superior asking to be allowed to visit his family. Another is a draft of a letter that a soldier wished to send to his wife back home. There's also a correspondence between a slave and his master.

Again, all this information, though incredible, comes from the perspective of the Romans. When it comes to the Britons, the tablets that have been translated only mention *Brittunculi* or "wretched little Britons" and note their fighting abilities. There are archaeological records of the native populations at the site, but that has received less attention than the records left by the Romans.

Other Constructions for Control

Though Hadrian's Wall is perhaps the most famous, other significant Roman structures are littered across Britain, including forts, roads, and smaller walls. The Antonine Wall was built farther north than the Hadrian's Wall during the reign of Emperor Antoninus Pius. However, the Antonine Wall was quickly abandoned in favor of Hadrian's Wall.

Roman forts, including those along Hadrian's Wall, were strategic military installations that also functioned as local administrative centers. They were used as the focal point of Roman presence in the more remote areas. The network of roads built to connect these structures, like Watling Street and Fosse Way, facilitated the easy movement of troops, trade, and information.

The construction of walls, forts, and roads considerably altered the patterns of settlement, trade, and military activities. The areas surrounding the forts became centers for large communities of both Britons and Romans, who all gathered together to find prosperity.

The legacy of Roman construction is still evident today. Hadrian's Wall is now a UNESCO World Heritage Site. Many modern roads lay on top of the old Roman roads. The ruins of forts and other structures are important archaeological sites that provide insights into the Roman military and administrative practices in Britain.

These constructions were crucial elements in the Roman strategy to control and manage the province. They served as obvious physical barriers and military outposts, but they were also a visual representation of Rome's social, economic, and political control over Britain. They left a lasting imprint on the landscape, echoing the lost era of Roman rule and its enduring influence.

Daily Life Under Roman Rule

One of the most notable and noticeable changes in Roman Britain was urban development. Towns and cities dotted the landscape. Some were developed on top of existing towns, but most were built from scratch. Urban centers were central to provincial life.

These centers were obviously Roman, as they were designed in the Roman style. They featured grid patterns for their streets, public baths, forums, amphitheaters, and temples. Roman cities, like Londinium, Eboracum, and Aquae Sulis, were new, bustling hubs of administration, commerce, and Roman culture.

Life in these urban areas was markedly different than in the countryside. The urban people enjoyed the amenities and entertainment that were typical of Roman life, including public baths. These baths were not just places for cleaning. People also went there to socialize and conduct business. Theaters and amphitheaters provided entertainment with plays, gladiatorial contests, and public spectacles.

Private dwellings were also built in the Roman style. In the cities, the wealthier inhabitants lived in townhouses called domus. They featured central courtyards and intricate mosaics. These homes were often inhabited by loyal Britons and Roman citizens. Britain became home to between thirty thousand and fifty thousand Roman soldiers and tens of thousands of Roman civilians. The domus were a clear and defined departure from the previous Iron Age roundhouses.

Changes in Rural Life

Rural areas did not remain untouched by Roman power; the changes just manifested differently. With the shift in agricultural practices and laws of land ownership, the rural areas were transformed. Villas run by wealthy landowners (both Roman settlers and Romanized Britons) became common in the countryside. They sat as large agricultural estates, and they were also symbols of Roman wealth and status. They often incorporated luxury features like hypocaust heating and incredibly ornate decorations.

In the rural areas of Britain, the Britons still lived in traditional Iron Age structures and maintained their pre-Roman lifestyle, at least for the most part. Their lives still revolved around agriculture, but the methods of work and who they worked for changed gradually.

Trade and Economy

Trade within Britain and with the rest of the Roman Empire expanded considerably. Roman Britain's exports grew exponentially. The mining operations provided the people with tin and lead, agricultural surplus allowed them to export grain, and new craftwork products became popular. Goods were not only leaving Britain. The demand for wine, olive oil, new pottery, and luxury items grew among the new Romanized elite.

Before Rome, the currency of the Britons was diverse. Barter and exchange systems were controlled by the individual tribes. The Britons in the southern and eastern parts of the island used gold coins before the arrival of the Romans, but this was restricted to the elite. Silver and bronze coins were far more common. The coins' size and worth varied among the tribes. In areas where coinage was less prevalent, bartering was common and accepted openly. Iron ingots were also used as a means of exchange. The introduction of Roman coinage standardized the money system, which led to an increased social hierarchy.

End of Roman Britain

By the 4th century, the Roman Empire was facing financial difficulties. The costs of maintaining their vast territories and armies were taking a major toll. Constantly increasing taxes was a heavy burden on the Roman people, who struggled to maintain their military personnel in all of the provinces at the same time. The Roman military underwent changes at the same time, as the dependence on legions gave way to a reliance on foederati (allied troops).

Combine the financial struggles with the political instability, and you have a boiling pot about to overflow. The constant change of emperors and the internal power struggles that came with that meant that the central authority in Rome was weak. A weak central authority made it harder and harder to govern and defend its many provinces, including Britain.

These weaknesses did not go unnoticed either. The Roman Empire also faced increasing threats from outside its borders. In particular, the Germanic tribes on the northern and eastern frontiers seemed ready to invade. The Roman military was stretched thin as they attempted to defend themselves from the Visigoths, Vandals, and other Germanic tribes. The threats caused them to pull military personnel from provinces like Britain to reinforce the troops that were under siege.

These weaknesses were also noticed within Britain. The local administration was competing with increasing uprisings and the growing power of the local chieftains, who benefited from their connections with the Roman Empire. As the economy declined and the Roman military presence declined, the Roman administration weakened, slowly eroding away Roman influence in the region.

Britain was included in those Roman frontiers that were under siege as well. The Saxons continuously raided the eastern coast. The Roman naval force could no longer defend the coastline it once dominated. The coastline became increasingly vulnerable to attack, which only eroded the power of the administration further. A great sense of insecurity and instability settled over the people.

A letter arrived from Emperor Honorius in 410 CE, officially ending the Roman occupation of Britain. He advised the cities of Britain to see to their own defense. This meant the Roman administration and the military had to withdraw to Rome or other areas to focus on defense. The Roman legions of Britain were called back to the heartland of Rome, and Britain was suddenly left to fend for itself against both internal and external threats.

This period after the Roman withdrawal was tumultuous. The island's social, political, and economic landscape was altered yet again, as factions warred and stability waned. A significant void in governance and law enforcement left a power vacuum that many were eager to fill. The Roman system had at least supplied a degree of stability for the past few centuries, and the sudden absence of that system led to uncertainty and confusion. Local chieftains and tribal leaders now found themselves with a new autonomy and power, which led to rivalries and a lot of infighting for ultimate control.

The Roman departure also led to a collapse of the economic system. Suddenly, the island, which had been connected to an extensive and global market system, had a more localized and barter-based economy.

The people no longer used Roman coins. The infrastructure that had been created, supported, and maintained by Rome fell into disrepair. The urban centers no longer enjoyed the trade that had supported them or the protection of the military, and many fell into disrepair or were abandoned completely.

Skills like stone building, advanced metalworking, and the use of Roman architectural techniques declined since there was no longer a demand for them. Many artisans and craftsmen left with the Roman fleet. The literacy and artistic expression that was fostered by the Roman education system also faltered in the absence of the Romans.

Britain became more vulnerable to threats since the people were not prepared to protect themselves. Saxons, Angles, and Jutes frequently sailed to their shores. The coastal areas were regularly raided, which eventually led to the Anglo-Saxon settlement of Britain.

New kingdoms and power structures eventually emerged in the absence of Roman rule. These were often based on tribal or ethnic lines and were the precursors to the later Anglo-Saxon kingdoms. The leadership and nature of these early kingdoms showed very little influence from the Roman structure that had been in place. There was a much greater emphasis on the traditional tribal and local Briton power dynamics.

Christianity had been introduced to Britain during the Roman period. The departure of Roman authority brought about a decline in the religion's impact on the Britons. Pagan practices experienced a resurgence in some areas. The Christian church in Britain had to navigate a new and difficult landscape until the Anglo-Saxon invasion occurred.

Chapter 5 – The Rise of Kingdoms

The withdrawal of the Roman administration and military left behind a society that had been under foreign rule for nearly four centuries. The Roman system of governance, which had imposed a degree of uniformity across Britain, disintegrated, leading to a return to more localized forms of rule. In the vacuum that ensued, power shifted to local tribal leaders and warlords. These leaders, who might have held positions under Roman rule or were local tribal chiefs, seized the opportunity to consolidate power and establish their dominions.

The nature and extent of political change in post-Roman Britain varied considerably. In the south and east, the influence of incoming Germanic tribes was more pronounced, leading to a greater degree of cultural and political change. In contrast, in the west and north, particularly in areas like Wales and parts of Scotland, the Roman withdrawal saw a resurgence of indigenous Celtic structures of power. These areas retained more of their pre-Roman cultural and political characteristics, although they were not immune to the effects of the broader changes occurring across the island.

In the areas where Celtic traditions remained strong, the post-Roman period was marked by a resurgence of native leadership styles and cultural practices. However, this resurgence was not a simple return to pre-Roman forms. The interaction with Roman culture and administration had left a lasting impact. The result was a merging of Roman and indigenous Celtic elements in governance, law, and social organization.

Identity in Post-Roman Britain

In those regions where the Roman authority was strong, you would think that a withdrawal would have a little cultural effect, but that would be wrong. Even in these areas, there was a resurgence of local Briton identities. However, the Romanized Britons had already adopted many aspects of Roman culture, which continued to guide their way of life after the collapse of Roman authority.

In the areas where new Germanic tribes were infiltrating (namely, the east and the south), new identities began to emerge. Native Briton, Roman, and Germanic cultural elements merged, forming the identity of the early Anglo-Saxon people. This fusion can be seen in aspects of their material culture, like art, burial practices, and everyday items.

The archaeological records show a shift in settlement patterns during this period. Urban living was no longer as appealing with the decline in the economy, and life shifted back to the rural lifestyle that had once dominated the island before the Romans. Roman-style architecture fell out of use, and a new mix of Germanic and Celtic architecture evolved.

Archaeological findings have been helpful in understanding the complexities of this era. Excavations of burial sites have shown a change in religious beliefs and practices. By looking at the variations in burial customs across different regions of Britain, one can see the coexistence and interaction of different cultural and religious customs. After Christianity spread throughout Britain, burials featured crosses and a lack of grave goods. The urban cemeteries shifted to the Christian practice of east-west orientation. In comparison, graves associated with the Anglo-Saxons before the spread of Christianity show the return of more pagan practices, with grave goods like weapons, jewelry, and everyday items. Cremation burials also made a reappearance with urnfields, grave markers, and mounds or barrows.

Archaeological evidence also supports the idea that trade with continental Europe did not die off completely. The island was not closed off from the rest of the world. Trade continued but on a much smaller scale than during the Roman period.

The Emergence of New Kingdoms

The power vacuum left by the Romans provided the perfect opportunity for the raiding Germanic tribes. The Angles, Saxons, and Jutes started to move beyond simply raiding the coastline to creating permanent settlements in Britain. These groups initially arrived as mercenaries or raiders but stayed and established their own kingdoms.

The earliest Anglo-Saxon kingdoms, which became known as the Heptarchy, included the kingdoms of Northumbria, Mercia, Wessex, East Anglia, Sussex, Kent, and Essex. They were by no means similar despite their heritage. Each kingdom developed its own distinct nature. Kent remained closely tied with the Continent and became a trade center. Wessex started off as a minor kingdom and eventually became the unifier of England. They evolved through warfare, alliances, and dynastic changes.

Welsh Societies

Gwynedd, Powys, and Dyfed in what we now know as Wales rose into powerful kingdoms when the Romans withdrew. Since this area was more remote, the kingdoms and tribes of Wales were better able to maintain their native Celtic traditions alongside the influence of Roman rule. The leaders of these kingdoms were local chieftains who continued to claim descent from the tribal leaders of pre-Roman times.

Welsh society prided itself on maintaining their ancestors' Celtic customs, language, and laws. The tribal social structure remained, strongly emphasizing kinship and clans. Although the tribes in Wales shared a similar cultural affiliation, the kingdoms themselves were not unified. They shared a culture that differentiated them from their Anglo-Saxon and Pictish neighbors, but they still fought for territory and power just like the others.

Pictish Societies

The Picts were the group of people that resided in what we call Scotland today. A distinct group in pre-Roman Britain, the Picts were often included in the hostile tribes that lay north of Hadrian's Wall. The scarcity of written sources, including those of the Romans, leaves our knowledge of the Picts minimal. The small archaeological record and some accounts from neighboring societies do provide us with some insights into their culture.

What we know the most about Pictish society is its unique art. Standing stones carved with intricate symbols are scattered all over northeastern Scotland. These carved stones are believed to have served two purposes: religious and commemorative markers.

The Picts had their own language, separate from the other Britons. It is not well understood, but it was documented as being different from the other Celtic languages spoken by the Welsh and the Scots. Considering the nature of the island at their peak, the Picts are believed to have lived in a tribal-based society, with their power centering around kinship groups and local chieftains, much like the Britons to the south.

Unique to the Picts and likely driven by their remote location, they resisted encroachment not only from the Romans but also from the later Anglo-Saxons. Until the formation of the Kingdom of Alba in the 9th century, the Pictish and Gaelic cultures maintained their distinct and unique way of life. The Gaelic language gradually replaced Pictish as the primary language in the kingdom. Gaelic place names and personal names became the norm when the people unified under a single kingdom, but one can still see the influence of the Picts in art.

Regional Differences

In post-Roman Britain, there were many regional differences as the island experienced changes and cultural interactions from multiple sources. These differences were largely shaped by the previous Roman influence, the impact of new settlers coming to Britain's shores, and the resilience of the indigenous people who held on to their ancestors' culture.

The South and East: Anglo-Saxon Influence

The regions to the south and east experienced regular raiding and then settlement by Germanic tribes. The Angles, Saxons, and Jutes eventually established several small kingdoms that marked the beginning of the Anglo-Saxon period in British history. The Germanic impact changed and added to the societal structure, language, and culture in these regions to some extent, setting them apart from other areas.

What would become the Anglo-Saxon kingdoms of Northumbria, Mercia, and Wessex developed their own distinct identities during the period after Roman rule. These regions were characterized by a mixture of Roman and Germanic elements. Eventually, the Germanic elements overshadowed the Roman elements, as more Anglo-Saxons settled in the area. The Anglo-Saxon social structure was hierarchical and somewhat similar to the Romans. At the top were the ruling elite, who were distinctly separate from free men and the feudal-like serfs.

The West

As mentioned earlier, the west of Britain, particularly what is now present-day Wales, was dominated by Celtic traditions. Roman culture influenced these areas far less than the heavily populated eastern coast. After the Roman withdrawal, it was easy for the traditional practices and structures to become popular again.

These kingdoms maintained a strong tribal organization, and their social and political structures were largely based on those that existed before the Romans' arrival. The Welsh language at this time was a direct descendant of the Brittonic languages spoken in Britain before the Romans and became a defining feature of these societies.

The North: Pict and Gaelic

In the northern parts of Britain, leading all the way into modern-day Scotland, one could find more traditional British cultures reviving and taking power. While the Picts maintained this system alongside other Gaelic tribes throughout Roman rule, others joined them after the Roman withdrawal.

Settlers from Ireland, often referred to as the Gaelic people, moved into the northern areas. Speaking Gaelic-Irish and coming from similar tribal-based societies, the Gaelic people and the Picts eventually merged into the Kingdom of Alba as their society continued to change.

Arthurian Legends

During this period of considerable upheaval, we find the development of the famous Arthurian legends. These legends have gone far beyond their historical beginnings to become a cornerstone of British mythology. The figure of King Arthur emerged as a beacon of hope and heroism during a time consumed by conflict, political fragmentation, and social upheaval.

Historical Context of the Legends

The chaotic and fragmented political landscape of warring small kingdoms set the stage for the Arthurian legends we're familiar with today. The character of Arthur first appears in historical records like *Historia Brittonum* and *Annales Cambriae* dating to the 9th and 10th centuries, respectively. They depict Arthur as a warrior rather than a king. This warrior stood fast and strong against the Anglo-Saxon incursions and fought alongside the Briton kingdoms.

In the *Historia Brittonum*, which was written in the early 9th century by a Welsh monk named Nennius, Arthur is identified as the leader of the Briton forces in the Battle of Mount Badon. He is said to have led the

Britons to victory against the Anglo-Saxons. He and his men are said to have slain 960 Anglo-Saxons in a single battle. In some cases, Arthur is said to have been the only one to strike down the enemy.

A century later, the *Annales Cambriae* was written. It depicts Arthur as a strong Christian leader who carried the cross on his shoulders as a shield for three days and three nights and then led the Britons into victory against the Anglo-Saxons at Badon.

Though the Battle of Mount Badon is believed to be a historical event, Arthur's involvement cannot be substantiated. Both of these texts were written centuries after the event. Scholars believe the battle took place on one of three possible dates: 493, 501, or 516. As such, the records linking Arthur as the victor date centuries later.

Nevertheless, this historical backdrop feeds into people's fascination with the Arthurian legends. After all, most legends start with a grain of truth.

Evolution of a Legend

In the 12th century, two centuries later, Arthur was transformed into the king we know today. Geoffrey of Monmouth's *Historia Regum Britanniae* is the first writing that shows Arthur as a ruler over the fictional kingdom of Camelot.

These myths and legends reached their peak in the medieval period with famous works by writers like Chrétien de Troyes and Sir Thomas Malory, who penned the famous *Le Morte d'Arthur*. This story shows when the grand King Arthur gained his Knights of the Round Table, the quest for the Holy Grail, and the tragic love story between Lancelot and Guinevere. It is the perfect example of how legends serve the values of the time with these new themes of chivalry, morality, and the human condition.

Their Significance

The enduring appeal of the stories of Arthur and how they were changed and adapted over the centuries is tantamount to their significance. The stories and legends began as a symbol of unity and resistance, and they provide a shared identity and a heroic past for a society that grapples with change and strife.

These stories evolved. To keep the myth alive, people added in new ideals and values to reflect new social mores and perhaps new aspects of life that troubled the people at the time. They held the stories of Arthur in such high regard that they had an effect on the people who heard them. The myths offered a way to discuss ethical and moral dilemmas, much like theater.

In our modern times, the Arthurian legends are still important. They are meaningful enough to be regularly reinterpreted and revisited in literature, film, and pop culture. These stories touch contemporary audiences just as much as those people in the past.

Chapter 6 – Spiritual and Religious Upheaval

In this chapter, we're going to dive a little deeper into the religion of the Druids to understand the profound effect the Roman presence and retreat had on spiritualism and religion in Britain.

The Druids were considered the intellectual elite of Celtic society. They were not just religious leaders; they were also highly regarded for their wisdom and knowledge. Many Druid leaders held multiple roles within society as priests, teachers, judges, and advisors to the elite. As religious leaders, they conducted the various rites and ceremonies required of them. However, the respect they commanded in Celtic societies was bestowed upon them because they carried their ancestors' knowledge and were believed to be the direct link between the people and the gods.

Due to the lack of a written language, the Druids were the keepers of all knowledge, including laws. As such, they presided over legal disputes, interpreting the laws of the people. They were considered the final arbiters in many matters. They worked alongside the tribal leaders to maintain social order and justice.

As the keepers of knowledge, the Druids were also educators. They mostly educated the elite, teaching subjects like religion, history, philosophy, and even astronomy. What little we know of the Druids shows a long life of training among their own. Training and learning could take twenty years or more. This was because they were required to learn and memorize centuries of information that had been passed down through their oral tradition.

Beliefs and Practices

As with most oral traditions, much of what defined the Druids has been lost in time. Their knowledge and belief systems were never written down, and with the advent and rise of Christianity, the Druids eventually died out. Today's Druidic practices are thought to be close to what the Druids practiced centuries ago, but there is no way to know for sure.

We know that the Britons and the Druids were deeply intertwined with nature, though. They revered natural elements and places like rivers, trees, and oak groves, all of which seemed to have been considered sacred. Archaeological evidence and the writings of neighboring peoples show this interconnectedness with nature and a belief in the immortality of the soul.

Most of our understanding of the Druids comes from Roman sources, and as such, they need to be translated and looked at with a discerning eye. The Romans depicted them as a people who sacrificed often, which is true to an extent. Their rituals, like many religions, made offerings and sacrifices to the gods to appease them.

While the Romans often claimed that the Druids participated regularly in human sacrifice, this is heavily debated. Archaeology does support the potential for human sacrifice through bog bodies. Specifically, the Lindow man suffered a violent death that included strangulation, a blow to the head, and a slit throat. Some have interpreted the location of his body and his injuries to mean he was ritually sacrificed, but again, this is highly debated and potentially influenced by the biased writings of the Britons' enemies, the Romans.

The Britons and Druids celebrated seasonal festivals that marked significant points, usually for agricultural reasons, throughout the year. These included festivals like Samhain, which marked the end of the harvest season; Imbolc, which celebrated the coming of spring; Beltane, which celebrated the arrival of summer; and Lughnasadh, which was the harvest festival. They were religious in nature but also important communal events.

Roman Influence and Druidic Resistance

As we have already established, the Romans brought a multitude of different ideas and ways of life with them, which included a new religion with its own pantheon of gods and goddesses. This was a direct challenge to the Druids and their traditions. The Romans looked down on the nature-based religion of the Britons. It differed too much from their structured pantheon and state-sponsored religion. Despite their polytheistic religion being tolerant of other deities, they clashed with nature-centric worship and, more so, the influential role that the Druids played in Celtic society.

The Romans were focused on subjugating the population, and the Druids' guidance of the local populations was concerning to them. The Druids had an incredible ability to mobilize the locals, especially against the Romans. Whether that happened frequently is a mystery. As we stated, most of what we know about the Druids comes from accounts written by Romans like Julius Caesar and Tacitus. And as the popular saying goes, history is written by the victors. Therefore, these writings and interpretations need to be viewed carefully.

Decline and Persecution

The Romans' conflict with the Druids started well before they even landed on Britain's shores. One of the most momentous events for the Briton Druids was the Roman campaign against the island of Anglesey (Mona) in 60 CE. Led by Suetonius Paulinas, this attack was on a known stronghold of Druidic power and, therefore, linked with Briton resistance to Rome. The Roman attack on the Druidic island was not only a military endeavor; it was also a chance to break down the power the Druids held over Britain. Tacitus wrote about this campaign in great detail and described how the Romans wanted to dismantle the power structures of the Druids.

They didn't only use their military prowess to fight the Druids, though that alone was quite successful. Their legal changes to the island, along with the cultural imperialism, undermined the Druids' authority and impact at every turn. The Druids held sway over the traditional societal structures. When the Romans came in and established their own administrative system, laws, and cultural practices, they slowly eroded away these traditional structures. All of these Roman beliefs and the eventual arrival of Christianity marginalized the Druids and their effect.

In spite of what it may seem, the Romans did not focus entirely on the Druids in their campaign. Their desire to diminish Druidic influence was part of a larger campaign against the Britons to suppress anything the Romans considered dissent or resistance. Because the Druids held major authority over the people, they were often seen as a focal point. They became an easy target. The Druids faced their own legal and social restrictions and, sometimes, outright persecution by Romans and those Britons who sided with Rome.

Even with all this conflict, the decline of the Druids' power was still quite gradual. This was most likely due to the fact the remote areas had little to no Roman influence. The actions of the Romans were not the only reason for this decline. Cultural and religious shifts undermined the Druids' status as well. Starting in the 4th century, the rapid spread of Christianity offered yet another religious alternative that was fundamentally at odds with both the Roman polytheistic religion and the nature-based pantheon of the Druids.

Christianity and Britain

Christianity began to rapidly take hold of the Continent and the islands of Europe in the 4th century. This process was a substantial transformation for the island of Britain, the Britons, and the Romans.

The exact arrival of Christianity in Britain is a contended topic among historians. The general consensus leans toward an introduction sometime during the Roman occupation. This was most likely related to the increase in trade and movement of people during this period, thanks to the new connections with the vast Roman Empire. It is plausible that the ideas of Christianity first arrived on the island not through priests but through Roman soldiers, traders, or administrators. The spread started slowly, with the first signs appearing in the urban centers where Roman authority was more pronounced.

Celtic cross.[23]

Archaeological discoveries help identify when early Christianity started to flourish in Britain. The most notable sign of Christian presence is the Chi Ro symbol associated with Christianity. In a Romano-Briton villa at Lullingstone, the Chi Ro symbol was found in stone during excavations, indicating that someone in this home had converted. The appearance of chapels and distinctly Christian burials in certain areas also points to the arrival and spread of Christianity by the 4th century.

The influence of Rome in the spread of Christianity in Britain and Ireland has been of considerable historical interest. Although the arrival of Christianity is fiercely debated, there is an agreement among scholars that the Roman Empire was directly connected to the arrival of Christianity in Britain. This is supported by the initial evidence appearing in the urban centers. However, archaeologically, there are few signs of Christianity in more remote areas. It is possible these signs could have simply been lost over time.

When it came to the Romans, the empire's stance on Christianity evolved considerably during the period of Roman occupation in Britain. Christians originally faced major persecution by Rome. However, in the 4th century CE, Emperor Constantine converted to Christianity, and the proclamation of the Edict of Milan in 313 granted Christians religious tolerance. This was a crucial turning point for the Christian religion, as a more open and flourishing practice spread throughout the empire, including Britain.

This acceptance was furthered by Emperor Theodosius in 380, when Christianity was officially declared the Roman Empire's state religion. This declaration swiftly led to the establishment of formal church hierarchies and the construction of churches across the empire. Combine this with the extensive trade networks and road systems of the Romans, and one can easily see how Christianity spread like wildfire.

Roman Christianity in Britain easily replaced the old pantheon. The organizational structure that followed the Roman model slid right in to replace the old religion. The church was hierarchically organized, mirroring society, with bishops playing a central role. Bishops often held significant sway in religious and civic matters of Roman Britain, much like the Druids of the Britons once had.

Christianity and Local Traditions

The Christian religion was quite adept at blending with pagan religions. The spread of Christianity was never a simple replacement of the old religions; it would better be described as a slow process of syncretism, the merging of Christian beliefs and practices with indigenous traditions. For instance, pagan traditions were transformed into the Christian celebration of the birth of Christ (Christmas). This process of syncretism was a pragmatic and effective approach to facilitating the acceptance of Christianity among the local peoples.

The process of syncretism was a gradual one, and the transition from traditional religious practices to Christianity was uneven. Some communities converted quickly, while others held on to their ancestral systems for a long time.

The Spread of Christianity after the Romans

The Roman withdrawal did not signify the end of Christianity in Britain. In fact, the period after the Roman withdrawal marked a new chapter in the religion's spread and impact.

Unlike the political vacuum that formed with the exit of the Romans, the spread of Christianity actually gained momentum and began to flourish. Embracing the religion had once been seen as a way to resist the Romans; with the Romans gone, a Briton could explore the religion with a more open mind. The growth during this time can largely be attributed to the abundance of missionaries. These missionaries came from local neighborhoods and abroad. They revitalized and spread the word of God across the island.

This process is most documented in the neighboring island of Ireland. St. Patrick was one of the most notable missionary figures and provides an example of what likely happened in Britain during this period. St. Patrick's efforts in the late 5th and 6th centuries were crucial in the establishment of Christianity in Ireland to the point where the island eventually became a center for Christian learning and missionary activity even though it was never ruled by Rome.

St. Augustine arrived in Kent in the late 6th century. St. Augustine was sent by the church in Rome to Christianize the Anglo-Saxons of Britain. Augustine and his missionaries were pivotal in the establishment of monasteries and churches throughout Britain, which became the focal points of religious life, education, and the spread of Christian beliefs.

One of the largest tasks these missionaries had was establishing monastic communities. These monasteries were more than just centers of worship; they were also part of the cultural life of the region. They were places of learning and where knowledge was preserved in writing. Through these efforts and by establishing themselves as part of the Briton community, monasteries became beacons of Christianity.

The monasteries held a lot of influence due to their role in the broader economic landscape of post-Roman Britain. They were involved in various forms of agriculture, which contributed greatly to local economies. Many people found work and prosperity in the monasteries. Their lands were worked by the monastic community, producing food for sustenance and trade. Monasteries became integral parts of the local and regional economies, often influencing trade and agricultural practices in the surrounding areas.

This period of missionary activity laid the groundwork for the eventual acceptance and integration of Christianity into post-Roman Britain until it became the dominant religion. The work of these early missionaries ensured that the Christian faith would grow and evolve while adapting to the changing social and cultural landscape, although that was not always for the better.

Chapter 7 – Art, Language, and Literature Pre- and Post-Roman Britons

In the next few chapters, we will be taking a look at parts of the Briton culture and comparing how they were before Roman authority and then after. The Romans had a meaningful impact on Briton culture, but it may surprise you how much of the traditional ways were preserved or enhanced by Roman influence rather than replaced.

Art and Craftsmanship Pre-Rome

The Celtic peoples, including the Britons, are well known for their artistic expression. The artistic and cultural landscape of Britain before the Romans was as distinct and diverse as the people who lived there. Briton art and craftsmanship was a union of local creativity and the external influence of the Celtic peoples of the Continent. The Britons are known for their ingenuity when it comes to their artistic expression during the Iron Age.

Much like their spiritual beliefs, the hallmark of pre-Roman Briton art is a deep connection to the natural world. Art was a form of aesthetic expression but also deeply engrained in their religious and social fabric. Intricate patterns were central in their artwork. These were often abstract and complex, with spirals and knotwork. They served both symbolic and ornamental purposes. Their bowls and beakers were decorated with spirals, chevrons, and zoomorphic figures.

The Celtic art tradition that began on the European mainland was quickly adopted in Britain. This style is known for its intricate patterns of knots, spirals, and geometric shapes, which could reflect symmetry but always reflected harmony with its fluidity and movement.

Celtic art in Britain was a fusion of styles developed on the island and those that came from trade and interactions or migrations with neighboring cultures. It showed an incredible understanding of balance and harmony, with negative spaces perfectly entwined with positive spaces to create a unified whole. This art graced decorative objects and their everyday, practical items.

Craftsmanship in pre-Roman Britain was equally remarkable. The Iron Age Britons were skilled metalworkers. They were particularly noted for their work with iron, bronze, and gold. Iron Age Britain saw the creation of elaborate jewelry, weaponry, and ceremonial objects that reflected the social status of their owners and the technical prowess of those who created them. The finer metalwork was often decorated with the Celtic art patterns mentioned above and was functional while also telling stories and beliefs.

Art of the Britons after the Romans

The art of the Britons was decidedly influenced by the Romans. As the Roman Empire declined, the Britons carved out a new and distinctive artistic identity that carried their old harmony and balance with new themes. This era saw a blend of Roman influences with the burgeoning native styles. This can be seen the most in metalworking and the new art of illuminated manuscripts.

Metalworkers continued to create objects that were functional and richly adorned with intricate and swirling designs. These designs featured newer geometric patterns, zoomorphic motifs, and symbolic imagery that reflect a melding of cultural influences.

Manuscript illumination was something distinctly new to the Britons, who were introduced to the written language by the Romans. The use of vibrant hues, elaborate borders, and illustrations on manuscripts took the same kind of art from carvings and metalwork and transferred it to the pages of books and scrolls. These were decorations but also told stories around the words on the center of the page.

These artistic developments were indicative of a society in transition. The people were reforming their identity after the departure of a colonizing force. They got to choose what cultural influences were important to them and create something new that was their own.

Language of Pre-Roman Britons

Language is one of the first places historians and linguists look for signs of cultural fusion. So many languages are a combination of original words and those borrowed from other cultures that they have encountered over time. The languages of pre- and post-Roman Britain are no different.

The Iron Age in Britain was predominantly characterized by Celtic languages, a branch of the Indo-European language family. The languages used by the Britons were part of a larger group of tongues spoken across western Europe. These languages are known to classical authors as Continental Celtic or Insular Celtic.

Continental Celtic includes the languages spoken by the Keltoi and Galatae. It was used widely from around 500 BCE to 500 CE and spoken from Gaul to Iberia to Galatia. Because the early Celtic peoples' cultures predominantly celebrated oral traditions rather than the written word, our knowledge of these languages is limited. The main sources of information, like much information about the early Celts, come from names of persons, tribes, and places that are mentioned in the writings of the Greeks and Romans. There are a small number of inscriptions found in Gaul and northern Italy by the Celts themselves.

Insular Celtic was found in what is now England, Scotland, Ireland, Wales, and the small area known as Brittany. Insular Celtic is further divided into sub-groups, such as Irish-Gaelic (often called Goidelic) and the language of the Britons (often referred to as Brythonic). The Irish-Gaelic of the 5th century is the precursor to more modern Scots-Gaelic through the colonization of the northern parts of Britain and the Isle of Man. The Briton languages were widespread over the island of Britain and the Isle of Man.

Even pre-Roman Britain adopted borrowed words into their own languages. The island was not closed off from the rest of the world. While their trade network was smaller, they regularly interacted with other cultures with their own languages and new objects. Traders from the Mediterranean brought weapons and coins that would have been something their language alone could not name. It was a period of discovery, settlement, traditions, and culture full of linguistic diversity.

The Briton Language after the Romans

The linguistic landscape after the Romans withdrew was complex. The predominant language among the regular people remained Brittonic, a form of Celtic, and it continued to evolve. Brittonic was still a part of the Insular Celtic group and eventually evolved into the modern Welsh, Cornish, and Breton languages. Breton was eventually found on the European mainland through migration, and these are the people who colonized Brittany.

Latin had been introduced by the Romans and was still used by the elite who resided in the more Romanized regions. As time passed, Latin gradually receded as a common language and remained more religious in nature. With the fall of Latin and Brittonic, the new Germanic dialects brought by the Saxons, Angles, and Jutes rose into greater use. This period marked the precursor to the creation of Old English.

Preserving their History

Pre-Roman Briton society was dominated by oral traditions and histories. There is some evidence of a type of written language, but it does not appear to have been widely used. Before the Romans, there was a rich oral culture among the Celtic tribes.

Oral traditions do not refer to methods of storytelling or entertainment. They were an integral part of the ancient people's everyday life and the transmission of knowledge. That was why Druids went through at least twenty years of study before gaining their role and position in society. These traditions encompassed a wide range of forms, including myths, legends, songs, and folklore, all of which were meticulously passed down from generation to generation.

The oral narratives of the Britons were deeply connected to their spiritual and religious beliefs. The Druids used these stories to impart moral lessons and to maintain societal norms. They taught about their understanding of the world around them, nature, the gods, and the cosmos. It reflected their worldview in which the natural and supernatural worlds were linked together.

Moreover, these oral traditions were in no way static like the written word. They evolved and adapted to the needs of the community with each retelling. A Druid put emphasis on certain aspects of a story to teach the lesson needed at the time. This fluidity allowed for the incorporation of more contemporary events and figures into older tales. These new elements were relevant to the newer generation, much like the Arthurian legends.

These oral traditions also served as a means of resistance and resilience during the Roman occupation. Despite the Romans pushing their own culture and language, the Britons maintained many of their own traditions. These oral histories provided them a way to preserve their cultural identity under foreign rule much better than written histories would have.

The transition from oral to written traditions began to take place more significantly after the Romans left. This was something brought on by the Anglo-Saxon invasions. However, the imprint of these ancient oral traditions can still be seen today in the remnants of Celtic languages, folklore, and cultural practices of Britain.

The Effect of the Romans on Literature

The Romans introduced their written language to Britain, which changed how the people kept records, ran their administration, and, eventually, literature. Latin was used for official purposes only, which may have been why the Anglo-Saxons had a more profound effect on oral traditions than the Romans. However, the Romans started changing a society where written documentation began to gain importance, especially among the elite. Oftentimes, in history, one can find the elite appreciating the written word since that kept the knowledge and, therefore, the power in their hands since the common people often did not have access to learning the written word.

This only applied to the Romanized regions, though. Many of the rural and remote areas maintained their original emphasis on oral traditions. This duality created a unique situation where the Briton traditions and the new Roman traditions not only coexisted but also affected each other.

When the Romans left, the area was open for new powers and new people to take charge. The Anglo-Saxons filled that emptiness. They influenced the prevalence of the written word, and their oral traditions began to blend with that of the Britons.

The transition from oral to written histories was greatly accelerated by the arrival of the Anglo-Saxons. They already had a strong tradition of the written language with their use of runes before they transitioned to the Latin alphabet. The period of Anglo-Saxon rule saw the creation of extensive written records like the *Anglo-Saxon Chronicle*, which detailed the history of the Anglo-Saxons in Britain.

Chapter 8 – Daily Life and Society

Pre-Roman Britain was typified by community layouts. These villages were the foundational units of society and reflected the Britons' way of life, cultural practices, and social organization.

The typical settlement would have been a cluster of roundhouses. These structures were generally made from timber frames with low wattle-and-daub walls and large thatched roofs. The circular design was structurally sound and an efficient way to maintain heat in a cooler climate. The size of their houses varied, which has often been interpreted as indicating the status of the individuals who lived there.

The villages were laid out organically rather than strictly planned. The roundhouses were often built close to each other. The Britons seemed to prefer small, tight-knit communities, often thought to be made up of kin groups. The center of the village might have been a communal space for meetings and gatherings. Where these villages were located was directly related to the agricultural land, water sources, and the defensive advantages in the landscape.

Agriculture, Craftsman, and Trade

As we have mentioned before, the Britons are a highly agriculturally based society. Most of these communities were based on farming and animal husbandry. The land around the villages was divided into fields for cultivation, pastures for livestock, and common areas for communal use and processing. The Britons practiced a mixed farming economy, which meant they grew crops like wheat, barley, and oats while rearing cattle, sheep, and pigs.

Craftsmen were an essential part of village life and were supported by the farmers. Artisans, such as potters and weavers, gained prevalence instead of families just creating what they needed. Metalworkers played a vital role within society as well, providing the community with essential goods.

Trade was an important aspect of this Iron Age society. Villages often engaged in the exchange of goods with neighboring communities or even foreign traders. Developing this type of society meant the people could enjoy a more prosperous way of life where they could focus more on one occupation instead of several. It also meant that a surplus was created by the farming class so they could support the lives of the craftspeople.

Briton Society

Large festivals, religious ceremonies, and communal feasts were common in the Britons' lives. The Druids were central figures in these communal activities, as it was their responsibility to maintain the norms and values of the people. These were not only religious gatherings. They served as opportunities for the exchange of information, ideas, goods, and marriage alliances.

Due to the nature of their tribal society, the threat of conflict was a constant concern. Violence was defined differently in Celtic societies, with a series of conflicts being completely acceptable and expected. Many villages prepared themselves for these expected conflicts by constructing defensive structures. Hillforts were commonly constructed in certain regions that provided refuge in times of war. These were often situated on elevated ground and fortified with earthworks and wooden palisades. We will talk more about hillforts later.

How Communities Changed after the Romans

The Romans introduced new architectural forms, urban planning concepts, and infrastructural developments to Britain. The Roman towns and cities are the most notable of these changes with their grid street layouts, public buildings, and fortifications that differ greatly from the Briton village structure. These urban centers were often built near existing Briton settlements, not only to bring the Britons into the Roman fold but also to attempt to control the populace.

These urban centers were strictly Roman. No aspect of Briton society was present, and those living there were expected to maintain the Roman way of life. They were completely symbolic of Roman power and "civilization" and were the antithesis of the Britons' way of life. They were a signal to the Britons to adapt and rise or maintain their way and fall.

Rural Britons under Rome

Many rural communities and villages retained their traditional structures throughout the Roman occupation. In these areas, one could still find clusters of roundhouses functioning in the typical agrarian lifestyle.

These communities, while maintaining their village lifestyle, did not remain completely untouched. Roman trade and culture affected their way of life but in a less obvious way. The demands of Rome and the new trade and market economy demanded that these people adapt to new farming techniques to produce more than they were used to. It was a matter of maintaining their society while serving a different lord.

Local chieftains and tribal leaders were under the overarching authority of Rome but still held power in these rural areas. The social balance remained largely intact with the traditional ways of the Britons as they served the empire. These tribal leaders built elaborate villas throughout Britain but retained far less power than they once held.

With the departure of the Romans, these rural communities and their leaders once again saw a rise in power. Local strongmen and tribal identities once again rose as the sole organizing principle of society. The decline of urban centers brought the focus once again on these individual polities.

The chaos that ensued in the political vacuum left by the Romans created a much more insular and defensive Briton society. The construction of hillforts and other similar defensive structures saw a resurgence. Communities sought to protect themselves from the internal conflicts of warring chieftains and external threats from the Germanic peoples.

Roles and Responsibilities among the Britons

Iron Age gender roles were complex and varied across the different communities and tribes. The evidence from the period comes from archaeological findings and stories and suggests a society where roles and statuses were influenced by a combination of tribal customs, economic functions, and possibly some ritualistic practices.

Warrior Elite and Gender Roles

Iron Age Britain was constantly in conflict, so the presence of a warrior elite is not surprising. Young adult males dominated the warrior class. Although men were primarily responsible for warfare and defense, there were exceptions.

The role of women in the Briton warrior class reveals the complexities and nuances of Celtic society. Contrary to many other ancient civilizations that relegated women to domestic roles, Celtic society and the Britons showed many instances where women had a more prominent place in society and even in warfare.

In Celtic mythology and historical accounts, stories abound where women are a part of the warrior class and fierce leaders and strategists. These stories are not fully fictional and support evidence of a societal structure that acknowledged the prowess and capabilities of women in warfare.

Boudica's story, while exceptional, suggests that women could step beyond traditionally viewed gender roles. It did not take Boudica long to gather her great force against the Romans. Even with the prevailing displeasure with the Romans, if women were viewed in only a domestic sense, then she would have faced much more difficulty getting the people to follow her into battle. The societal structure of the Britons allowed for such things.

It is important to stress that though there are instances of women doing exceptional things like Boudica, they were exceptions rather than the norm. The majority of women in Briton society, as far as we can tell, likely served roles that were more traditionally aligned with domestic responsibilities. However, the mere fact that women could ascend to roles of power, even under exceptional circumstances, speaks volumes about the society of the Britons.

Warriors were trained in combat and strategy and were known for their ferocity and courage. The presence of warrior women in Celtic lore and in the accounts of battles against the Romans indicates a society where martial valor was a revered trait, regardless of gender.

Female Roles in Briton Society

These views of women are supported by the evidence of females and even children partaking in performative rituals that involve violence. These rituals were thought to be symbolic ceremonial dismemberments or transformative practices. They could have included sacrifices. A central theme in Celtic belief systems was fertility, death, and rebirth, and it's thought that women and children might have played a large role in reenactments of these themes or in symbolic acts representing the cycle of life. At Danebury and Maiden Castle, archaeologists uncovered the remains of women and children that showed signs of a violent death and dismemberment. These Iron Age sites might provide evidence that these people were part of sacrificial rites or rituals.

It is important to note that the exact nature and significance of these roles are not fully understood. They are subject to interpretation based on archaeological evidence, of which there is little, and the accounts of the Romans, which could be potentially biased.

The Harper Road burial in London dates to around 50 to 70 CE and reveals a woman buried with objects that reflect high status and power. It included items that suggest that she was connected to both the Iron Age Briton way of life and the Roman Empire, which is supported by the dates of the burial and the location. This evidence also indicates that Briton women could hold positions of significant influence and prestige.

Health and Social Inequalities

Bioarchaeological data collected from two Iron Age Briton cemeteries shows an absence of evidence for abuse against children, older people, and women. In fact, despite the obvious social hierarchy, the skeletal data shows very little difference in health between higher-status and lower-status individuals. Status in these burials was determined through the orientation of the grave, animal symbolism, and grave goods. Certain animals represented different statuses. The horse represented power and nobility. Birds were often associated with someone who held spiritual and shamanistic status. Boars were often associated with warriors.

Skeletal markers suggest that the diets of the higher- and lower-class individuals were very similar. The only difference between the groups was the evidence of harder labor among the lower classes compared to the higher classes. This is not to say that there were no disparities in health between the classes; they simply are not as marked as in other societies.

However, this changed after the Roman conquest. There is a marked increase in burial evidence for inequalities explicitly linked to differences in age, sex, and status after the Romans arrived. Skeletal remains show that more abuse appears to have occurred against women, children, and the elderly. Much more observable and probably harder-felt inequalities occurred, which was most likely due to enslavement. In fact, post-Roman occupation shows an overall decline in health and evidence of abuse in these vulnerable groups, mostly females. It seems the potentially performative ritual violence continued and increased based on evidence of disarticulated body parts found in obviously sacred spaces to the Britons, but there's much debate regarding the interpretation of these remains.

Briton Family Dynamics

The core of Briton society, as we know it, was tribal. Multiple tribes were scattered across the landscape, each of which was led by their own chieftain or king. These tribes served as political entities and familial units. Kinship played a crucial role in defining social relations, inheritance patterns, and leadership structures. The Britons' concept of family extended beyond our recognition of the nuclear family, encompassing a wider network of relatives. Loyalty to one's tribe and family was paramount. The desires of the individual were almost nonexistent in relation to the family.

In Briton families, it seems that both men and women had defined and complementary roles. While society was predominantly patriarchal, with men holding most of the leadership roles, women in certain tribes enjoyed considerable rights and respect. Women could own property, engage in trade, and sometimes even lead tribes. This level of female autonomy was notably different from the Roman model and surprised many Roman historians, hence our knowledge of it.

Tribal leaders and chieftains were often selected based on their lineage. The role of a leader was often passed down within a single family. This hereditary principle underpinned the tribal hierarchy. Leadership was ensured to remain within a particular family or clan. This concept of inheritance and succession was about power, but it was also about maintaining the spiritual and cultural continuity of the tribe.

Children within Briton families were raised with an emphasis on the community and family. From a young age, boys and girls were taught the skills necessary for their future roles within the tribe. Boys often learned hunting, warfare, and farming, while girls were taught weaving, cooking, and other domestic skills. However, as we have mentioned, this did not preclude women from learning to fight or men from engaging in domestic activities. The survival and success of the tribe often required versatility and adaptability from all its members.

Family life was inextricably linked to Briton religion and spirituality. Many tribes practiced a form of animistic or nature-based spirituality. A family's connection to their ancestors and the natural world was a key aspect of their religion. This spiritual dimension influenced aspects of their daily life. Agricultural practices revolved around nature and its rhythms. Rites of passage marked momentous life events like birth, marriage, and death.

Marriage seems to have served both personal and community affairs. Some marriages served to strengthen alliances between families and tribes to ensure stability, mutual support, and cooperation. Others could be what we term a love match. It seems that many marriages were arranged with an element of personal choice and affection. The dowry system was common, where both the bride's and groom's families contributed to the union.

How the Romans Affected Family Life

Because Briton society was organized by family, the immediate impact of Roman rule was the introduction of Roman law and administrative systems. These tribal and kinship relations were replaced in some areas by a new order with a more centralized system. Roman law emphasized patriarchy and paterfamilias (the male head of the family), which could have potentially altered the existing power dynamics within Briton families. Tribal leaders and kings no longer held sway unless they adhered to the Roman way of life, which meant their families no longer held power as they used to. Roman officials and local elites, who were often coopted from the Briton aristocracy, gained prominence over the family unit.

In those regions closer to urban centers and military settlements, these changes to family dynamics would have been felt harder. These regions saw those traditional Briton family structures undergo changes while they adapted to the more nuclear family concept of Rome. They would have been encouraged, if not forced, to set aside their familiar loyalty to the extended family to instead support their immediate family, breaking apart a cohesive tradition.

The Roman economic system would also have played a crucial role in reshaping family dynamics. With family and the concept of family loyalty a large part of society, the shift to Roman currency, trade practices, and property laws would have influenced the way families engaged with the economy. Briton families that fully embraced these changes could find the potential to rise in social status.

Societal Expectations among the Britons

If we dig deeper into the tribal society of the Britons, we find that the tribes were independent. The island was not a cohesive mix of small kingdoms; instead, it was a scattering of families that often fought among themselves for power and, more importantly, prestige. It was a very different system than that imposed by the later Roman administration.

Pre-Roman Britain was fragmented. Numerous tribes governed their own small territories. These tribes constantly changed because of alliances, conflicts, and power struggles. Leaders were chosen by lineage, but their ability to lead in war became far more important. A chieftain's authority was not only political but also held significant religious and social implications.

Since warfare was a common aspect of tribal life, a strong chieftain or king needed to prove himself (or herself) a skilled and competent warrior. Inter-tribal conflicts over resources, territorial disputes, and personal vendettas/revenge were frequent. Martial prowess became a feature that was highly valued. Societal expectations required leaders with strong skills and every able-bodied member of the tribe to be trained in combat.

Although the tribes were hierarchical, this was mitigated by their sense of communal responsibility. The wealth and resources of the tribe were often shared. The chieftain had a major but not absolute claim over the people. At the same time, it was the chieftain's or king's responsibility to make sure all of their people were taken care of. You can see this mentality in the burial remains from the period, where grave goods and burial practices were far more indicative of status than differences in diet and health. The community felt a strong sense of mutual dependence and cohesiveness. The people of the tribe were expected to contribute to the health and welfare of the entire tribe. This could be accomplished with farming, craftsmanship, or other means of production.

When speaking of societal values, it seems that honor and loyalty were paramount. Personal bravery in battle was obviously highly esteemed in this warrior culture. Feats of valor were often the path to social prestige and respect. Most of society and laws revolved around the concepts of maintaining the honor of the family and remaining loyal to the tribe.

Roman Influence on Briton Society

The more centralized and hierarchical structure imposed by the Romans obliterated the tribal-based society in many areas. The Britons that did not hold Roman citizenship, called Peregrini, still lived their traditional way of life. However, certain restrictions were put in place by Roman law. These restrictions controlled who could own land with a Latin title and who could serve in the Roman legions to gain prestige.

After the Romans withdrew, the traditional way of life gained new momentum. However, there were massive numbers of soldiers, mercenaries, nobles, officials, and even farmers who declared themselves as kings. Even those not trying to claim power for themselves didn't necessarily want to return to the previous tribal-based societies; rather, they wanted to establish a new centralized rule reminiscent of what had been introduced by the Romans.

Briton Agricultural Practices

We have mentioned agriculture before; it would be hard not to since it was such a large part of Briton life. The agricultural practices of the Britons were both simple and sophisticated for their time. The landscape of pre-Roman Britain was much different from what we see today. Large parts of the country were covered in dense forests that would disappear during the Middle Ages. The Britons had to clear sections of woodlands in order to create space for their fields and villages. They used simple iron tools that included the adze (a curved blade set at a right angle to the handle) and ards (a type of simple plow). The ard was particularly momentous since they could now take advantage of heavier soils compared to earlier plows.

The Britons mostly grew cereals, with barley and emmer wheat being the most common. The British climate restricted what they could grow, and these cereals were the best suited for the colder and wetter summers. They used small plots, often referred to now as Celtic fields. These small fields were rectangular or curvilinear in shape, depending on the nature of the surrounding landscape. These fields were indeed small compared to our modern farms, with most being less than an acre since they had to manually plow them. Each field was part of a larger, communal patchwork of cultivated land. They did not fence in their fields; instead, they surrounded them with banks or ditches.

The Britons also grew legumes like peas and beans. Whether they understood it or not, these crops would help enrich the soils by fixing nitrogen, an agricultural practice still used today. This rudimentary understanding of crop rotation and soil fertility was important for sustaining agriculture in a period where there were no synthetic fertilizers. It is also believed that they cultivated smaller crops of flax for the purpose of making linen and various herbs and vegetables. Our knowledge of the specifics of these smaller gardens is limited due to the scarcity of archaeological evidence.

Each season throughout the year was marked by specific agricultural tasks. The spring was the time for sowing crops besides winter wheat. Summer was spent tending the fields and their herds of cattle, sheep, and pigs. The late summer and early autumn were harvest time, which could mean prosperity or famine, depending on the weather. Winter was a quieter time for more domestic work like weaving and other jobs that could be done in the home.

Farming was a communal effort, with the families working their plots and sharing equipment like plows and oxen. The entire community came together for harvesting. The chieftains and kings often had larger estates that would be worked by dependents, tribal members, and even slaves. These leaders determined the distribution and storage of any surplus produce. It was on their shoulders to support the tribe in times of harsh winters or crop failure.

Their farming methods were effective for their time and needs. They managed to sustain their communities and even create surpluses in good years. The introduction of iron tools was a noteworthy advancement that greatly improved their efficiency.

Rome's Great Influence on Agriculture

To understand the power of Rome on the Britons' agricultural practices, let's imagine what it would be like to introduce modern machinery to a workshop that uses manual tools. The Romans brought with them the heavy plow called the carruca. This was an incredible advancement for the Britons and the tough clay soils of southern Britain. The Britons' lighter plows cleared more land than their predecessors, but the Roman plows furrowed deep and readied more land for crops than could be accomplished before.

The Romans also introduced a wider variety of crops with newer types of wheat, spelt, rye, and oats. They introduced grapes for winemaking and viticulture. The British weather made this difficult, as the Mediterranean vines struggled in the colder, wetter climate. The orchards, however, flourished with an abundance of apples, pears, and cherries. They introduced a new concept of crop rotation that decreased crop failures due to maintaining more soil fertility. The Romans were able to maintain a more stable food supply.

Although the British climate was wet, that did not mean their fields were abundantly productive. Next to the new plow, perhaps the second-best Roman contribution to agriculture was the concept of irrigation. This opened up more land for cultivation that would not have been considered before. The Romans built aqueducts and canals for their baths, fountains, and fields. In the wetter parts of Britain, this also meant turning wet, marshy land into sustainable and arable fields by drawing the water away.

The smaller scattered farms often gave way to larger Roman-style villas. These sprawling estates became the epicenters of agricultural activity and were often owned by Romanized Britons. They were homes but also statements of the wealth that came with adopting the Roman way of life. These estates were fueled by a mixture of slaves and free tenant farmers.

The Romans also introduced new breeds of cattle, sheep, and pigs that were larger than their British counterparts. They produced more meat, wool, and leather, providing the surplus needed for the massive trade networks Britain was now connected to.

The construction of roads made it easier to move people and the military across the country, but they also made it easier to move goods. Grains, meats, and other produce could easily and quickly travel over these well-maintained roads, not only connecting villages and urban centers but also trade ports. Despite these networks of roads, the influence of Roman agricultural advancements did not sweep the country. The more remote areas like those of modern-day Wales and Scotland were still dominated by the traditional Iron Age farming practices.

Roman Changes to the Economy

The Roman economy was another world compared to that of the Iron Age Britons. The Roman Empire was characterized by a complex economy that was monetized, commercialized, and highly integrated. They introduced their economy to the island of Britain and might have been the most profound change experienced by the Britons. A market-based economy brings more prosperity but often leads to more hierarchical complexity with larger gaps between the different levels of society.

One of the most significant changes they made was introducing a single monetary system. Roman coinage became widely used, which facilitated an increase in trade and commerce. This institutional monetary system also allowed the implementation of a taxation system. Taxes were a crucial aspect of Roman economic control and a bone of contention between the Britons and the Romans. Roman taxation in Britain involved direct taxes on the land and the people, as well as indirect taxes on their goods and trade.

Although the Britons exploited the mineral sources of the island for their intricate metalworking, the Romans considerably developed the mining and metallurgy industries. They extensively mined gold, silver, lead, and tin at a much greater level than the Britons. These mining operations supported the local populace and Rome's trading network. Mining was one of the reasons the Romans created the British province. Towns developed around these mining locations, bringing more urbanization into previously remote areas.

While the Britons had an international trade network, it was in its infancy compared to what the Roman Empire had built. Britain became fully integrated into the vast trading network of the empire. The people of the island benefited from importing goods like wine, olive oil, and luxury items from other parts of the Roman world. They exported surplus grain, wool, and metals.

The Romans also brought more crafts industries. After the arrival of the Romans, there were more pottery-making facilities, glass production, and textile manufacturing. These industries were often the center of new towns, which later became economic and administrative centers.

The impact of the Roman economic system was felt more in the south and east of Britain than anywhere else. Roman control and influence were not capable of extending farther north and west, although it was not for lack of trying. The Romans encountered incredible resistance in these areas and eventually considered it not worth the effort, considering how well the rest of the province was fairing.

Chapter 9 – Warfare and Defense Tactics of the Britons

We have touched briefly on the emphasis on warfare in Iron Age Britain already. Military affairs were deeply entrenched in Briton society. In the absence of a centralized government like the one introduced later by the Romans, each tribe was responsible as its own self-contained military unit.

Briton Military vs the Romans

The Roman invasion of 43 CE presented an interesting study of the clash between two distinctly different military cultures. The military organization, training, and equipment of the Briton warriors were inferior to that of Rome, but even with that, they often triumphed and showed considerable resilience and ingenuity.

In the face of the Roman invasion, the fragmented nature of Briton society was both a strength and a weakness. In order to stand a chance, the tribes needed to form coalitions, and at the same time, each tribe had its own methods and styles of warfare developed over time to fight each other. This made joining forces against Rome difficult. At the same time, it is harder to conquer a society that has no centralized government to overturn. It requires intensive military strategy and numbers to overcome and subsume all the different polities.

Rome's military operated under a highly structured and unified military system. The Britons' approach to warfare was more reactive and inconsistent due to a lack of cohesion. Some tribes chose to resist the Romans fiercely, while others chose to submit and avoid conflict.

Briton warriors were trained from a young age. This was not like the formal training received in Rome, though. The skills they needed for combat were taught and learned through hunting, controlling inter-tribal skirmishes, and engaging in mentorships. Young men were taught to handle weapons like swords and spears and to value stealth, tracking, and ambush. They hunted their enemies like they hunted their prey. These skills were crucial to their more guerilla style of warfare.

This type of training is what led to the warrior ethos that was centered around individual prowess, one of the few individual aspects of their society. Briton warriors were known for their fierce and passionate fighting. They were fueled by the need and the drive to, first and foremost, protect their family. Many written records speak of their charges into battle with a zeal that was awe-inspiring and terrifying. However, ferocity and terror only went so far. They often lacked the discipline and coordination compared to the Roman legions. Their style might work well against other tribes, but the Roman legions were another enemy entirely.

Iron swords and spears were the primary weapons the Britons used. The sword was prized for its versatility in close combat. They used shields made from wood, which sometimes were reinforced with metal or leather. They served as a defensive weapon but also signified a warrior's status.

Where the Britons rose above the Romans was with their use of war chariots. These chariots were the hallmark of Briton warfare and were used with great effect against the Romans in the early stages of the invasion. They allowed for more rapid movement across the battlefield, supporting their more hit-and-run style of combat.

Armor was almost nonexistent. Many tales speak of the Britons and other Celtic warriors entering battle with little protection. According to historical accounts, they were often simply "clad in skins." This lack of heavy armor aided in greater mobility and supported their quick style of combat and guerilla tactics. However, it did leave them vulnerable to the more equipped Roman soldiers.

The Britons, like other Celtic peoples, were adept at using their natural environment against their enemies. They employed their hit-and-run tactics, ambushes, and night attacks to catch the enemy off guard. The Romans were not familiar with the British landscape, and the Britons used this to their advantage. These tactics might not have been as effective on the battlefield, but they were helpful in smaller engagements and in causing disruptions to the Roman supply lines and their reconnaissance efforts.

In open battle, the Britons often found themselves at a disadvantage. The disciplined formations and superior equipment of the Roman legions often outmatched the Britons with their more chaotic and individualistic fighting style. The famous Battle of Watling Street during Boudica's rebellion is the perfect example of this. While Boudica and her forces found many victories in their rampage against the Romans, their first encounter in open battle quashed their rebellion instantly.

Over time, the adept Briton leaders learned from the Romans and adapted their tactics. They started to adopt more organized formations and strategies, though these changes were not widespread or uniform.

Impact of Roman Tactics and Warfare on the Britons

One of the most profound changes in the Roman administration was the formation of a formal and hierarchical military structure. The Romans brought this concept of a standing army, organized into legions with a clear chain of command. This structure was a sharp departure from the Britons' approach, where warfare was largely a part-time occupation for tribal warriors. Because of Roman influence, some Briton warriors began to understand and adopt aspects of the more organized approach to military affairs.

Roman military training was rigorous, systematic, and continuous. They focused on discipline, stamina, and combat skills. The Britons, in comparison, were more sporadic and less formal with their training methods and became exposed to this new concept of warfare as an occupation. With warriors gaining prestige and status in their own culture through battle, it is easy to see how this concept would have been appealing. The Romans used this to their advantage by creating laws that would require Britons to adhere to Roman life and gain citizenship in order to take on this occupation.

The Romans introduced new types of weapons and armor. The Roman gladius (short sword) and pilum (javelin) were far more advanced than the typical long swords used by the Britons. Roman armor offered better protection with chainmail and plate armor. Compared to the leather or simple animal skins that the Britons wore, this was far superior protection on the field of battle.

The Romans also developed feats of engineering when it came to warfare. Though the Britons were incredible engineers, none of that knowledge had been applied to the battlefield. The construction of Roman forts, roads, and defensive walls, like Hadrian's Wall, demonstrated their advanced strategies in both offense and defense. The Britons primarily relied on hillforts for protection.

Roman tactics covered several scenarios, ranging from open-field battles to siege warfare. The Britons' guerilla-style warfare only served certain scenarios and proved useless when engaged in open battle. The Britons used chariots in war, but the Romans introduced the concept of a more traditional cavalry. Roman cavalry units were used primarily for reconnaissance and rapid engagement and were a new element to the Britons. It was a simple shift for the Britons to go from chariots to more formal cavalry units.

The Roman military machine was not just about physical warfare; it was also a psychological tool. The discipline, order, and might of the Roman army were intended to awe and intimidate. For the Britons, this presented a new psychological dimension to warfare, where morale and discipline became just as important as physical prowess.

How Britons Waged War

There are only a few documented engagements between the Britons and the Romans, the most famous being Boudica's revolt. Despite their crushing defeat at the Battle of Watling Street, the conflict has continued to live in history as a symbol of resistance against oppression. The Britons were vastly outnumbered and outmaneuvered, but even so, they fought with a raw courage that has become synonymous with the Britons' legacy.

Briton military strategy was often shaped by their immediate needs and tribal dynamics rather than grand strategic designs. Tribal chieftains, who were respected both as leaders and warriors, were the linchpins of this strategy. They rallied their warriors, not just with the promise of plunder or territory but also with appeals to tribal loyalty and shared heritage.

By the Battle of Watling Street, it is believed that Boudica's numbers reached as high as 230,000 to 300,000 warriors. Historians continue to state that these reports should be looked at with a healthy amount of skepticism. Suetonius Paulinus, having regrouped his forces, commanded an army of almost ten thousand men. Considering these vastly different numbers, you can understand why historians advise us to be skeptical regarding the numbers reported by writers like Tacitus. When they were writing to further the Roman agenda, they were more likely to exaggerate a Roman victory.

Suetonius Paulinus stationed his ten thousand soldiers at a narrow passage, now referred to as Watling Street, with woods behind them to cover their flank. In front of them was a wide plain. Most agree that the Romans were heavily outnumbered. Even if the Roman soldiers were lined up only one deep, they would not have extended past Boudica's line. This strategic positioning forced Boudica to attack from the front, putting her at a distinct disadvantage considering Briton war tactics. Despite being poorly equipped, they expected a victory, as the Roman reports claimed that wagons full of families were stationed at the far end of the field. However, the Britons suffered a resolute defeat. Tacitus claims that Boudica poisoned herself after this incredible loss, but others attribute the loss to complacency and say that Boudica later died from illness and was given a lavish burial.

Another hallmark of Briton resistance took place in what is now modern-day Scotland around 83 CE. The Battle of Mons Graupius was documented by the famous author Tacitus, through whom we learn a lot about the Britons and Celtic peoples. Being a Roman, his writings are often interpreted as exaggerated, but they still share a wealth of knowledge. This particular campaign was launched by Gnaeus Julius Agricola (who happened to be Tacitus's father-in-law) against the Caledonians of the north. This tribe happened to be the last unconquered Briton tribe and regularly avoided open conflict with Rome. As such, Rome changed tactics and went for their granaries immediately after the harvest. The Caledonians had a choice: engage in battle or starve over the winter.

If Tacitus can be trusted with numbers, the Romans possessed a formidable force with eight thousand allied infantry, three thousand cavalry, and Roman legionaries in reserve. Estimates for the exact size of the Roman army range from seventeen thousand to thirty thousand. The Caledonian army was said to be over thirty thousand strong and held the higher ground, with their forces maintaining a tiered horseshoe shape up a hill for maximum field coverage. On the level plain between the two armies stood the Caledonian chariots.

After some missiles were fired, the Roman infantry attacked and cut down the lower tiers of the Caledonians quickly. The upper tiers attempted to flank the Romans but were beaten to the punch; they were flanked by the Roman cavalry. The remaining Caledonians were expertly pursued through the woods. Tacitus reports that 10,000 Caledonian people died that day compared to only 360 Romans. Even with the remaining twenty thousand Caledonians successfully evading pursuit in the woods, Agricola was declared the victor and claimed that he had finally subdued all the tribes of Britain. Not only was this greatly exaggerated, but some even argue that this battle never happened.

The Britons' Fortifications

When it comes to Briton ingenuity in defense and settlement, hillforts stand out as their monumental creations. Hillforts dotted the landscape in many regions from around 1000 BCE until the Roman invasion.

The construction of hillforts was another example of how the Britons used the natural landscape to their advantage. Points of naturally elevated ground were sought out since they offered strategic vantage points over the surrounding area. They were ideal locations for surveillance and defense. The choice of location was never random. It was carefully considered to ensure maximum visibility, defensibility, and access to essential resources like water.

The design of these forts evolved over time to cater to the needs of the people, changes in social structure, threats, and the available technologies. Early hillforts were relatively simple. They were built on naturally elevated ground and surrounded by a single rampart and ditch. As the Iron Age progressed, there was an increase in complexity. The ramparts were constructed from earth or stone. A combination of the two slowly became more prevalent. Some hillforts developed multiple lines of defense that included networks of ditches, banks, and wooden palisades. Some hillforts even built stone walls.

Although a hillfort's primary purpose seems like it would be for defensive purposes, hillforts were not military structures. They were the homesteads of powerful leaders and were designed to provide a place of refuge for their people when needed. The size and complexity of a hillfort directly reflected the power and wealth of the chieftain who controlled it. These forts became focal points of the local communities, as it was a place where they could trade, gather, and conduct rituals.

Some scholars propose that the hillforts housed agricultural surpluses, especially in the fertile regions. Surplus and food storage were often targets in warfare, so protecting the people's food would have been paramount for survival. Some excavated hillforts have shown evidence of granaries, which support this idea.

Initially, the primary threat to these communities would have been other local tribes vying for power and prestige. As the Iron Age progressed, new people began to arrive on the island, presenting new dangers. New challenges meant new strategies were needed.

In response, these hillforts became more complex and formidable. The introduction of new building techniques and materials, partially brought about through contact with mainland Europe, led to stronger and more durable structures. Some hillforts were even refurbished and expanded during times of heightened threats well into the Roman invasion.

The decline in the use of hillforts is closely linked to the Roman occupation of Britain. Most hillforts posed little defense against the advanced tactics and siege technology of the Roman military. Combine that with the shift in Roman governance and the emphasis on urban centers and networks of roads guiding travel through the landscape, and you can understand why the people's focus shifted away from traditional forms of living, especially among the elite.

While some hillforts were abandoned during the Roman period, others were refurbished and integrated into the new Roman landscape. Hillforts that were abandoned during this time were sometimes reoccupied after the Roman withdrawal to house the new elite who found themselves at war yet again.

Chapter 10 – The Britons and the Wider World: The Anglo-Saxons and Becoming "English"

During the Iron Age, the Britons were not cut off from the rest of the world. Their network of relationships varied from friendly trade with neighbors and seafarers to hostile incursions. All of these interactions played a role in shaping the cultural, economic, and political landscape of the Britons well before the Romans arrived. The Celtic peoples are well known for resisting conquest by taking the pieces of the cultures they encounter that they like and making them their own.

Neighboring Tribes

There is no denying that the Britons gained themselves a reputation for being a violent society, much like the neighboring Irish tribes. Though there was conflict, it was not as bad as historians and the Roman and Greek writers made it out to be. Today, historians try to bring focus away from the disparaging writings of that time and focus more on archaeological interpretations of a people who have been grossly misinterpreted thanks to Roman propaganda.

The interactions between the different Briton tribes were complex. The larger tribes, like the Iceni in the east, the Brigantes in the north, and the Silures in the west, no doubt went through tumultuous times with each other. In a culture where warrior prowess was valued and needed for advancement, there would have been skirmishes and raids to display that prowess. Most of these cultures, much like the Irish and the Native Americans, had strict rules for conflicts that controlled when this violence could occur and what could happen.

Despite these more violent encounters, alliances were common. They came and went, though, depending on common enemies or a need to strengthen economic ties. With so much land that could not be tilled or turned to pasture with the tools they had available, usable land had to be acquired in order to support a growing population.

Conflict between tribes was just as common as cooperation was. The most common disputes seemed to be over land, resources, and power, and these often led to skirmishes and minor wars. These conflicts remained local and limited, unlike their later confrontations with Rome. Regardless, they were still important when it came to shaping the culture of the Britons.

Trade

Trade was imperative and happened between neighboring tribes and distant cultures. Not every tribe had access to all the natural minerals, but they still participated in the beautiful metalworking that the Iron Age is known for. These tribes could either trade for the minerals they needed or trade for finished products. Many tribes traded widely, exchanging their local resources like tin, iron ore, and agricultural surplus for imported goods, whether imported from other areas of Britain or outside the island. Evidence of trade routes has been discovered that link Britain and Ireland to the Mediterranean and beyond.

Trade is important from an economic standpoint, of course, but there is also a cultural aspect. Through trade, the Britons were exposed to new ideas, technologies, and artistic styles. You can see this in the Mediterranean influences found in later Briton art and craftsmanship.

During the late Iron Age, the Britons' connection to more distant cultures grew. There was an increase in the presence of Roman merchants and mercenaries, who were hired to help with tribal conflicts. They were exposed to the Roman culture well before Julius Caesar landed on Britain's shores. Roman goods like pottery, wine, and olive oil were already shown in the archaeological record before the Roman conquest.

The effect of the Celts, a widespread cultural group across Europe, was evident in Britain. The La Tène artistic style, characteristic of the European Celts, found its way into Briton art, indicating a shared cultural heritage or at least substantial cultural exchange.

The arrival of the Belgae from the European mainland in the 1st century BCE is another example of the Britons' interaction with distant cultures. The Belgae, possibly fleeing the expansion of the Roman Republic in Gaul, settled in southeastern Britain, bringing with them new cultural and military practices.

Northern Neighbors

The Britons and the Picts were perhaps the two most prominent groups in ancient Britain. The relationship between these two groups seems to have been much the same as between the other tribes. There was a combination of conflict, cultural exchange, and even cooperation.

The Britons, for the most part, cover the tribes living in what is now England and Wales, but this may be oversimplified. Some historians now consider the Picts to be Britons, as they were direct descendants of Bronze Age Britons inhabiting the northern parts of the island.

The Picts are the people and tribes that inhabit what we now call Scotland. Their name is likely derived from the Latin word *Picti,* which means "painted people." They were named this by the Romans because of their practice of painting their bodies with lime and possible tattooing. There is not much evidence to differentiate whether they practiced tattooing or simply painted designs on their skin for conflict. Notwithstanding the basic similarities, they were distinct from the Britons of the south in terms of culture, language, and societal structure. This is why there is a debate on whether they should be classified as Britons.

Much like the relationships between the southern tribes, the relations between the Britons and the Picts often involved conflict. The Picts have been labeled as fiercely independent people who frequently clashed with their neighbors, but that could be propaganda. Remember the Caledonians? They often worked hard to avoid conflict with Rome. We cannot say for sure if that was because they knew the Romans were a more experienced opponent or because the tales of the violence in the tribes were exaggerated. The conflicts that occurred would have most likely revolved around the need for land, resources, and political control.

Despite the conflicts, there was a degree of cultural exchange between the Britons and the Picts. This exchange was likely facilitated by trade and intermarriage. Artistic influences, particularly in metalworking and stone carving, suggest a level of interaction that went beyond mere conflict. The Picts were renowned for their symbol stones, which exhibit artistic styles that might have been affected by their southern neighbors.

When faced with a common enemy, the Picts and the Britons were known to join forces. This is most especially noted in the conflicts with Rome. There is evidence to suggest regular alliances between the southern Britons and the northern Picts throughout the Roman occupation.

The Picts, being above Hadrian's Wall, were saved from severe Roman influence, giving historians and archaeologists an insight into their lives. Over time, both the Britons and the Picts faced external pressures that reshaped their societies. The Britons contended with Anglo-Saxon invasions, as the Picts faced challenges from both the Vikings and the emerging Scottish kingdom. These pressures eventually led to the decline of Pictish independence and the assimilation of Briton territories into emerging medieval kingdoms.

The Opening for the Anglo-Saxons

The period after Rome withdrew from Britain is often referred to as the dawn of the Early Middle Ages. It heralded a monumental shift in power within the political sphere.

The Romans didn't suddenly leave Britain; it was a gradual affair. Starting early in the 5th century, several phases of migration took place, which made the problems they had been facing on the island that much worse. Infighting among those who wished to replace the Romans at the top of the hierarchical ladder was prevalent.

By 410 CE, the Romans were officially gone, but the leadership crumbled, as the Romans had abandoned the people, left no plan, and established no ruler for those who remained behind. Without any unity on the island, the instability opened the door for new people to enter into the turmoil and fight for power. Before anyone really realized it, a group of people had established their own settlements on the island, giving them the needed foothold.

The Arrival of the Anglo-Saxons

The Anglo-Saxon invasion spans from the late 4th century to the early 7th century. It was not at all a quick process like with Rome, which might have been the reason for its eventual success. The influx of Germanic peoples from the regions we now call Denmark and northern Germany may have traveled along the coasts first as raiders, but the richness of Britain called to them. They saw an opportunity to thrive with better soils, warmer weather, and vast mineral resources.

Their initial forays were largely opportunistic. They capitalized on the weakened state of Rome and then on the weakened and distracted state of the Britons after Rome's departure. These coastal raids were profitable. They specifically targeted the areas where the Romans had accumulated considerable wealth. The raids were frequent and devastating.

The frequent raids eroded away the settlements on the coast. These Roman settlements could not recover and were abandoned or went into disuse. As more of these settlements fell and became less profitable, the Germanic peoples, including the Angles, Saxons, and Jutes, began to look for footholds to facilitate raiding farther inland. The eastern and southern shores of Britain bore the brunt of these early attacks. Archaeological evidence shows the establishment of a series of beachheads from which they staged further raids.

There were many motivations for these raids. Their home regions were becoming vastly overpopulated and also suffered from considerable political unrest. Raids were a way for lords to gain more power and wealth, which would allow them to remain at the top. The more successful raiders might have seen that Britain could provide them with bigger opportunities than they could ever gain on home soil.

The process of settlement was sporadic. A series of waves brought Anglo-Saxons who raided and left, those who decided they might stay a while, and then those who decided to make the island their home. These settlers started to carve out their own territories for themselves, taking advantage of the disunity that plagued the island. Families and larger groups replaced the smaller raiding parties.

This led to regular conflicts with the existing Briton and Romano-Briton populations. Being successful warrior societies themselves, the Germanic tribes established a dominant presence in various parts of Britain. The nature of their integration with the local Briton populations remains a subject of historical debate. Theories range from violent displacement to a more gradual assimilation and intermarriage.

The first settlements were placed to take full advantage of the local resources. These settlements were no longer designed for raiding; they needed to support a small population instead. The settlements were strategically located on fertile land, near water sources, and with natural defensible positions nearby. The nature of their relations with the local Britons varied from region to region. Some regions showed obvious signs of violence during this period, whereas others showed more interaction with cultural exchange.

No matter how it happened, the new Anglo-Saxons settled and thrived. They brought new customs, languages, and social structures. These new ideas eventually imprinted themselves on the local inhabitants in some way.

The success of the Anglo-Saxon invasion of Britain could easily be attributed to their similarities with the traditions of the Britons. Unlike Rome, the Germanic tribes organized their society into small kingdoms and tribes that carried their own hierarchy and laws. Family and kinship ties provided their central social structure and affected everything from legal disputes to land ownership. It is easy to see from our perspective how quickly the non-elite of the opposing groups would have settled into a more cooperative relationship once they realized how similar they really were.

One of the more enduring impacts of these new people was the introduction of what would become Old English, which eventually led to our modern English language. As the Anglo-Saxons gained more power and control, the Celtic and Latin languages gradually disappeared in many areas. Place names, many of which are still used today, reflect the Anglo-Saxon influence on the island. The layout of fields, villages, and even road systems in many parts of England today still reflect the organization brought to the island by these Germanic tribes.

The Formation of Kingdoms

We have mentioned the Anglo-Saxon kingdoms previously, and the trajectory of the Anglo-Saxon kingdoms is outside the scope of this book. However, these early kingdoms signified the end of the era of the Britons. Once these kingdoms gained power, very little remains of the Britons to follow through history. In fact, the Anglo-Saxons themselves saved the term mostly for the people who lived in what is modern Wales.

Northumbria

Northumbria stretched from the Humber to the Forth. While most recognize the name Northumbria, they do not know that it formed out of the union of two lesser and early kingdoms named Bernicia and Deira. Due tot Brittonic names and archaeological evidence, it is believed that while the kingdom was ruled by an Anglo-Saxon lord, the people were Britons. Located in what is now northern England and southern Scotland, Northumbria became the center for Christian scholarship and art. It is from this kingdom that we received the beautiful Lindisfarne Gospels.

Mercia

Rising to power in the central region of England was Mercia. Mercia was, at one time, the most dominant Anglo-Saxon kingdom. Over time, its power extended even farther south and east. Because of its expanding power, it was often in conflict with its neighbors. Mercia is a good example of the new governance and military power of the Anglo-Saxons.

Wessex

Wessex is perhaps the most famous Anglo-Saxon kingdom. Wessex rose to power later in the Anglo-Saxon period thanks to leaders like King Alfred the Great. Alfred's reign was pivotal in sending Britain on the path to becoming a unified England.

East Anglia

East Anglia had access to the North Sea and rich farmlands. With the immediate sea access, this kingdom developed as a trading hub with continental Europe. It is best known for its wealth and artistry, which is witnessed in the famous Sutton Hoo ship burial found there.

What Happened to the Britons?

"What happened to the Britons?" is a question that opens a window into a complex chapter of British history. The fate of the Britons varied considerably across the different regions that made up these early Anglo-Saxon kingdoms.

In some areas, the arrival of the Anglo-Saxons led to the displacement of the Briton communities. Archaeological and historical accounts suggest that many Briton populations moved west and north to avoid the Germanic incursions. While forced migration due to conflict is a viable reason, there also could have been voluntary relocations due to the tumultuous political and cultural landscapes.

However, the interaction between the Anglo-Saxons was not always conflict and displacement. There is plenty of evidence of the Britons being subsumed into the Anglo-Saxon settlements. Over time, many Britons adopted the Anglo-Saxon customs and language, leading to a blended culture that eventually formed the early English identity.

In regions like modern-day Wales and Cornwall, the Briton identity persisted. These areas might have found it easier to maintain their Briton identity since they had not been as influenced by Rome. With a stronger personal identity left to them after the Roman occupation, it might have been more difficult for the Anglo-Saxons to exert their own authority there.

Even with the strength of the Anglo-Saxon kingdoms, there were substantial holdouts of Briton culture. Briton kingdoms formed in several locations. Notable among these Brittonic kingdoms were Gwynedd, Powys, and Dyfed in Wales and Strathclyde and Rheged in what is now Scotland and northern England. These kingdoms stood against the Anglo-Saxon expansion and often cooperated in warfare to fight against their common foe.

The legacy of the Britons endured through these kingdoms. The Welsh language is a direct descendant of the language spoken by the early Britons. Elements of Briton culture, mythology, and folklore survived here and blended with both the Anglo-Saxon and the later Norman culture.

Conclusion

The time of the Britons up to the Anglo-Saxon invasion and rise to dominance is a period rich in cultural, political, and social intricacies. The era of the Britons is pivotal to the creation of not only modern England but also the cultural identity of the entire island today. It is often overshadowed and ignored in favor of the more documented and vibrant developments during the Middle Ages and modern history. Despite this, the Britons are a crucial part of the foundational layers of Britain.

Starting with the earliest Celtic inhabitants, we set the stage for a unique and fascinating cultural development. The intricate patterns of Celtic art and the myths and legends that survived centuries of oral traditions speak volumes about their worldview and lasting legacy for all of Britain.

Even during the few centuries under the control of one of history's greatest empires, the Britons survived and thrived, saving parts of their heritage. They rose up against a talented foe despite all the odds stacked against them. They had fought them before—they had to know that their superior numbers did not mean much against a professionally trained military—but they were inspired and driven to try anyway.

Roman roads, cities, and institutions left not only a mark on the physical landscape but also on the people themselves. Despite being considered an inferior people, the Britons showed the Romans otherwise. The Romans, in the face of their self-proclaimed superiority, never stayed totally or completely unchallenged. In spite of the Roman efforts to subjugate the Britons in any way possible, the Britons held out in regions all over the island.

Even when the Romans left, the Britons fought to endure. In this period of uncertainty, upheaval, and obscurity, they remained and transformed. The power vacuum left by the Romans ignited a period of realignment, a period where Briton leaders fought for dominance once again. Inspired by their past and their traditions, this era gave rise to heroes who stood the test of time, like King Arthur.

As the shadow of a new enemy loomed over the island, the Britons stood at a crossroads once again. One era of conquest shifted into another. The resilience and adaptability of the Britons ensured that their legacy would still be felt and that they would survive yet another attempt to consume them. Some stood strong against the wave, while others saw no reason to fight and blended into the new. They all would continue to create the wonderful cultural fusion that defines Britain today.

Part 3: The Battle of Britain

A Captivating Guide to One of the Most Critical Battles of World War II

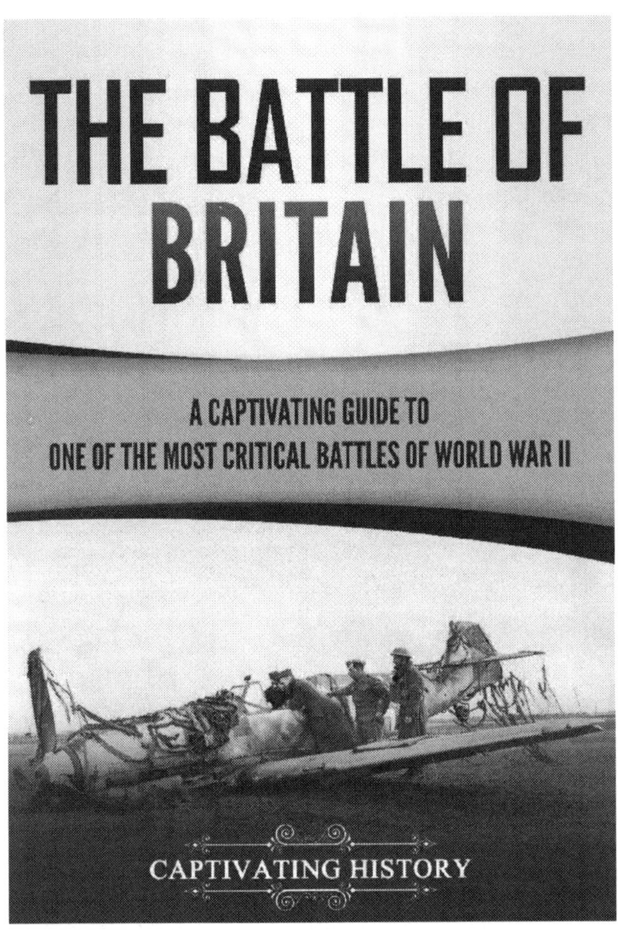

Introduction

There is almost no way to overstate the importance of the Battle of Britain. It was exceptionally important in 1940, and in many ways, it's exceptionally important now.

There is an entire book genre called alternative history, which might be better understood as "what-if history." In these books, authors take a specific event or period in history and reverse or alter the outcome. One of the most common scenarios is what would have happened if General Robert E. Lee did not order Pickett's Charge at the Battle of Gettysburg or what would have happened if Hitler had been admitted to the Academy of Fine Arts Vienna.

Another favorite topic in alternative history is the Battle of Britain. Despite the many variations on the what-if question, the result would always be the same: Hitler would win World War II and control all of Europe and the USSR to the Urals for at least ten years, if not longer. Think about that. Aside from the idea of personal freedoms being erased from the lands where Hitler's regime ruled, it's likely that millions, perhaps *tens of millions* more people, would have been killed in war and the gas chambers.

That is not to say that other Allied victories were not important. The Battle of Stalingrad and D-Day were extremely important, but strong arguments can be made that Hitler would have been defeated even if those battles had been lost. It's hard to make the same case for the Battle of Britain.

Only one of the famous "Few" (the fighter pilots who won the Battle of Britain) is still alive as of this publication. However, the "can-do" spirit of the men of WWII is very much alive and well. In July 2022, 103-year-old John "Paddy" Hemingway was reunited with a Hawker Hurricane fighter plane, the same type he flew in the summer and fall of 1940.

This book covers the period from the fall of France through September 15th, 1940—now known as Battle of Britain Day. The story of the Blitz, the bombing attacks on English cities that came after the Germans realized they would not be able to invade England, is a story for another time, though it will be mentioned throughout the book and in its conclusion.

Chapter 1 – Sausages?

In March 1935, Winston Churchill was a political has-been. A hero of the Boer War in South Africa in the last year of the 19th century, he had ridden his fame into the House of Commons in 1900. Over the course of thirty-five years, Churchill's political career had gone from highs to lows so many times that people lost count. Like his father before him, Churchill had initially seemed to be destined to become prime minister. In 1935, he still seemed to be following in his father's footsteps, as he was heading toward failure.

Churchill's father, Randolph, had been considered one of the greatest speakers in the House of Commons and a brilliant politician. However, due to a combination of a hot temper, a massive ego, and the syphilis he had contracted as a young man, his behavior became more and more erratic, both publicly and privately. At the end of his life, his once-brilliant career lay in shambles.

Lord Randolph Churchill in 1883. His son Winston was ten at the time this picture was taken [24]

When Churchill gave a speech to Parliament on March 19th, 1935, many people throughout Great Britain believed his career was on the same trajectory as his father's had once been. From 1934 onward, Churchill began to warn Britain that the new German leader, Adolf Hitler, was beginning an arms production program that could only have one purpose: avenging Germany's defeat in World War I. This made Churchill decidedly unpopular with many people, such as the public, opposition parties, and Churchill's own Conservative Party, whose leader, Prime Minister Stanley Baldwin, was convinced that a policy of disarmament was a way to lasting peace and would revive the consumer economy of Britain.

Churchill rose to give his speech amid a clamor of shouts and catcalls telling him to sit down; many already knew the reason he had stood up was to deliver yet another speech on the dangers of Hitler's rearming of Germany, which was a violation of the Treaty of Versailles. This treaty ended WWI, and Churchill believed Germany's rearmament was being done secretly. "I am reliably informed that the working population of Dessau, a small town near Leipzig, increased last year by 13,000 people. And why was that? What is manufactured in Dessau that requires such an enormous influx of workers? Lager beer? Lederhosen? Sausages? ... Aircraft."

Churchill's speech angered most of the men in Parliament, particularly Stanley Baldwin, the party leader and prime minister. He was upset at Churchill's opposition to him and because his facts and figures seemed so exact. He had to be asking himself where Winston was getting his information.

The information was readily available. Departments in the Ministry of Defence and the intelligence apparatus of Great Britain were gathering it, but Baldwin and his supporters either didn't want to know what was becoming increasingly clear, or worse, they had turned a blind eye to it. Many in the Conservative Party (and in England, in general) had come to believe the Treaty of Versailles had been too hard on Germany.

What Baldwin did not know was that Churchill was not completely without support in Parliament and in the bureaucracy. In his over thirty-five years in Parliament, Churchill had cultivated many relationships and supporters. What's more, like his father, he had held some of the most important positions in government. Some of the offices Churchill held were directly related to defense: Secretary of State for Air (1919–1921),

Secretary of State for War (1919-1921), Minister of Munitions (1917-1921), and, most illustrious of them all in a nation that, for centuries, had depended on its navy for safety, First Lord of the Admiralty (1911-1915).

Churchill had connections in almost every part of the British government, especially in the defense and intelligence departments, and a small group of his supporters had begun warning him about Hitler even before the Nazi leader had taken control of Germany in 1933. Even though Churchill was out of office, meaning he did not have a role in the government outside of being a member of Parliament, he received classified information from people who believed that Hitler and Germany were becoming a threat.

A Quick Summary of the Years between 1918 and 1933

The battlefields of World War One fell silent on November 11th, 1918, at 11 a.m. "The eleventh hour of the eleventh day of the eleventh month," as students used to remember it. (By the way, not enough Americans know that November 11th was Armistice Day, lasting from 1938 to 1954. It then became known as Veterans Day.) The German Army still occupied much of northwestern France and virtually all of Belgium, but the army's ability to fight was wearing down rapidly. The German population was also tired of war and beginning to starve because of it.

Almost until the very end of the war, German newspapers and government speeches repeatedly stated that a German victory was "right around the corner." So, though many Germans, especially in the cities, knew the war was not going well, many others believed what they were being told—that is until they were told the war had ended.

Still, the armistice was supposed to be a ceasefire. The Germans were hopeful that an agreement could be reached that was acceptable to both sides. At least, that's what many Germans thought.

However, the German General Staff and its two chiefs, Paul von Hindenburg and Erich Ludendorff, knew the German Army had been defeated or shortly would be. They suggested that a group of German politicians should enter into talks with the Allies to discuss terms to end the war. Most of the men sent to negotiate with the Allies were members of the rising Social Democratic Party (SPD), which called for liberal socialism.

Unfortunately for the Germans and especially the Social Democrats, the Allies were not in the mood to negotiate. The German delegation was given preliminary terms of a "peace treaty" (which really meant "terms of surrender"), and they were shocked and appalled. They had expected to be negotiated with, not dictated to. Hindenburg and Ludendorff knew the German military's position was untenable. If talks were rejected, the Allies, who were now backed by millions of fresh American troops, would be inside Germany in weeks, if not days. Aside from the overwhelming strength facing them, many German troops had already gathered their things and headed home. The German front lines didn't exist in any meaningful way after November 11th.

Over the course of the year, the Allies argued and bargained with one another over the final terms of what would become known as the Treaty of Versailles. There were many terms in the treaty, not all of which had to do with Germany, but most of the terms had a direct effect on the breakout of World War II.

For our purposes, the most important terms of the treaty are as follows. 1) Germany could not have an air force of any kind. 2) Its army was not to exceed 100,000 men. 3) And its navy was limited to small coastal defense boats. No submarines were allowed.

World War One had cost Europe millions of lives, and in the minds of the Allies, Germany was responsible for most of those. This sentiment was clearly stated within the treaty and became known as the war guilt clause.

Many in Germany were appalled by the terms of the Treaty of Versailles, but in 1919, when the German delegation signed it, there was nothing Germans, individually or collectively, could do about it. There was a great deal of resentment toward the treaty, and much of that resentment was aimed at the Social Democrats, even though they were also angered by the harsh terms handed down to them by the Allies.

On the extreme right wing of German politics, the politicians (and, to a great extent, their party) who signed the treaty came to be known as the "November Criminals." Hindenburg and, to a lesser extent, Ludendorff were not seen as the men who recommended approaching the Allies but as the representatives of what many saw as the only stabilizing force in the country: the army.

Starting as early as the 1920s, the German General Staff began making plans for the country's eventual rearmament. Taking the lead on this was General Hans von Seeckt, but many other officers, including some who would become famous during WWII, worked to subvert the terms of the treaty in any way possible.

(For much more information on the Treaty of Versailles and how it contributed to the rise of Hitler, please check out Captivating History's *Treaty of Versailles*.)

Many German right-wing parties, including the Nazis, had paramilitary groups. Many of these groups' core members were WWI veterans who trained younger men in self-defense and the rudiments of military life and combat. Since they were not officially the German Army, this was not a violation of the treaty, though the real army kept a close eye on them, as it did not want to lose its position.

After Hitler came to power in 1933 but before he repudiated the Treaty of Versailles, the German Navy (Kriegsmarine) got around naval restrictions on battleships by building what became known as "pocket battleships." These battleships displaced less water than the limit set by the treaty but were still large and well armed, though lacking a bit in the armor department.

How the Germans got around the restrictions surrounding an air force is of the most interest to us here, and it is also the most fascinating aspect of the secret German plans to rebuild their military.

The most well-known part of this German program involved the Soviet Union. The Germans fought Russia from 1914 to 1917. In 1917, Lenin led the communist Bolsheviks to victory and took Russia out of the war, although the official treaty with Germany wasn't signed until 1918. Though Germany occupied a lot of Russian lands until the war ended, Germans helped Lenin return to Russia from his exile in Switzerland to lead the revolution. This was not done out of friendship or any type of agreement with Lenin's policies. Germany simply realized it was in its best interest to aid Lenin, as he would likely take Russia out of the war if he won.

What's more, once the Soviets were in power, they fomented communist revolutions throughout Eastern Europe and Germany. In Germany, from 1918 to 1920, a low-level civil war was fought between German communists and the paramilitary groups of the German right wing, which ended in defeat for the communists and included what today would be considered war crimes. Despite this, both the Germans and the Soviets had an abiding hatred toward Britain and France, albeit for entirely different reasons. How does the old saying go? "Politics make strange bedfellows."

In the mid-1920s, the German Army and the Soviets struck a deal. For reduced prices on finished and advanced German machine parts, as well as technical advice, the Soviets allowed the Germans to use Soviet planes to train German pilots. The Germans also worked to design and develop their own warplanes. One of the men integral in this effort was future German Field Marshal Albert Kesselring, who had been an infantry officer in WWI but transferred to the German air force, or Luftwaffe, after Hitler's rejection of the Treaty of Versailles. Kesselring commanded a German air fleet in Poland in 1939 and in France in 1940. Later in the war, he was given an infantry command, performing real miracles of defensive action from North Africa to Sicily to Italy. Many of the older pilots who flew in the Battle of Britain had been taught to fly in the Soviet Union.

By definition, a secret program is limited to a relatively small number of people. It would not do for the Germans to ship a large number of young men in their late teens and early twenties to the Soviet Union for pilot training. The risk of the secret getting out would have been too great. However, there was another way in which the Germans could get around the restrictions on flying: gliders.

In the 1920s, especially in the hilly or mountainous regions in the central and southwestern parts of Germany, private gliding clubs began. Sponsored and equipped by some of the richest men and families in Germany, these gliding clubs were extremely popular. You have to remember that human flight was only about twenty years old at the time. During the war, pilots of all countries became exceptionally famous and were called the "Knights of the Air" for their exploits. The most famous of these "knights" was, of course, Manfred von Richthofen, also known as the Red Baron. The man who took over Richthofen's command when the Red Baron was shot down in April 1918 was Hermann Göring, then an attractive, dashing figure and a war hero in his own right. You might already know that Göring headed the Luftwaffe throughout WWII.

Many of these gliding clubs were subsidized or completely funded by the German Army. Those that weren't still had strong ties to the military. The Treaty of Versailles placed no restrictions on gliders, and since gliders provided a basic understanding of flight and flight controls, they were perfect for teaching a new generation how to fly. Through these gliding clubs, hundreds of men were ahead of the curve when Germany was able to develop a modern air force. One of these men would become famous during the Battle of Britain, not only for his skill in the air but also for a famous incident that involved him telling off Göring during the battle. This man's name was Adolf Galland.

Hitler came to power in January 1933. One of the key pillars of his election platform was the repudiation of the Treaty of Versailles. He did not feel strong enough vis-à-vis the Allies (meaning Great Britain and France) or secure enough at home to move forward with the bolder elements of his program.

After Hitler weakened his rebellious SA "Brownshirt" paramilitary and secured control of the armed forces in the summer of 1934, Hitler felt strong enough to face the Allies and move forward with his plans to rearm Germany. On March 16th, 1935, the Führer announced that Germany was henceforth going to ignore the arms and defense restrictions placed on Germany at the end of WWI. However, he was careful to follow that announcement with another, stating that he would respect the borders drawn up after WWI, would be willing to engage in arms limitation talks on an equal basis with other nations, and would be happy to host such a conference in Germany.

What was the reaction in Britain, France, and the United States, the prime authors of the Treaty of Versailles? There hardly was one. Many in England had come to believe the Treaty of Versailles was too harsh on Germany. Many believed the treaty's economic provisions had contributed to a weakened Germany that was ripe for communism to spread and had contributed to the worldwide depression that began in 1929. What's more, a considerable number of British politicians had come to believe that a strong but westward-leaning Germany would be a check on Soviet power. Hitler's intense anti-communism beliefs gave these politicians hope that Germany would indeed prevent Soviet expansion in Europe.

Not long after Hitler's announcement, Britain and Germany signed the Anglo-German Naval Pact of 1935, which allowed Germany to have a navy but limited it to 35 percent of Great Britain's naval power. Though it doesn't sound like it, this was a "win" for Hitler. Essentially, he went from having no navy to a rather large one with the stroke of a pen. (Hitler later repudiated this treaty as well, in 1939, on the verge of WWII.)

The French were not as sanguine about German remilitarization. It was their countryside, not England's, that had been occupied by the Germans in 1914. The French suffered more combat losses and sustained many civilian deaths. France's most productive agricultural and manufacturing areas fell under German control in 1914 and remained in their hands until the end of the war.

Additionally, many of the French wanted revenge for their humiliating defeat in 1871 at the hands of Prussia, which would eventually become the German nation. The strategic and economically important regions of Alsace and Lorraine, which border Germany, had been annexed by the Germans in 1871. The Treaty of Versailles gave the regions back to France, but the French still desired to make the Germans pay.

However, the French were in a pickle since they relied on their alliance with the United Kingdom for defense. With many Britons taking a neutral stance against the idea of German rearmament, the French sensed they might not be able to count on Britain.

In 1930, the French began to build that now-infamous line of fortifications known as the Maginot Line. Though the Maginot Line has been greatly criticized in the years since France's defeat in 1940, the actual fortifications (at least those built on the Franco-German border) were a marvel of modern technology.

There were thousands of these defensive structures built on the Maginot Line. Estimates for its construction run from five to nine billion US dollars as of 2022.[25]

In the two years or so just before the war, France built an extension of the Maginot Line to cover parts of its border with Belgium. Both the

French and British were concerned that doing so might signal to the Belgians that the Allies were planning to leave them to fend for themselves should the Germans invade again. The Belgians were mollified when it was made clear to them that the Allies would move into Belgium to meet the Germans in the event of another German attack.

Unfortunately, the French neglected to fortify an important part of their border, electing to save money by not building fortifications inside the thick Ardennes Forest. Of course, the Germans concentrated their main thrust there in 1940. Though many Americans scoffed at this oversight, they fell for almost the exact same thing in 1944 in the Battle of the Bulge, where new and battered troops held the line because the Allied high command did not believe the Germans were capable of attacking in the forest, especially in winter. Both nations were wrong, but the French paid a much higher price for their error.

However, back in 1935, the idea of war was far from the minds of most people in England and France. The Great Depression ground on into its sixth year, and people fervently prayed that there would never be a war such as WWI again. The war left a profound scar on France and the United Kingdom. The British had fought not only in France but also in Africa, Turkey, and other parts of the Middle East. Though their number of dead and wounded were less than that of France, as a ratio of their pre-war population, the British suffered a higher death and casualty rate. To this day, the British call the men of WWI the "Lost Generation."

Adding to the emotional toll were the thousands of men who came home wounded in body, mind, and spirit. Throughout Britain but especially in the crowded cities of England, limbless men with hollow eyes haunted the streets. Many of those without physical wounds suffered what we call post-traumatic stress disorder or PTSD. World War I involved artillery shelling on an almost unimaginable level, which caused thousands of men to shake, twitch, and seize up, some to such a degree that lifetime hospitalization was their only choice. The sight of some of these men and knowing that many more suffered in silent emotional anguish as a result of their experiences caused many in the British Isles, from coal miners to politicians, to dread the idea of another war.

As a result, the British reduced their military expenditures throughout most of the post-WWI period. This was not a particularly dangerous policy in the 1920s, for the only real enemy the British had in Europe was Germany, and in the 1920s, Germany was decidedly not a threat. Keeping the levels of their forces up in their colonies around the world while reducing them at home was not a dangerous proposition for the British in the 1920s. After all, the budget for the Royal Navy, England's protection from invasion since 1588 (the year the Spanish Armada was defeated), was still adequate, and Britannia still "ruled the waves," as the popular song went.

To sum up, many British did not view Hitler's rearmament program as an immediate danger to Great Britain. Some even saw it as a good thing since they believed the Treaty of Versailles was too harsh on the Germans and that the Germans could be "useful" against Soviet aggression.

Hitler with Göring (in vest) and influential Nazis Martin Bormann (wearing hat) and Baldur von Schirach.[26]

Not everyone in the British government was so relaxed about the possibility of German rearmament. Though they were in the minority when Hitler came to power and for some time afterward, a few British politicians and quite a number of military men were alarmed by the idea of a remilitarized Germany under Adolf Hitler.

These men, with Churchill being foremost among them, had watched Hitler's rise with alarm. The street violence, the talk of German racial superiority and anti-Semitism, and Hitler's willingness to shed the blood of his own supporters in the 1934 Night of the Long Knives pointed to a larger problem. They had also read his book, *Mein Kampf*, and listened to his speeches. In their view, the book was a literal indication of what Hitler planned to do. His speeches, both before and after his rise to the chancellorship in 1933, were oftentimes angry, vitriolic rants that fired up the German population to seek revenge against the "November Criminals," the Jews, the French, the communists, the Russians, and more. Hitler spoke of "friendship" with Great Britain, whose population he regarded as Germanic, but this friendship would be on his terms. He thought Germany should control Europe. England would keep its colonies and strong navy, but if England stood in the way of his European hegemony, it, too, would fall victim to German might.

Many Britons heard and read these statements but decided to hide their head in the sand, hoping that Hitler's rhetoric was aimed at gaining the people's support. It was thought by many in the United Kingdom that Hitler would see reason and "mellow out" when he came to power. And even if he did rearm Germany, there was always the Royal Navy to protect them.

The Changing Nature of War

It's an old adage that nations do not plan for the next war but plan for the last one. In other words, nations assume the next war will be much like the one they had just fought. This is especially true for the victors in a conflict. It has happened throughout history, so you would think that people would learn by now, but through a combination of arrogance, bureaucratic inertia, and a sense of resting on one's laurels, armies tend to begin the next war by using the same tactics and strategies that won the last one. Usually, that's a bad idea, but hindsight is always 20/20, and looking into the future is quite difficult.

For most of the 1920s and early 1930s, both the British and French were guilty of this faulty thinking. The British had a rightly-earned confidence in the Royal Navy, and the navy would again prove vital in WWII, just not in the way the British had imagined. The French also had confidence, as they had the Maginot Line and a tenacious army that had proven itself in WWI. The British also relied on the strength of the French Army to prevent adversaries from reaching the shores of the English Channel.

Though the Royal Navy had many functions, its prime mission was to prevent the invasion of the British Isles. However, the only realistic route for any invader was to cross the English Channel. By 1940, the British Admiralty realized that positioning ships in the Channel to prevent an invasion was foolish. The narrowness of the passage prevented the maneuvers of large fleets. Powerful new types of coastal guns could also target any fleet.

The British luckily began to correct their errors before WWII began. Had they waited even three months longer to begin their rearmament, history might be completely different.

Over the course of the 1920s and into the 1930s, military thinking began to change, at least in some places. Ideas about land warfare began to evolve. Men like German General Heinz Guderian, French General Charles de Gaulle, British military theorist Basil Liddell-Hart, and American General George Patton realized the tank, which had been developed toward the end of the First World War, would change the way wars were fought.

On the Western Front but, to a degree, on all the front lines, WWI turned into a defensive battle of attrition due to developments in weaponry, such as the machine gun. Many military men realized that static defenses were almost obsolete with the development of the tank and the modern warplane. Used separately, these weapons could be quite effective. Used together in close coordination to overwhelm the weakest part of an enemy's line before moving rapidly into the supply and command areas behind the front line to sow destruction and confusion could win the next war. That was what happened when the Germans attacked Poland in 1939 and France (along with Holland and Belgium) in 1940.

In WWI, two oft-overlooked weapons were deployed: the long-range bomber (long-range for the time) and the Zeppelin. Though both sides deployed these weapons, their use by the Germans is most remembered. Though German and Allied bombers could carry substantially more bombs in comparison to WWI fighters, which could only carry one or two, their range was quite limited, and they were largely confined to raids at or closely behind the front lines. Though bombers were employed in growing numbers throughout the war, it was not until

British recruiting poster, 1915/16.[27]

1917/18 that bombing raids became common, at least in France and Belgium, though their damage was relatively limited.

Zeppelins, such as the famous post-WWI *Hindenburg*, were bags of lighter-than-air gas held together by a metal frame and propelled by four or six engines attached to the command gondola. German Zeppelins (although there were Allied airships as well) carried two to three tons of bombs over the English Channel and over London and Paris beginning in 1915 and continuing almost to the war's end.

There were only about fifty Zeppelin raids on England over the course of those three years. The raids killed about 1,500 people, which, when compared to the over forty thousand people who perished from the German air raids in WWII, was minor. The raids also did comparatively little damage. However, when the Zeppelin raids began and to a degree afterward, they caused panic and affected morale, though not to any permanent degree. They also caused widespread criticism of the government for a perceived lack of defenses.

The Zeppelins and bombers of WWI, on a practical level, were quite ineffective. They were extremely inaccurate, vulnerable to fighters, and relatively expensive to make. However, after the war, air strategists understood that improvements in airplane and engine designs, targeting, and much else would bring new technologies to these weapons, which might make them effective.

In the case of airships, the framed Zeppelin was phased out and replaced by the frameless "blimp." And it would be England that employed them to a greater degree in WWII, using them as observation platforms and as tethered "air obstacles" to prevent low-level fighter attacks on important targets. As a weapon, the airship became obsolete by the time WWI was over, but the bombers' role in warfare was just beginning.

In the years between the world wars, forward-thinking officers in the major powers (including the United States) began to develop ideas about what aerial warfare in the future might look like. The best-known men to work in this area of thinking were Italian General Guilio Douhet and American Commander William L. "Billy" Mitchell. Walther Wever from Germany and Sir Hugh Trenchard from Britain were also influential military thinkers.

In brief, Douhet's premise was that strategic bombers would be the weapon of the future. He is famous for writing that "the bomber would always get through," which turned out to be partially correct. While Douhet understood the importance of the bomber, he did not foresee the improvements in air defense and fighter technologies that World War II would bring.

Billy Mitchell is famous for two reasons, at least in American military history. First, Mitchell was the first to understand the importance of air power at sea, both as a means of defense and, in the form of the aircraft carrier, for attacking. Mitchell famously illustrated the importance of air power at sea and the obsolescence of the battleship when he flew bombing missions over target ships in 1921. Mitchell is also known for being extremely outspoken in his criticism of the United States Navy for building battleships throughout the interwar period.

Hugh Trenchard was responsible for laying the groundwork for what the Royal Air Force ("RAF") would become in 1940. He was appointed head of the Royal Flying Corps in 1918. After the war, he established the command structure and much of the organization of the RAF. (As a note, the "RAF" was the amalgamation of the Royal Flying Corps and the Royal Naval Air Service in 1919.) He also helped to convince Winston Churchill about the future importance of air warfare.

Walther Wever was second-in-command of the Luftwaffe from 1933 to 1936, when he died in a plane crash. Wever was a proponent of Douhet's theories about the bomber and had begun planning for a German long-range heavy bomber fleet, similar to what Britain and the United States were developing. His death changed the trajectory of German aircraft production before and during the war, for Hermann Göring, having been a fighter pilot during WWI, believed more in the production of fighter planes and medium bombers to support combat operations than he did in Wever's idea of strategic heavy bombers. The only German heavy bomber in mass production during the war was the Heinkel 177, which carried too small a payload for its size and was never used to any great effect during the war.

Wever was one of the first to put down on paper what became the framework for the strategic air doctrine, which took hold during WWII and afterward. Ironically, the Western Allies adhered to this framework to a greater and more efficient degree during the war than the Germans. These elements are still among the bedrock principles of strategic bombing today:

1. To destroy the enemy air force by bombing its bases and aircraft factories and to defeat enemy air forces that are attacking targets
2. To prevent the movement of large enemy ground forces to decisive areas by destroying railways and roads, particularly bridges and tunnels, which are indispensable for the movement and supply of forces
3. To support the operations of army formations by impeding the enemy's advance and participating directly in ground operations
4. To support naval operations by attacking enemy naval bases, protecting naval bases, and participating directly in naval battles
5. To paralyze the enemy armed forces by stopping the production of armaments factories

Chapter 2 – Blitzkrieg

Guernica, Spain, after a German Condor Legion air raid, 1937.[28]

The name Guernica, a city in Spain, might strike a chord with you. The bombing of the town in the Basque Country of northern Spain is depicted in the famous painting by Pablo Picasso. A casualty of the Spanish Civil War, Guernica was bombed by the Condor Legion, a group of German fighter and bomber pilots sent by Hitler to aid Spanish fascist General Francisco Franco in his struggle against the Republicans. The Republicans were largely supported by the Soviet Union, though small numbers of

British, French, and American troops aided the Republican effort as well.

The bombing of Guernica set off even more alarm bells in Europe about Hitler's intentions, for he had openly promised that German troops and pilots were only in Spain to train Spanish fighters under Franco. The death toll in the bombing was put anywhere between two hundred to two thousand people killed (in the confused and highly politicized times, a hard number was difficult to determine). In addition, much of the town was destroyed.

The Condor Legion's participation in Spain gave the Luftwaffe its first chance to test its planes, men, and combat theories, which aided the Germans in their upcoming campaigns in Poland in 1939 and Western Europe in 1940. Many of Germany's top fighter pilots and commanders in the Battle of Britain took part in aerial combat in Spain, such as Werner Mölders, Adolf Galland, Hajo Herrmann, Hugo Sperrle, and others.

Werner Mölders, the first man in history to down one hundred enemy planes. Mölders was killed in a plane crash in 1941.[29]

On September 1st, 1939, Germany began WWII by attacking Poland. Poland's hopes rested on a possible French offensive against Germany's western borders to draw off attacking German troops. A small offensive in the Saar region of Germany resulted in the French driving about eight miles before they stopped, as they lacked resolve and feared they were being baited by the Germans. Not a single German soldier or plane was diverted back to the Western Front, and Poland fell in five weeks. It had no chance, as it had been invaded by the Germans from the west and the Soviet Union from the east. Poland's soldiers fought hard but were outnumbered and outgunned. Their weapons were also outdated. When pitted against the two totalitarian countries, Poland was doomed.

However, in a way, the air campaign against Poland fooled the Germans, but this was not realized until after the war. It had nothing to do with the Poles and their resistance but had everything to do with German overconfidence and misreading the results of their efforts.

There's no doubt the Luftwaffe was dominant in the skies over Poland. The record bears that out, and the victory gave German fighter pilots a sense of superiority. Confidence is not a bad thing, as it is needed by any fighting force. However, in Poland, the German fighters were fighting against relatively unskilled pilots in outdated planes.

As for the German bomber fleet, the planes rained death indiscriminately over Polish cities and towns. Warsaw was the most frequent target, not just because it was Poland's capital. It was also Poland's most populous city, and Hitler wanted to terrorize the population into submission. Whether or not the Poles were cowed by the bombing is debatable, but much of the city was destroyed.

The problem for the Germans was that their bombing campaign in Poland led Göring and others to believe their bombers were adequate enough to "do the job" against any adversary. However, they were not. Many of them were too lightly armored and slow. Their bomb loads were too small for the intense war that was to come, yet Göring insisted on building more and more slow and vulnerable bombers. One of Göring's favorite weapons and one of the main tools of Nazi terror in the skies over Poland and later France was the Junkers Ju 87 dive bomber, which famously had sirens attached to its wings to terrify defenders and civilians alike.

On April 9th, Hitler invaded Denmark, which was unsurprisingly overrun in a day, and Norway. German forces attacked Oslo and the airfields of southern Norway, along with important towns up the Norwegian coast. In the south, paratroopers were used for the first time in a combat situation, illustrating to the British the importance of air defense around important installations. The British and French responded by sending ships and troops to major northwestern Norwegian towns and resource-rich areas. The fighting was hard but typically ended in the

Germans' favor. Hitler attacked Holland, France, and Belgium on May 10th, forcing an Allied retreat from Norway.

Germany's operation, codenamed Fall Gelb ("Case Yellow"), included an attack into Holland and Belgium, which the Germans hoped would draw the best divisions of the French Army and the entire British Expeditionary Force ("BEF") into Belgium. The Germans also gave the impression of planning a full-scale attack along the Maginot Line to hold up French troops on the Franco-German border.

Once the Allies moved into Belgium, the German trap was sprung. Seven *panzer* (tank) divisions rolled through the "impassable" Ardennes Forest and, in short order, trapped the BEF and much of the French Army in Belgium. Allied attempts to break through to these forces from the south failed. Soon, over 300,000 British soldiers and a considerable number of French troops had their backs to the English Channel. Their only possible escape route was the Channel.

Though historians agree the "real" Battle of Britain began on July 10th, 1940, in a way, the battle can be said to have begun over the northern coast of France a few weeks prior. The RAF, along with elements of the French Air Force (Armée de l'Air), flew thousands of sorties (a sortie is one individual mission by one plane) over Pas-de-Calais, the northern French coast closest to England.

The battle over France did not go particularly well for the RAF. Though their planes were a relative match for the German Bf 109 fighters, their pilots, for the most part, were not. The RAF pilots had a great fighting spirit, which they would show on a daily basis in the much bigger battle to come, but they were inexperienced. The fatigue the pilots, their ground crew, and their commanders felt was intense, and though morale was high among the pilots, they were aware the fight over Pas-de-Calais was a losing one and that they were there to cover a retreat never before seen in British history.

What's more, their tactics, which had been only somewhat modified from those used in WWI, were outdated and lacked flexibility. The RAF learned quickly, but that would not happen until the Battle of Britain was underway some weeks later. We will tell you more about the tactics of the RAF and the Luftwaffe in the coming chapters.

By contrast, the morale of the men, crew, and commanders of the Luftwaffe could not have been higher. They had gained experience in Spain and won every battle they had been in since then, Britain was next, and in the minds of nearly every man in the Luftwaffe, all the way up to Göring and Hitler, there was no doubt they would soon clear the skies over England as well.

Propaganda magazine of the Luftwaffe, 1942.[30]

Two figures or groups usually come to mind when talking about the Battle of Britain: Winston Churchill and the young pilots of the RAF collectively known as "The Few," but there were so many more people that contributed to Britain's victory. Other than military studies majors and history professors, one crucial name is often overlooked: Air Chief Marshal Sir Hugh Dowding (1882–1970).

Dowding was the officer in command of RAF Fighter Command throughout the Battle of Britain. Dowding's forward-thinking was one of the prime reasons the RAF was ready for the Luftwaffe when it came across the English Channel.

In the next chapter, you'll learn more about the planes that flew over England, the innovations that took place during the fight, and Dowding's role while the battle raged, but for now, it's enough to say that even before the battle started, Dowding's personality and confidence saved England in spite of Winston Churchill.

Churchill didn't panic about what was happening. Panicking was not in his nature. However, sometimes his fighting instinct got the better of him, and he continued to cling to a position to almost the bitter end (in this case, sending virtually all of Britain's fighters over the Channel). His stubbornness had gotten him into political trouble during WWI, contributing to the political isolation he faced during the late 1920s and 1930s. However, his tenacity turned out to be one of Britain's greatest assets during WWII.

While the BEF struggled to hold the line around Dunkirk on France's coast, the Royal Navy and seemingly every private boat owner in England headed over the Channel to rescue the men on the beaches. Meanwhile, the RAF fought a desperate battle with the Luftwaffe.

Most of the losses sustained in the Battle of France took place in the crowded skies over Pas-de-Calais in late May and early June. The RAF lost 959 planes (477 fighters and 381 bombers), and over 900 aircrew members were killed, missing, or taken prisoner, 300 of which were pilots. The Luftwaffe lost 1,129 planes to the RAF and the French. Another three hundred were temporarily put out of action. Just under 1,100 German aircrew members (including pilots) were lost. Nearly 1,400 aircrew members were wounded, and nearly 2,000 were missing (killed in action, missing, taken prisoner, or simply dead and not discovered). The French lost 574 planes. The losses were incredible, especially for a campaign that only lasted about eight weeks, but the Luftwaffe could afford to lose more planes than the British because they had plenty more.

During the Battle of France, especially during the retreat and evacuation at Dunkirk, the RAF flew almost non-stop. Many RAF bombers attempted to interrupt the German advance in any way they could. However, it was the fighter pilots who played a crucial role as the Battle of France drew to a close. They were tasked with preventing the Luftwaffe from turning the beaches of Dunkirk into a slaughterhouse.

As the battle raged, Churchill believed that more squadrons should be sent to France. After it was clear that was unrealistic (as there was nowhere safe in the closing pocket around Dunkirk to base them), he called for more fighter planes to be sent over the Channel each day. Luckily, Dowding had a good enough idea of the Luftwaffe's strength in the area, and he also knew the strength of the British forces. He created an estimate of the number of fighter planes Britain would need to have a chance of defeating the Luftwaffe in his homeland.

Churchill wanted to bring the fight to the Germans, but Dowding knew the battle in France was already lost, both on the ground and in the air. Churchill knew this too, but his desire for victory, his love of France, and his hatred of the Nazis blinded him, for a short period, to the bigger picture. Eventually, Churchill realized that despite a surge in British aircraft production from 1938 onward, the Luftwaffe could bring many more planes to a fight than the RAF could. Dowding knew if Britain's extra planes were shot down, the skies over England would be filled with German planes.

Though Dowding was a stiff, somewhat arrogant man (whose nickname among the pilots who loved him was "Stuffy"), Churchill liked and respected Dowding. "Stuffy" was one of the few men who would openly and strongly tell Churchill that he was wrong. In this case, Churchill was wrong, and he eventually admitted the strength of Dowding's argument. Fighters would be sent to France in limited quantities, just enough to keep the German troops off the beaches, while the rest would stay at home.

This was one of the most pivotal decisions that affected the coming battle. The attrition rate in France had been very high. Had the RAF continued the air campaign across the Channel, it's likely there would not have been enough fighters to fend off the Germans when they came to England.

Air Marshal Sir Hugh Dowding at the time of the Battle of Britain.[31]

Chapter 3 – Sealions and Spitfires

Why did Adolf Hitler and Hermann Göring begin their air campaign against England? First, they were who they were. Both men were megalomaniacs. However, Hitler likely did not want to fight England before his invasion of Poland, but since the British had "dared" to stand up to him, a battle was inevitable. Peace feelers had been sent to the British via Italy's leader, Benito Mussolini, and been rejected outright. Churchill's (and Britain's) defiance was summed up in his famous "Their Finest Hour" speech, which was given on June 18th, 1940. His speech was not hyperbolic; he spoke the truth when he told the British people and the world what was at stake:

"What General Weygand called the Battle of France is over. I expect that the Battle of Britain is about to begin. Upon this battle depends the survival of Christian civilization ... if we fail, then the whole world, including the United States, including all that we have known and cared for, will sink into the abyss of a new Dark Age made more sinister, and perhaps more protracted, by the lights of perverted science. Let us therefore brace ourselves to our duties, and so bear ourselves that, if the British Empire and its Commonwealth last for a thousand years, men will still say, 'This was their finest hour.'"

Churchill in 1941.[32]

Hitler's grand plan, which he had laid out in his book *Mein Kampf,* was to secure what he called "living space" (*lebensraum* in German) for the German people. This living space was to be in Eastern Europe, especially Russia and Ukraine. Some historians believe Hitler never wanted to go to war against Britain for racial and ethnic reasons but that opposing political systems and international goals made it necessary. For years, Hitler had loudly proclaimed his belief that Germany's defeat in WWI happened because it had fought a two-front war against Russia in the east and Britain and France in the west. If Hitler attacked the Soviet Union with Britain at his back, he would find himself in the same situation he had so vehemently criticized. What's more, he could never direct all of Germany's power against the Soviets, and he would need it. At least, that's what he believed in 1940.

The problem for Hitler was the English Channel and the Royal Navy. No invasion force would be able to get even close to England if the Royal Navy wasn't somehow neutralized. Though the German Navy (Kriegsmarine) had grown powerful under Hitler, it was no match for the British. The only possible way for Hitler to negate the Royal Navy's power was to control the air over the Channel and southern England. If the

Germans could destroy the RAF, then Germany's many fighters and bombers might be able to prevent the British from sailing into the Channel from the headquarters of their powerful Home Fleet base in the Orkney Islands off the northern coast of Scotland. If Hitler were to land a powerful force in southern England, it might be possible for German ships to brave the Channel to resupply them. Some German troops could be supplied by air as well.

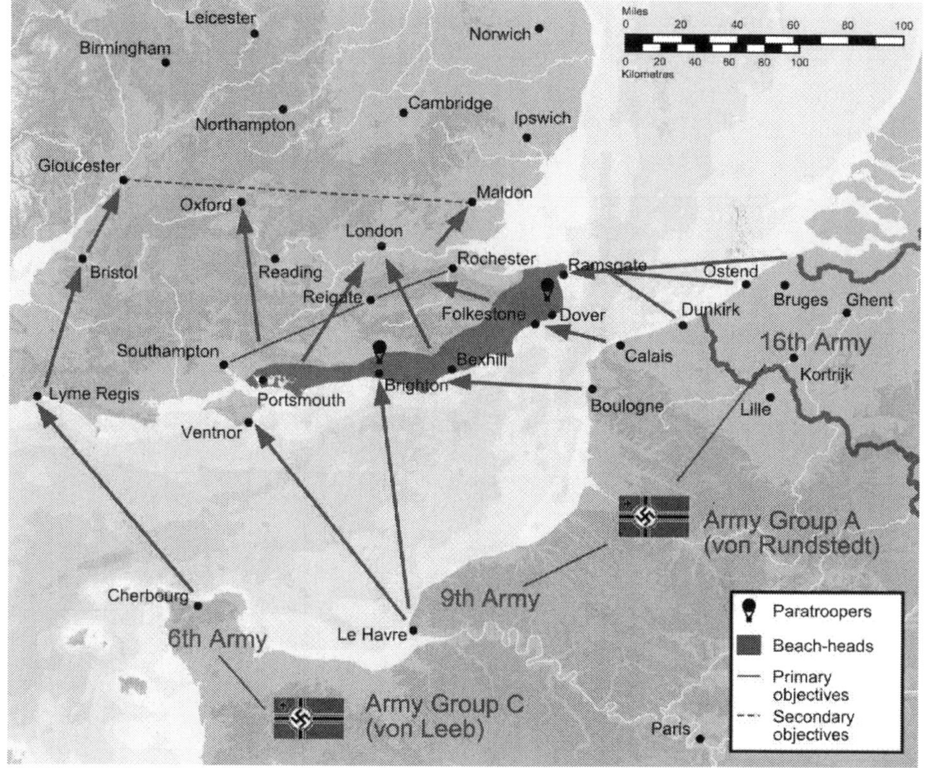

Operation Sealion, Hitler's plan to conquer England.[33]

The future of both nations would be decided in the air over the Channel and southern England. How big were their respective air forces, and what planes did they fly?

RAF Strength at the Start of the Battle of Britain

The Royal Air Force mustered an estimated nine hundred fighter planes at the beginning of the battle, though the Germans believed it had half that. While the battle raged over England, a number of British bombers launched attacks against German targets in France and Germany. The RAF's "Bomber Command" was small compared to what it would become in two years, not to mention by the war's end, numbering about seven hundred, but many of these planes were woefully outdated and quite vulnerable.

Despite the Germans' best efforts in the coming battle, British warplane production actually grew during the Battle of Britain. This was due in part to the British decentralizing their production. Aircraft parts were produced in a large number of smaller factories and then shipped to a smaller number of central finishing locations, many of them out of the range of German planes or, in one amazing case, underneath a stately and unassuming old manor house, much like that seen in the TV series *Downton Abbey*. The British desperately needed this production; during the battle, they lost an estimated 1,700 planes.

Women made up a large portion of the workers making warplanes in Britain[34]

Luftwaffe Strength

The principal German airbases used in the battle were in France and Belgium, though there were also airfields in Holland. The Luftwaffe's medium bombers, with their longer range but relatively small payload, occasionally raided the coastal areas of central and northern Great Britain from bases in Norway.

Altogether, Göring's Luftwaffe had nearly 1,100 single- and twin-engine fighters, 1,260 long-range bombers, just over 300 dive bombers, and a number of reconnaissance planes. The Germans had a nearly three-to-one advantage going into the battle, but numbers do not tell the entire story, for the British had a number of advantages over the Nazis, including the fact they were defending their homeland.

The Planes

The most numerous and well-known German fighter plane was the Messerschmitt Bf 109 (sometimes referred to as the "Me 109"), of which the E-4 variant was the most used during the Battle of Britain.

Bf-109e painted in Werner Mölders's regalia[35]

The Germans flew a variety of planes during the Battle of Britain: the Dornier Do 17 bomber, the Junker Ju 87 dive bomber, the slow Heinkel 111, and the much-vaunted but highly disappointing Messerschmitt Bf 110 twin-engine escort fighter. The most numerous and effective German fighter was the Bf 109. The most effective German bomber, a plane rated highly by both sides, was the Junker Ju 88 medium long-range bomber.

The Bf 109 had many similarities to the popular British Spitfire. Their top speeds and ranges were about the same. They cut a similar profile, at least to the untrained eye, but there were significant differences in performance that made each plane unique.

The Bf 109 was better armed, carrying one 20mm cannon in each wing and machine guns in the fuselage and, at times, in the nose. The Bf 109 had a faster rate of climb and dive than the Spitfire and the Hurricane, the most numerous British fighters. This led German pilots to carry out swift, diving attacks on unsuspecting British planes and climbing away before the RAF could catch them. Ideally, the German approach would come with the sun behind them, leading to the important RAF motto, "Beware the Hun in the sun!"

The men of the Luftwaffe could not always come out of the sun, and oftentimes, the RAF were waiting for them. Many times, the Germans were "bounced," or attacked by surprise. When neither side could exploit the element of surprise, a dogfight ensued. When that happened, the fighter pilots of the Luftwaffe had to watch their gas gauges very carefully, for they were far from home in machines that were definitely not fuel-efficient.

Though historians consider the Battle of Britain to have formally ended in September when Hitler canceled his invasion plans, the Germans continued bombing British cities for months afterward. Their bombers were often escorted by fighters, though most of their attacks came at night. Hundreds of German planes were forced to "ditch" (crash-land) their planes in the Channel, and that's if they were fortunate. Most times, German pilots who crashed in the Channel and survived were picked up by British ships and were out of the war for good. British pilots forced to bail out of their planes were often back in the air the same day if they had been fortunate enough to avoid injury.

When a dogfight ensued, Spitfire pilots had a decided advantage over the Bf 109. They were much more maneuverable. Adding to the Luftwaffe's woes was the fact that when the Bf 109s turned too fast, especially in a dive, it had a habit of going into an almost uncontrollable spin. Experienced pilots could handle the plane, but inexperienced German airmen had a steep and sometimes deadly learning curve. If that was not enough, 5 percent of all Bf 109s in the battle were lost because their landing gear was too close together and did not always adequately handle the weight of the plane when they returned to occupied Europe.

Ju 88 over France, 1942.[36]

The Ju 88 had been designed just before the war began and was Germany's most effective bomber. It was fast, versatile, and rugged and could dive more rapidly than one would believe, looking at its size and design. However, it was poorly armed, which left it vulnerable. It could also only carry two thousand pounds of bombs. Other German bombers had a similar payload but often made up for this by carrying lighter but more numerous incendiary bombs.

The last Hurricane that fought in the Battle of Britain in flight, 2017[37]

Few people outside the world of aviation history know that during the Battle of Britain, there were more Hurricanes deployed than Spitfires. By the time the battle started, the Hurricane was on its way to becoming obsolete and was due to be phased out as more Spitfires and other British and Allied fighters became available. However, it showed its abilities during the Battle of Britain and was easy and fast to build. It continued to come off British assembly lines until 1944, with improvements being added along the way. Because it was less maneuverable than the Spitfire and was a bit slower than the Bf 109, the Hurricanes were largely assigned to attack enemy bombers and leave the dogfighting to the "Spits" during the Battle of Britain. Despite some real disadvantages against the Bf 109s, experienced British pilots engaged the premier German fighters often and were successful. Over half of the 1,200 German planes shot down during the battle were claimed by the more numerous Hurricanes.

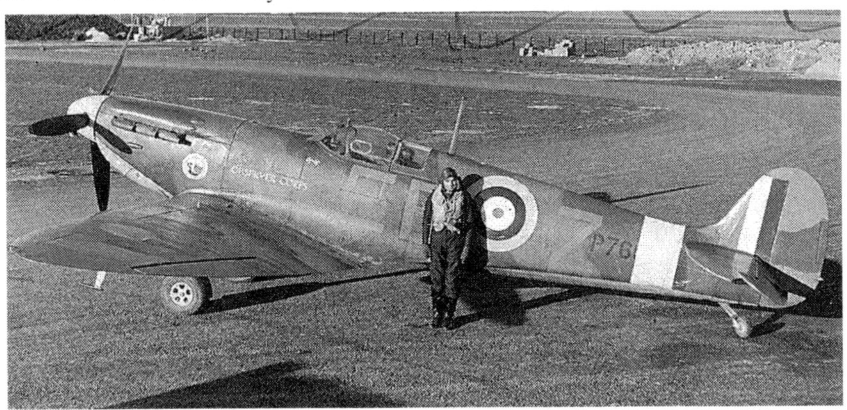

Spitfire Mk IIa of the Observer Corps, late 1940.[38]

There were many good and even great fighter planes in WWII, but the word "iconic" is saved for these four: the North American P-51 Mustang, the Japanese "Zero," the Bf 109, and the Supermarine Spitfire. Some might include the Messerschmitt Me 262, the first truly operational jet fighter, and perhaps the gull-winged US Vought F4U Corsair.

We have already told you a bit about the Bf 109, and you will learn more about this German icon later in the book. Had the battle gone against the British, the Messerschmitt plane might have found itself more famous than the Spitfire.

For the first part of the war in the Pacific, the Zero was seen as the ultimate dogfighter and developed a fearsome reputation, though American technological developments allowed US fighters to leave it in the dust by late 1942, if not before.

Many regard the P-51 as the best all-around fighter of WWII. It was fast, maneuverable, well armed, and well armored and was built for many tasks. By the end of the war, the Mustang's operational ceiling was over forty thousand feet, higher than virtually any Axis plane. Overall, the Mustang was an amazing plane, but perhaps its most outstanding quality was its range. With wing-mounted drop tanks, the Mustang could escort Allied bombers from take-off to landing, beginning in London, flying over Berlin and other German targets, and returning home. The Mustang also escorted American bombers based in Italy over the Alps and into southern Germany, Austria, and Romania.

The Spitfire's elliptical wings gave it added maneuverability and a unique profile.[39]

The British Spitfire was a brilliantly designed plane with exceptional maneuverability and a ceiling close to that of the Mustang. Even today, it is widely regarded as *the* symbol of British resistance during the Battle of Britain. Remaining Spitfires sometimes take to the skies of England during air shows. Traffic frequently slows to a crawl to watch them taxi or do a low "fly-by." Not only are the Spitfires truly iconic, at least in the United Kingdom, but if one asks any British WWII pilot (and many pilots today) what the most beautiful plane they had ever seen was, almost all of them would answer, "That's easy: the Spit."

Chapter 4 – Supporting Cast

The Battle of Britain would not have lasted long if both sides did not have extensive supply and repair teams. In both areas, the British had a slight advantage.

The Germans invaded Denmark and Norway in April 1940. France and the Low Countries were attacked in early May. For many German air force units, there had been little rest, and they certainly had not had the time to build modern defense facilities in the many airfields they either captured or built right after the invasion. Many of the advanced French airbases had been destroyed by German attacks or by the French before their surrender. While the Germans made many of the needed repairs and rebuilt former French bases, they also operated from numerous makeshift airfields that had been cleared out of forests or farm fields. Many of the runways were little more than wide dirt tracks that could easily turn to unusable mud when it rained heavily.

German ground crew refueling a Me 110 "Destroyer." [40]

The Germans also had long supply lines reaching hundreds of miles back into Germany. Gasoline, ammunition, parts, new planes, anti-aircraft guns, food, and much more had to be trucked through northern France to the coast. Bases in Norway, which were used by bombers and their fighter escorts to attack important targets in central and northern England and southern Scotland, were also dependent on these long supply lines.

However, this was 1940, when Germany ruled the skies over Europe, not 1944, when the reverse was true. For the most part, the Germans were able to bring supplies and materiel to their airbases safely, though nighttime raids by RAF Bomber Command began almost as soon as the Battle of France was over. Many people do not know this, but RAF Bomber Command lost more pilots and crew than RAF Fighter Command did during the Battle of Britain. Over seven hundred men were killed, and a large number were captured.

The German ground crews were experienced and had been working together for quite some time. However, they were tired. They needed leave, proper housing, and proper rest after the Battle of France. Most did not get it, and it's likely that their "tiredness" turned into exhaustion as the Battle of Britain wore on. The German crews missed important flaws in aircraft, and turnaround times for damaged aircraft to be combat-ready again became slower and slower.

British ground crews had a number of advantages. First and most importantly, they were working because their country was about to be invaded. Second, most of them were near their homes and families. The British supply lines were very short, and for the most part, gasoline, oil, and needed replacement parts got to the repair crews quickly.

Though the British ground and repair crews were not experienced like their German counterparts, they learned quickly. They had to. Their country and culture were on the line. Many British fighter planes returned to base full of holes or with damaged airframes and engines. British ground and repair crews had to learn on the job.

What's more, even undamaged planes would return after a relatively short time due to running low on fuel or being out of ammunition.

Bf 109 that ran out of fuel as it crossed into France. This pilot was lucky.[41]

Looking at movies of WWII aerial combat, especially those that came out during or shortly after the war, you might think the fighter planes had a virtually unlimited supply of ammunition for the cannons and/or machine guns they carried. Nothing could be further from the truth. The Bf 109s, Hurricanes, and Spitfires all carried about the same amount of ammunition. If their pilots leaned on the trigger and fired a long burst of ten to fifteen seconds, they would be out of ammunition. And just like that, they would be useless in the fight. Good fighter pilots learned that very short bursts fired from close range were the best way to maximize ammunition and increase their chances of a kill. The learning curve was steep for inexperienced pilots, most of whom were British.

But as they gained experience, British crews and pilots became so efficient that it was common for RAF pilots to take off to meet incoming German planes coming over the Channel. They would run out of ammunition, gas, or both but then take off again to catch the same German planes heading toward home.

As you can imagine, the Germans had to be more cautious with their ammunition, and the fighters, especially those escorting German bombers, could not be lured away by British pilots, for this would leave the bombers open to further attacks by other British fighters. It also greatly increased the likelihood of them crash-landing in the very cold English Channel.

Chapter 5 – British Early Warning Systems

In times of war, we often hear something like, "Before the enemy could be attacked, their early warning systems had to be destroyed." In many military conflicts today, it's imperative for an attacking air force to jam, confuse, or destroy an enemy's air defense systems. Modern air defense is multilayered and likely includes elements the general public has no knowledge of, but one thing is clear: most of the time, those "early warning systems" do not include people on the ground looking up in the sky with binoculars.

In WWII, it did. Even late in the war, when radar was more common, an important element of air defense was observers. There are many famous pictures of coastal and other British observers scanning the sky with powerful and not-so-powerful binoculars.

This famous picture was taken before the Battle of Britain (you can tell by the lack of damage around St. Paul's Cathedral in the background; the neighborhood largely went up in flames during the battle. It is likely a posed shot to remind the British people that every possible measure was being taken to keep them safe.[42]

Much has been made of Britain's use of radar during the Battle of Britain. Unfortunately, if you watch certain popular documentaries, you might get the idea that the Germans didn't know about this British invention. However, they did. The British responded to public rumors that the new radar towers were "death rays" by putting on a public demonstration of radar in 1934. There were articles about radar. The Germans intentionally bombed a few of the British radar towers. What the Germans didn't know was how much more powerful and accurate Britain's radars were than their own and how quickly the British could repair damaged equipment. The Germans themselves had begun to deploy radar in certain areas by the time of the battle, but they were short-range and not very accurate.

One typical trait of the Germans in WWII was arrogance, as they believed their technological developments were superior to those of Britain and the United States. In a number of cases, such as jet technology and the "V" missile program, they certainly were, but in many areas, the Germans were far behind, most obviously in the technology to build nuclear weapons. Since the war, many studies have determined the Nazi atomic program was much further away from discovery than believed during the war. The German attitude seemed to be the British radar must be either inferior or comparable; in other words, they believed British radar was not very good.

Another way the Germans showed their arrogance was in their belief that their codes, generated by the famous Enigma machine, could not be broken. They were eventually broken. By the time of the Battle of Britain, a growing amount of German radio traffic was being read by the British in their ultra-secret base at Bletchley Park and sent to air defense.

Radar, which is the acronym for "Radio direction and range finding," was developed in the 1930s. Great Britain, Germany, and the US all had programs devoted to the research and development of radar by the late 1920s. Ironically, most of the groundwork for the radars of WWII was laid by the German physicist Heinrich Hertz and Scotsman James Clerk Maxwell in the late 1800s.

The word "radar" is actually an American acronym and only came to be used in 1940. The British called their systems "HF-DF" (for "high-frequency direction-finding") or "huff duff," at least at the beginning of the war. The British military's codename for the radar systems placed around the southern and western coasts of England and Scotland was "Chain Home" or "CH."

Basically, radar systems work by sending out or relaying electromagnetic waves (radio signals). The radio signals sent by radar are short pulses, much like that of a bat flying above an insect-filled field. These signals hit objects as they travel, particularly metal objects. The signals are then reflected back to their point of origin to receivers. The data is analyzed to determine the characteristics of the reflection. Is it big? Moving fast or slow? How high? How far is it from the transmitter or receiver?

Though the Chain Home radars served the British very well during the battle, their signals were not good enough to single out individual planes in a sky full of aircraft. However, with hard-won experience, the size of the radar's signal, which resembled a large ball or wall of static, would tell the British the almost exact size of the incoming German strike.

The large Chain Home towers could detect objects 120 miles away, but there was a weakness the Germans failed to recognize and exploit. Chain Home could only detect planes flying over three hundred feet. The Germans flew relatively high because they believed they were safe from detection. However, the Germans were playing right into British hands. Flying low often makes spotting aircraft from the ground more difficult, for objects flying low and fast are only visible for a moment compared to those flying at a high altitude.

Had the Germans begun to fly low, at least at the start of the battle, they might have realized the weakness present in Chain Home, but flying low was dangerous over the sea, and the thicker air meant greater fuel consumption. At any rate, the British began to install shorter-range (fifty miles) radars lower to the ground to pick up low-flying planes. Unsurprisingly, these systems were codenamed "Chain Home Low."

Chain Home station at Poling, Sussex, England, on the central southern coast.[43]

Additionally, British radio stations could pick up the radio signals of large numbers of German planes in France as they switched on and tested their radios. This also gave an advance warning of a large German raid in the making and allowed for British air defenses to go on some form of alert.

When Chain Home detected a radar signature coming from the European coast, the relevant information would be sent to RAF Fighter Command headquarters at the 16th-century manor of Bentley Priory on the northern outskirts of London. Auxiliary operations rooms functioned throughout Britain on a contingency basis. The information coming from the radar station was raw, meaning it was not interpreted. The radar station operators simply sent the data they were receiving to RAF Fighter Command. It was the job of the men and women in the famous "filter rooms" (also known as "operations rooms") to determine whether the radar signal came from friendly planes returning from a mission. (At the time, "Identification, friend or foe," known as IFF, technology was in its infancy. The identification of a radar signal was usually double-checked with known missions and RAF radio transmissions.)

The WAAFs

Watch any movie, TV show, or documentary about the Battle of Britain, and you will undoubtedly see a depiction of one of the filter rooms. These were manned by both men and women. The men were members of the RAF. The women were called WAAFs (Women's Auxiliary Air Force). In 1940, WAAFs already numbered in the tens of thousands. In 1943, the number of women in the WAAF was 180,000, but it began to decline slightly afterward. It would not be unrealistic to say the Battle of Britain might have been lost if not for the work of the WAAFs.

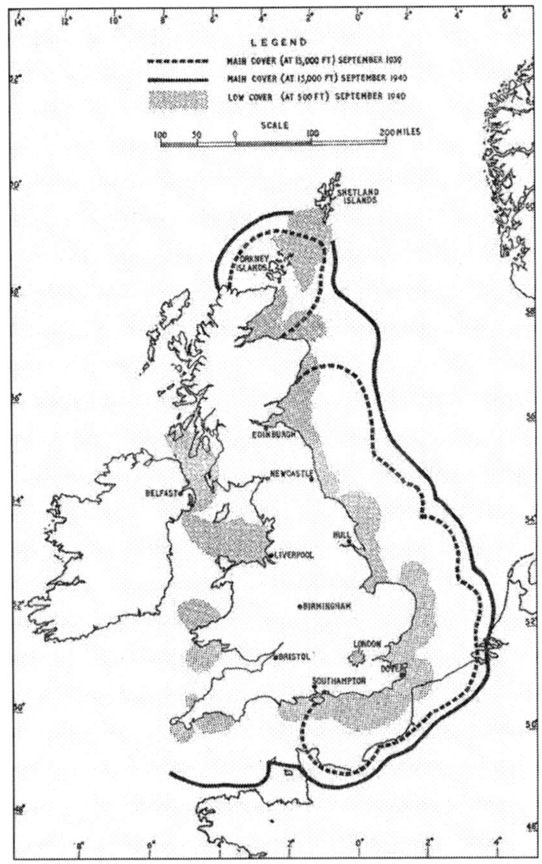

Chain Home's coverage of Britain.[44]

Though the popular image of the WAAFs is of them working around a table during the Battle of Britain, the women of the WAAF had a variety of duties. About a dozen of them ended up being trained for and carrying out clandestine operations for the Special Operations Executive ("SOE"), one of Britain's secret intelligence branches. The SOE's task was "to set Europe ablaze," to use Churchill's words. SOE agents were flown or dropped behind enemy lines to gather intelligence, coordinate resistance movements and activities, sabotage enemy efforts, and much more. If SOE agents were captured by the Germans, they were subjected to the most brutal torture, regardless of their gender. Volunteers were informed of this at the beginning of their training.

The work of the WAAF volunteers was vital to the SOE, but only a small number of women were selected. Before the war, WAAFs were mainly utilized, as you might imagine, given the time and circumstances, for cooking and driving. However, as more and more men were needed for duty at or near the front lines, the role of the WAAFs grew. One of their new roles was radar plotting. They were also trained in photo reconnaissance interpretation, an important job that grew in importance as the Allied invasion of Normandy approached in 1944.

WAAFs in operations room with plotting table.[45]

WAAFs were also responsible for the maintenance of the blimps used by the RAF during the war. The blimps were known as barrage balloons and were often seen in the pictures and newsreels of the time. A barrage balloon was exactly what it sounds like. It was a large gas-filled blimp-shaped balloon tethered to the ground by a metal cable. They were flown at important buildings, installations, headquarters, and airfields, and their purpose was to discourage or prevent low- or mid-level air attacks. No pilot wanted to hit a barrage balloon.

Initially, British barrage balloons might not bring down a German plane. However, the British soon deployed the "double parachute ripping" balloon. When struck, the mooring cable of the DPR balloon would set off a charge, which would release the cable and open two parachutes. The enemy plane would be slowed to the point where it stalled and fell out of the sky.

German dive bombers were more prone to strike the balloons, but they were so ineffective that the Germans pulled them out of the battle. From that point, barrage balloons were generally useless since the enemy's medium bombers could fly above the ceiling altitude of the balloons.

Still, Britain continued to make them, and many of the balloons, especially in the London area, were effective at bringing down or rerouting the winged German V-1 "buzz bombs" later on in the war. During the Battle of Britain, there were some 1,400 barrage balloons in England, with about 350 of them over London alone.

Barrage balloons over Buckingham Palace during the battle. The royal family, including the future Elizabeth II, refused to leave, endearing themselves to the British after scandals in the late 1930s.[46]

A significant number of WAAFs were pilots, and as the war progressed, they became an integral part of the British war effort, flying finished planes from the factories to airbases around the nation.

However, during the Battle of Britain, the lasting image of the WAAFs was cemented into history as plotters laying out incoming German planes and plotting the flights of British fighters racing to meet them. This was not a simple job and did not mean the women were simply "taking notes" and plotting the information they received in their headsets. Oftentimes, the people they were receiving information from were WAAFs who were listening to the radio transmissions from the radar stations and from the Observer Corps on the coast.

The information went to RAF Fighter Command headquarters at Bentley Priory and was plotted on the large table there. Depending on where the detected German planes were heading, information would be sent to the responsible fighter bases around England and southern Scotland.

At Bentley Priory, male RAF officers monitored communications (as a redundancy measure to prevent mistakes) and reported up the chain of command. Top officers would communicate with the fighter bases and send them out to meet the enemy. The staff at Bentley Priory, including Hugh Dowding, were the brains of RAF Fighter Command, as they sent out signals to the various limbs and muscles of the RAF.

The plotting rooms were the final stages of an intricate process. Each WAAF there would be responsible for a certain defined area. They would receive messages in their headsets and sift through the information to make it manageable. As the WAAFs sat in their low wicker chairs with drawers full of organized plastic symbols while wearing their headsets, they would place the information on their metal or wooden racks.

As the raid progressed, the German planes divided to attack different targets or perhaps attack the same target from different directions at different times and altitudes. Some German formations might have been decoys of a sort, attempting to lure RAF fighters away from the main focus of their raids or to otherwise confuse RAF Fighter Command.

The pressure was high for men and women in the plotting or "Ops" rooms. Plot something wrong, and the men in the air or civilians on the ground could die. If having many voices in your ears was not enough (supervising officers could cut in at any time with new information and instructions), the room was constantly busy. As the battle began to grow in intensity, the WAAFs and everyone else in the plotting rooms had to deal with the distinct possibility of being killed or wounded in a Luftwaffe raid. Helmets were on hand when incoming German flights seemed to be heading straight at them.

Corporal Daphne Pearson, 1911-2000[47]

One of the WAAFs, Daphne Pearson, was awarded the George Cross (Britain's highest award for gallantry not in the face of the enemy) when she ran out to assist a wounded RAF pilot whose bomber had crashed. The bomber was still full of live bombs. The pilot had crawled a distance away from the aircraft when one of the 120-pound bombs aboard his plane exploded. At that moment, Corporal Pearson dove on top of him to shield him from shards and other materials that fell from the sky. She waited like that until a stretcher crew came to take him away, then ran to the remains of the bomber to see if there were any survivors. The co-pilot and bombardier had been killed, and the radio operator died as she approached.

Airfields and Bases

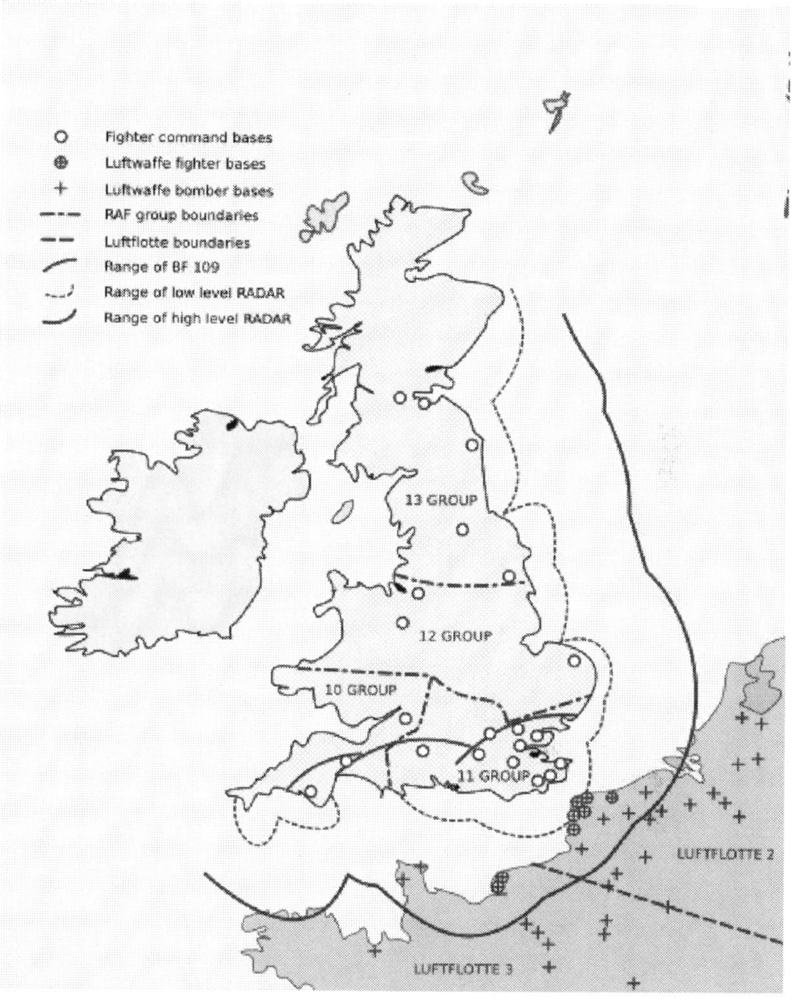

RAF Fighter Command and Luftwaffe sectors with Bf 109 and radar ranges.[48]

The most active area was the sector covered by Group 11 of RAF Fighter Command. It was tasked with defending the southern coast, which included London, along with the airbases and radar stations closest to occupied France.

However, there were times when 11 Group and RAF Fighter Command were stretched so thin that the other groups would have to send relief. The most well known of these instances was on September 15th, 1940, the day Luftwaffe Commander-in-Chief Hermann Göring proclaimed as *Adlertag* ("Eagle Day"). Churchill was at 11 Group headquarters that day, as he knew that a huge raid was planned for the 15th from intercepted German communications. As the raid began to take shape and move over England, Churchill, in the operations room some fifty feet underground with 11 Group's commander, Air Vice Marshal Keith Park, looked at the plotting table and asked Park, "How many more [fighters] have you got?" Park replied, "None. I am putting in my last." When Churchill later wrote his famous Nobel Prize-winning account of the war, he wrote of that moment, saying, "The odds were great; our margins small; the stakes infinite." After nearly an hour of combat, reinforcements from nearby groups arrived.

There were six fighter groups in Britain: 9, 10,11, 12, 13, and 14. No. 9 Group covered northwest England and Northern Ireland. No. 9 Group's area was very seldom raided, so new and inexperienced pilots were stationed there to get on-the-job training.

Some of the more well-known airfields include Duxford (where the Imperial War Museum is today), Debden, Hornchurch, Biggin Hill, Uxbridge, Tangmere, Lympne, Hawkinge, and Manston. These are some of the more famous names, but almost all of the airfields played a critical role.

Air Vice Marshal Keith Park, a New Zealander and veteran of sea, land, and air combat in WWI. He was known as the "Defender of London." [49]

Chapter 6 – Warm-ups

The Germans began to test RAF Fighter Command's defenses beginning in June by attacking British shipping in the English Channel. At the time, there was a fierce debate within the British government and military about the wisdom of sending shipping through the Channel. Most of the ships carrying goods through the Channel were not bringing supplies from overseas; most of the ships were carrying goods and resources from other parts of England and Great Britain (meaning Scotland and Northern Ireland). To many in Britain, this was foolhardy. The supplies on those ships could have more easily and quickly been carried on the extensive British railway system.

However, some within the government and most of the higher commanders of the Royal Navy insisted that keeping ships moving through the Channel was important. It wasn't important strategically or tactically. Economically, it didn't make sense either. But war doesn't always make sense. For reasons of civilian morale and national honor, as well as to send a message to Germany and Britain's allies that the Royal Navy would never be driven from the English Channel, shipping continued, though it would slowly abate as the battle gained intensity in July.

This presented the Luftwaffe with great opportunities, as it could test RAF Fighter Command's responses (time, numbers, etc.), sink ships and their cargo, hone their skills, evaluate the enemy, and hopefully win a prestige victory over both the Royal Navy and Royal Air Force.

The Luftwaffe learned a number of important lessons, but it misinterpreted important results of the battle, which would, in the long run, cost them deeply. One of the first lessons it learned was that its vaunted Ju 87 "Stuka" dive bomber was already obsolete, even though the war had only begun one year prior.

The Stuka had terrorized the Poles, Belgians, French, Dutch, and Norwegians. In Poland in September 1939, the Stukas were virtually unchallenged in the air. Along with escorting Bf 109s, the Ju 87s destroyed many important targets on the ground and helped the German Army break through Polish lines in coordinated attacks as part of the famous Blitzkrieg. The same happened with Germany's victims in the spring of 1940, though the French possessed better fighter planes than the Poles. The Germans felt invincible by June 1940, and the past successes of the Stukas led their pilots (and, most importantly, Hermann Göring) to believe they would inflict much damage on the British.

A later Stuka variant, 1943.[50]

They were wrong. Compared to the Spitfire and Hurricane, the Stuka was slow and too lightly armed. Despite the British having some serious flaws in how they formed to attack (at least at the beginning of the Battle of Britain), Stukas fell to the British fighters by the dozen. British coastal guns and armed merchantmen soon took a toll on the Nazi dive bombers as well. Though the Luftwaffe sent Ju 87s over England at the beginning of the battle, it soon realized that its once-feared plane, first flown in 1935, was woefully out of date. The planes were eventually pulled from the battle. The Stuka regained some of its reputation as an anti-tank aircraft on the Eastern Front and in anti-partisan activities over the USSR and occupied Europe, but by 1944, it was clear the Stuka's time was done.

The Battle Begins

History books tell us the battle began on July 10th, 1940, and ended on September 15th, 1940. Battles rarely begin and end so suddenly, and the Battle of Britain was no different. For weeks before July 10th, the Luftwaffe had been probing Britain's air defenses. The way in which the RAF reacted was of more interest to the Germans than most of their prospective targets.

Looking back, the closer to July 10th we get, the more German probes there were. The types of German sorties began to change as well, going from mostly reconnaissance to a mix of recon and night-bombing raids on airfields, ports, and factories. On June 18th, a raid of one hundred German bombers flew over a wide area of Britain from north to south and even west into Wales. At the time, this was considered a large raid. Later Luftwaffe activity would show that it was just a "warm-up."

By the end of June, the Luftwaffe had "visited" Britain eight more times. The British were just getting a taste of what was to come, although these raids resulted in dead and wounded civilians. All of these raids came at night, but on July 1st, the first large daylight raids on Britain took place, surprisingly in Scotland and Yorkshire.

The Attacks on the Channel

From the second half of June to July 10th, the Germans mustered their strength on the eastern Channel coasts. They expected the order from Hitler to destroy the RAF to come at any time. Until then, they attacked British ships in the Channel.

The Royal Navy was not sending large battleships, cruisers, or aircraft carriers through the narrow waterway. No, those ships had more important duties than to help merchantmen deliver their wheat, coal, or whatever else they might be carrying. And if worse came to worst, the British would need their large, powerful warships to try to prevent a German invasion of their country.

Many of the merchantmen went through the Channel alone or in small convoys, trying to stay as close to the British coast as was safely possible. This made it easier and safer for the RAF to provide cover. The anti-aircraft gun batteries also provided some protection from German attacks.

Remember, the RAF had argued with the Royal Navy over whether British ships should be sent through the important waterway at all. Over the course of the Battle of Britain, a shift in power within the military gradually occurred. For centuries, the Royal Navy had been the guarantor of British safety. The navy had been a symbol of British power, and in 1940, it still was. Many more conservative thinkers within the navy believed that it would continue to be the preeminent branch of the British Armed Forces for the foreseeable future.

There is no doubt the Royal Navy played an incredibly important role in Britain's survival during the early years of the war. Even after the threat of invasion was gone, the Germans attempted to bring Britain to her knees through the U-Boat War, which at times threatened the UK with starvation. The oil and gas needed to continue the war came by ship, and those ships were protected by the Royal Navy.

However, the Battle of Britain and the bombing campaigns against Germany in the years to come showed the Royal Navy was not the only branch of the British military. It can be argued that by the end of the war, the RAF was the more influential of the two branches, at least in the relatively close quarters of northwestern Europe.

Churchill was not an inflexible thinker, but at the beginning of the war, he leaned toward the navy and supported its opinion that shipping should continue through the Channel. It was left to the RAF, more specifically, Hugh Dowding and RAF Fighter Command, to work out how.

German attacks on British ships presented the RAF with a dilemma. An Englishman of the time might refer to the situation as "quite a sticky wicket" or comment that they were between "a rock and a hard place." The RAF was outnumbered in the summer of 1940 by a lot. The leadership knew the enemy was going to launch attacks against it soon, but what was it to do? Let the Germans prey on the merchantmen in the Channel without opposition?

Dowding and his group and wing commanders debated what to do, and their decision would affect not only the battle over the Channel but also the larger battle to come. They determined the minimum number of RAF planes they would send over the water, which would depend on the number of ships and the number of attacking German planes detected by Chain Home and the Observer Corps. As the raids continued, the RAF got a relatively good idea of how many planes it could send while still marshaling its strength for what it believed would be a massive German effort in the near future.

British calculations on how many planes to send took into account the size of the German raid, which was information they gleaned from radar and radio interceptions. Dowding also had to calculate what he knew about German fighter production and how many British intelligence officers were believed to be in France. At that time, just after the fall of France, resistance movements in France were few and far between, and what communication there was between Britain and France was limited at best.

Additionally, RAF Fighter Command had to constantly be aware of how many of their own fighter planes were being built, lost, and repaired. And they had to solve the big question: when the Germans began to fly over England in force, what would be their main targets? How many planes should be sent to meet them as opposed to another potential target? And how many British fighters could the RAF afford to lose?

The answer to that last question was very few. There were two ways for the RAF to make up for its disparity in numbers: be very aggressive and be better pilots than the Germans. The RAF was always the former, and those who survived got to be just as good or better than their enemies.

The fight over the Channel has come to be known by the German word for it: Kanalkampf. At the end of June, there was rough weather over the Channel and on the Channel coasts of both France and England. This threw off the German timetable by a few days, and the first big raid on shipping over the water took place on July 4th, 1940. Over the course of the next few days, the Luftwaffe picked up the frequency and size of its raids.

From July 4th to July 6th, the Germans attacked convoys passing through the Channel with a small number of Stukas. Remember, at the very start of the battle, the Luftwaffe did not have an honest appraisal of how the Stukas might fare in a fight with British fighters. They should have, for the specs on the plane were public, and accounts of the plane's capabilities had been communicated to the British by their Polish and French allies. After a number of Stukas had been shot down or seriously damaged by British fighters, the Ju 87s had to be escorted by a number of fighters, which changed German thinking about whether the Stukas needed to be used against England at all. Also, on July 4th, German fighters flew over the south-central English county of Kent, hoping to catch British fighters by surprise while they were on their way to the Channel or lure them away from the attacks taking place over the water and destroy them.

It did not take amazing technology for the Germans to know when a British convoy was sailing through the Channel. The vast majority sailed from east to west and had to pass through the narrowest part of the Channel, the Straits of Dover, opposite Cap Gris-Nez near Calais on the French side of the water. The distance across at this point is twenty miles, and on a good day, a person standing on one coast can see the other side.

The peaceful, present-day view across the Channel.[51]

The German fighter "sweeps," as the sorties of Bf 109s were called, forced the RAF to deal with a dilemma within a dilemma. The ships sailing through the Channel carried vital supplies and needed protection. However, if it appeared the German fighters were looking to attack an area where an important British installation was located, such as a Chain Home tower, for instance, then fighters would have to be scrambled. The Germans would then realize that something nearby was precious to the British and needed to be sought out. Imagine a huge deadly game of cat and mouse.

Between July 7th and 8th, the pace and strength of the raids hitting the ships in the Channel and the important ports on the southern English coast increased. A number of ships were sunk, and many more were damaged. The German strategy of attacking ships and ports succeeded in getting a response from RAF Fighter Command, but the British tried to ignore German fighters roaming inland as much as possible, as they knew the Germans were trying to tempt the British into engaging in a fight.

A couple of days later, on July 10th, Göring sent huge formations of planes over England. That date is now recognized as the real beginning of the Battle of Britain.

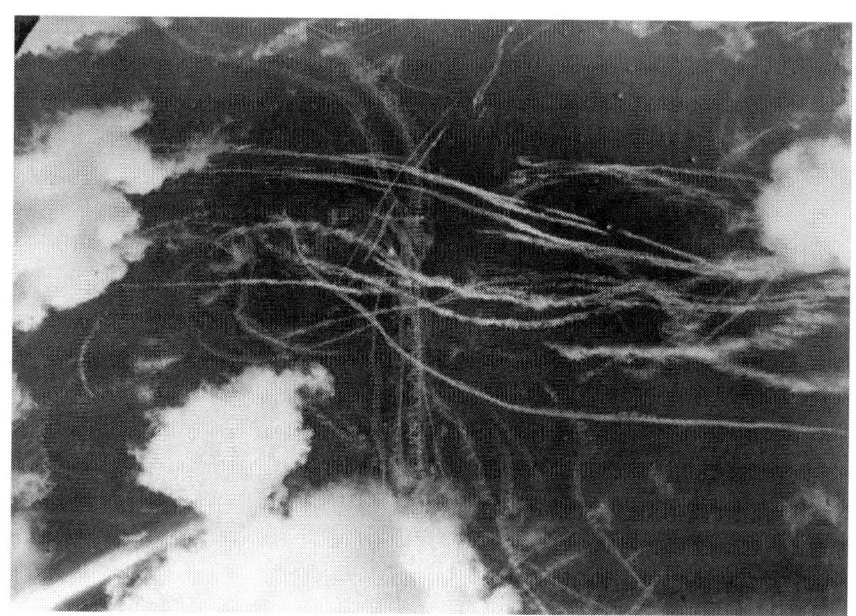

Vapor trails from a dogfight over England, 1940.[52]

Chapter 7 – Tactics and Command

In Chapter 5, you learned a bit about Britain's defense organization and how the nation was divided into sectors, with a "Fighter Group" being responsible for each one. Each Fighter Group contained roughly between a dozen and two dozen or more squadrons, depending on their location. Fighter Group 10 contained ten squadrons, whereas Group 11, whose responsibility was the London area, contained twenty-seven squadrons at the start of the battle. Though most of the squadrons were comprised of Hurricanes or Spitfires, there were a number of squadrons that were made up of older, obsolete planes like the Defiant and the Blenheim, both of which were reassigned to night-fighter duty during the battle and phased out as soon as possible.

An RAF squadron contained an average of twelve planes, at least in ideal circumstances. At the start of the battle, squadrons would form into four V-shaped groups of three called "Vics." The tactic was a holdover from the 1930s when an erroneous assumption by the RAF was made, which cost many RAF pilots their lives at the start of the battle.

Before the war, the RAF believed it would more likely face massed groups of bombers rather than significant numbers of enemy fighters. This mistaken belief had more to do with how the British believed the next war would be fought than it did with simply overlooking German fighters. When you hear or read something about the fall of France being a complete and utter shock, you should believe it. When devising their defensive structure for southern England, they didn't take fighters too much into account because it was felt they would be flying from bases in

Germany. The planes would have to fly over the Low Countries or northern France and would not have the range to reach England. The successful invasion of France forced RAF Fighter Command to change how it looked at the coming battle, but the Battle of France was over so quickly that there was not enough time to retrain British fighter pilots in new tactics.

"Necessity is the mother of invention," as the saying goes, and during the battle, RAF pilots began to change their tactics because the Vic formation was costing them dearly. There were a number of reasons for this. First, the squadron leader flew at the front of the foremost Vic. He was responsible for spotting incoming enemy formations. Before the war, this would have been easier, as the massed firepower of the squadron could have been brought to bear on the enemy. However, German fighters flew in loose formations, often called a "finger-four" in English.

The Vic was the basic unit of another strategy debated before, during, and after the war called the "Big Wing." Proponents of the Big Wing believed that massed units of fighters concentrated on one enemy would provide overwhelming firepower. The main advocate of the Big Wing was Group 12's commander, Air Vice Marshal Trafford Leigh-Mallory, an ambitious WWI fighter pilot who often argued with both Keith Park and Dowding over tactics. After the Battle of Britain was over, Churchill replaced Dowding with Leigh-Mallory, as the prime minister found himself in agreement with Leigh-Mallory and his supporters, which included one of the heroes of the battle, Douglas Bader. Bader had lost both his legs in a flying accident in 1931. Nine years later, he shot down twenty-two confirmed German planes (the number was likely more) and then survived a German prisoner-of-war camp. He lived until the age of seventy-two, dying in 1982.

Douglas Bader in 1941 by Cuthbert Orde.[53]

The problem with the Vic formation was that it meant two wingmen had to concentrate on keeping a close formation. The most serious and deadly byproduct of this was that RAF doctrine called for the squadron to move as one, which meant the British fighters, at least at the start of the battle, took too long to turn and covered too much distance while doing it. Meanwhile, Luftwaffe fighters, acting separately but in a coordinated fashion, would tear them apart. Not only was the Vic formation deadly, but it was also wasteful and frustrating, especially for the Spitfire pilots, who knew they had a fast and highly maneuverable airplane at their fingertips.

At times, British fighters would have another fighter flying above and slightly behind the Vics. This pilot, called Tail End Charlie by the British (a nickname that saw a lot of use by the Americans in WWII as well), was supposed to be a relatively invisible spotter for the Vic, but within a very short time, the Luftwaffe was on to the tactic. Being Tail End Charlie was akin to flying a suicide mission.

The RAF commanders on the ground knew the Vic formation was deadly yet continued to insist their pilots fly in the formation. Their logic was new pilots were coming to the battle every day, and that was the formation they had been taught. Knowing that Hitler could only invade England before the summer was out in mid-late September, the RAF commanders believed teaching these new pilots a new tactic in the middle of the battle would be worse than continuing to fly it.

However, as losses mounted, RAF pilots switched tactics themselves. As for the new men, they would have to "learn on the job," and they did. Though the proponents of the Big Wing would eventually win out, the Vic became a thing of the past before the Battle of Britain reached its climax.

The Germans

The German "finger-four" actually resembles a hand laid on a flat surface. The finger-four would divide into two, with each pair being called a *Rotte* ("pack"). The entire formation was called a *Schwarm* ("swarm"). Each *Schwarm* had a commander, as did each *Rotte*. The *Rottenführer* ("pack leader") scanned the skies for their targets ahead, above, and below, while the *Katschmareks* (an old German military nickname) scanned from side to side and behind. From time to time, the *Katschmareks* or the entire *Schwarm* would weave and change positions, doing so to get a better view of what might be approaching, especially from behind.

The German squadron was called a *Staffel* (plural: *Staffeln*) and generally consisted of the same number of planes as their RAF counterparts. The *Staffeln* made up the *Gruppe* ("group") or *Geschwader*.

Like the RAF group structure, the number of *Staffeln* in a *Gruppe* or *Geschwader* varied but usually numbered three or four. Next up the chain were groups of *Geschwader*, each named according to their function. The *Jagdgeschwader* were the fighters. *Kampfgruppe* were formations of bomber squadrons. There were also reconnaissance and pathfinder groups. The flying corps or *Fliegerkorps* consisted of three or four *Geschwader* or *Gruppe* formations. Above them all was the *Luftflotte* or "Air Fleet, which was the command of all operations. *Luftflotten* is the plural.

Kesselring, pointing with his field marshal's baton, with Reichsmarschall Herman Göring at right.[54]

The *Luftflotte* commanders reported directly to Göring. *Luftflotten* 2, 3, and 5 were involved in the Battle of Britain. In command of *Luftflotte* 2 was a man who originally had been an infantry commander and helped create the secret program to rebuild the Luftwaffe between WWI and WWII. This was Albert Kesselring, whose *Luftflotte* cleared the skies over Poland and acted in close support of the Blitzkrieg, both in Poland and France. Kesselring, known to his men as "Uncle Albert" for his care of them, was known to the British and later the Americans as "Smiling

Albert" for his toothy grin. Albert Kesselring was a military genius who often goes overlooked in history books. Not only did he command an air wing, but in 1941, he was transferred to Italy and took command of all German land and air forces in Italy, coming very close to destroying British supply lanes in the Mediterranean in early 1942.

After Erwin Rommel had been recalled to Germany to begin preparations for the Allied cross-Channel invasion (and to avoid the disgrace of being in command when North Africa fell to the Allies), Kesselring took command and fought a stubborn retreat to Tunisia, where he organized a masterful retreat of Axis forces to Sicily, despite Allied command of the air and sea. He did the same in Sicily, fighting the Allies tooth and nail until he was forced to organize yet another retreat across the Strait of Messina to mainland Italy, right under the nose of the Allied armies. Kesselring was the overall commander of German forces in Italy until the end of the war, and he made that campaign one of the most miserable and costly in the entire Allied war effort.

Despite Kesselring's role in the Battle of Britain, many in the British and American military respected and actually liked him after meeting him once he finally surrendered his armies on May 1st, 1945, despite an order from Hitler forbidding it. Though troops under his command treated most Allied prisoners well, Kesselring was convicted after the war for war crimes committed against Italian partisans and civilians under his command. However, his sentence was commuted, partially due to pressure brought by the British military and Winston Churchill himself.

Hugo Sperrle was in command of *Luftflotte* 3, which was based, like Kesselring's command, in Pas-de-Calais. Sperrle looked like the stereotypical German general, and his image or one resembling it was used in many Allied propaganda posters depicting Germany's evil behavior in WWII. Sperrle's command was drastically reduced in number during the Battle of Britain, and it never was brought up to full strength again. Sperrle and *Luftflotte* 3 were still in France when the invasion of Normandy occurred in June 1944. His inability to repulse Allied air power (which would

Hugo Sperrle.[55]

have been an impossible task for any German commander at that stage of the war) resulted in his transfer to reserve command officers. He never saw the battlefield again.

Hermann Göring

The story of the Battle of Britain is not complete without a short biography of Hermann Göring, who was, in many ways, Hitler's number two man for most of the war. Göring held the unique title of Reichsmarschall ("Marshal of the Empire") and was one of the most public and popular Nazi leaders until he began to lose.

Göring was famous long before Hitler and the rise of the Nazi Party. While Hitler was slogging through the mud of WWI's Western Front as a corporal and runner, Göring was flying high above it as an officer. Toward the end of the war, he was the commander of the famous Flying Circus, which was originally led by the famed "Red Baron," Manfred von Richthofen.

Before the war and for its first year, Göring had the respect of most of his men, especially the fighter pilots. He had lived their life. He was an ace pilot, having shot down twenty-two enemy planes and winning Germany's highest honor at the time, the Pour le Mérite. His men respected him for his skill in the air, but during both WWI and WWII, he was not well liked. He was very handsome as a young man fighting in the First World War, and combined with his role as an ace and commander of the Flying Circus, he grew increasingly arrogant and dismissive of others.

After WWI, Göring got involved in right-wing nationalist politics, meeting Adolf Hitler in Bavaria. In 1922, Göring heard a speech given by Adolf Hitler and soon after joined the Nazi Party. Göring's fame was a boon to the Nazis, and his house became sort of a Nazi meeting place, with meetings hosted by Göring's Swedish wife, Carin.

In 1923, Göring was at Hitler's side when the infamous "Beer Hall Putsch" took place, which was Hitler's attempt to overthrow the government. A number of Nazis were killed and wounded when the army broke up the attempted coup. Göring was seriously wounded, and when he was declared an outlaw and a wanted man by the Bavarian authorities, he fled to Carin's home in Sweden. By the time he arrived, he was badly addicted to morphine, which caused a violent change in him. He was forcibly committed to an asylum to recover. He returned to Germany in 1927 after an amnesty was announced. Though he, at times, kicked the habit, he was addicted for most of the rest of his life. Despite this, Göring was incredibly shrewd and intelligent. At the end of the war, as an Allied prisoner, the clear-headed Göring at times ran rings around the prosecution.

As the Nazis rose to power, so did Göring. He held a number of posts, including being the Prussian head of police, which gave him great power after Hitler became chancellor. He was also given command of the Luftwaffe when Hitler announced the repudiation of the Treaty of Versailles. For a time, before the rise of Himmler and before Göring began to lose his luster after the Battle of Britain, Göring was the most powerful man in Germany after Hitler. As the war turned against Germany and Allied bombers began to bomb German cities and other targets, Göring was blamed. People began to call him "Meyer" after a statement he made early in the war. "Meyer" was a popular German character, somewhat akin to Charlie Brown, for nothing goes right for him. Göring said, "If one enemy bomb falls on Berlin, you can call me 'Meyer.'" Many people also called him "Der Dicke" or "Fatso," although never to his face.

Göring was also appointed head of the Nazis' Four Year Plan to revitalize the German economy. He was intimately involved with the massive slave labor program that grew during the war and played a central role in the allocation of resources during the Holocaust. As Hitler's designated successor, Göring was also the man that signed off on much of the Nazis' "Final Solution" and was found guilty of crimes against humanity after the war. He committed suicide in his cell before he could be hanged.

Chapter 8 – "Wir fliegen gegen England!" ("We fly against England!")

"We fly against England!" was one of the German battle cries during the Battle of Britain and the title of a 1941 best-selling book in Germany (which naturally put a positive spin on the battle). On July 10th, 1940, the battle began with the largest raid yet.

Not having that much success over the last few days in their effort to draw large numbers of RAF fighters into battle, the Luftwaffe sent a combined force of twenty-seven medium bombers, the Dornier Do 17 "Flying Pencils" (named for their thin shape), escorted by twenty-four Bf 110s and twenty-four Bf 109s to attack a large British convoy heading south into the Channel. The Germans believed that such a large formation of their planes would have to draw British fighters into the sky, and it did.

In response, RAF Fighter Command sent elements of four different squadrons to meet the threat, comprised of twenty-four Hurricanes and six Spitfires. There were thirty British planes versus seventy-five German planes. With very few exceptions, this was the way the Battle of Britain would be fought.

The battle did not begin auspiciously for the Luftwaffe. Nine of their planes were destroyed, while the RAF lost one fighter, two crash-landed, and two were seriously damaged in the air but managed to return home. One British ship was sunk. Generally speaking, this was how the battle would go; the British would shoot down more Luftwaffe planes than they lost, but the Luftwaffe had more planes to lose. For the first part of the battle, the British lost a higher percentage of their planes, though the Luftwaffe lost more numerically.

British production would increase throughout the battle, and by September, British factories were putting out more planes than they were losing. Regardless, the Germans began with a decided advantage. But as the battle continued, British production grew while Luftwaffe production lagged. In July, the British assembled nearly five hundred planes. The Germans, whose economy was still in many ways on a peacetime schedule, produced virtually none. What's more, at the height of the battle, civilian workers in Britain were repairing damaged aircraft at an amazing rate of speed, sometimes as pilots waited to take off again. A very large number of German planes that sustained heavy damage either crashed in Britain or the English Channel, making them a complete loss to the Luftwaffe.

On July 19th, the British sent nine convoys through the Channel. In response, the Luftwaffe sent large numbers of fighters and bombers. In almost constant dogfights throughout the daylight hours, the RAF lost more planes than the Germans.

Even though it was militarily illogical for the British to send so many convoys through the Channel, politically, it had to be done, especially if England wanted to show the world (especially the United States) that it could hold its own. As the raids increased over the next week, the Admiralty and a number of politicians put pressure on the RAF and especially Hugh Dowding to devote more planes to the fight over the Channel. He did not want to do this, as he knew the real fight was yet to come. Still, he compromised with the Royal Navy and assigned a standing number of patrols over the Channel and its ports.

Before the war, Dowding and his staff made very detailed calculations of the number of fighters he would need to hold the Germans off. He had just about that many when the navy began to pressure him for more planes. He could not afford to lose them in what he viewed as a fight that could have been avoided. Even at this early stage of the battle, RAF Fighter Command was flying nearly six hundred sorties a day. It's also important to remember that the pilots of both sides would get tired to the point of exhaustion many times during the battle. Luckily for the RAF, Fighter Command gave its pilots rest days when it could. The Luftwaffe did not, and as the battle reached its climax, pilot exhaustion and error became an important factor.

One thing the fight over the Channel did was give the RAF pilots more experience. They began to tear up the book on a variety of things, one of them being the optimal range of their guns. Their handbooks told them that the best range to harmonize their guns (the point at which fire from the machine guns in their wings would converge) was six hundred yards. Wind, airspeed, and distance all conspired to make six hundred yards inefficient. The pilots of the RAF ordered their guns to be "zeroed in" at 250 yards, making them more accurate, powerful, and effective. The RAF began flying much more aggressively, attempting to come very close to the enemy for maximum accuracy and damage.

Before the battle, the RAF introduced an incendiary bullet to their crews, which aided in marksmanship and increased damage. Pilots also experimented with a variety of loadouts for their guns, with experienced pilots carrying two guns with incendiary rounds, two with armor-piercing rounds, and two with standard bullets. The RAF found that the combination of closely harmonized guns and incendiary bullets would frequently mean the difference between damaging a German plane and destroying it.

The RAF also introduced changes to propeller technology, which increased the fighters' speed and gave the Germans a nasty surprise. However, one thing was holding the British pilots back: the Vic formation. This was doing harm in more ways than just the loss of planes. The RAF was actually making and repairing more planes than it lost, but it was losing veteran pilots at a high rate. The Vic was one of the main reasons for that since the Germans knew exactly who the flight leader was in each formation. Planes could be made in days. Fighter pilots, at least ones who stood a chance in the air, could not. Since Dowding was holding the main part of his force back to defend the attack he knew was coming, less than 50 percent of RAF pilots had any combat experience.

Some of the most experienced pilots were not British. There were pilots from many countries in occupied Europe, especially Poland, Czechoslovakia, and France. Large numbers of Canadians, Australians, and New Zealanders flew for RAF Fighter Command as well. There was also a small number of American volunteers, who called themselves the Eagle Squadron, but most flew within RAF squadrons with the British. The Polish 302 and 303 Squadrons shot down 203 German aircraft while losing only 29 pilots in the process. The 303 Squadron was actually the most effective RAF squadron of the entire battle, shooting down 126 Nazi planes in just 42 days. Interestingly, their top pilot, Josef Frantisek, who shot down seventeen Germans, was not Polish but Czech. After the war, Dowding wrote that he believed that without the contribution of the Poles, the battle might have been lost.

Polish 303 Squadron Hurricane showing the number of "Little Hitlers" (as the Poles called their enemies) that had been shot down.[56]

Chapter 9 – "Adlerangriff"

In the last days of July and first days of August, Luftwaffe communications spoke about a coming *Adlerangriff* or "Eagle Attack" or "Eagle Offensive." British officers who read these intercepted messages knew the "Eagle Attack" could only mean one thing: the expected massive attack on England. This belief was reinforced by reports coming from France via reconnaissance planes and other sources, including isolated reports coming from the ground in France.

There was only one person with more power in Germany in the summer of 1940 than Göring: Adolf Hitler. At the end of July, the Führer gave Göring free rein to begin his all-out attack on England any time after August 5th. The Germans had amassed almost all of their available aircraft on the Channel coast and were ready to go any time after the 5th, but bad weather rolled in. The skies were not clear enough to begin the massive assault until the 13th, which became known as *Adlertag* or "Eagle Day."

The British enjoyed another advantage not already mentioned. Their radar could detect flights of German planes massing over the Channel sometimes fifteen minutes or more before the Luftwaffe headed over the water. In clear weather, formations could sometimes be seen with the naked eye. What's more, during the first part of the battle, the German fighter and bomber groups were not as coordinated as they should have been. Fighter and bomber pilots could not talk to each other, and the high command would often send fighters to rendezvous with the bombers before the bombers had even left their bases. This meant more German planes were in the air for a longer time, which inadvertently gave RAF

Fighter Command more time to prepare. This extra time in the air also wasted immense amounts of gasoline, something the British had a ready supply of but which the Germans had to send hundreds of miles from the heart of Europe.

There is an oft-repeated myth about the Battle of Britain that the Germans did not know about radar. The Germans did not only know about radar, but they also had their own. Fortunately for the British, German radar was not as good as theirs, even though the Germans thought it was.

On August 12th, the day before *Adlerangriff*, the Germans made a concerted effort to knock out as many of the British radar stations as they could. If successful, this would give the Luftwaffe a distinct advantage in the coming battle, which would begin in earnest the next day. Four Chain Home installations were targeted by the Luftwaffe: three on the southeastern coast below London and one on the Isle of Wight. One of the Chain Home Low stations at Dover was also targeted.

At 7 a.m., the Germans flew a series of sweeps with a total of two hundred fighters. Their job was to be decoys and lure as many British fighters as possible away from their targets. An hour and a half later, sixteen Me 110 twin-engine fighters took off from Calais. These planes were from a highly trained squadron of fighter-bomber pilots called Erprobungsgruppe 210. (Loosely translated, the name means "Test Group 210," and it achieved a unique distinction during the battle, as four of its members received the Knight's Cross of the Iron Cross, one of the highest decorations that could be bestowed during the war. Erprobungsgruppe 210 received more than any other unit).

Four of 210 *Gruppe*'s planes were sent to Dover to attack the Chain Home Low stations, and while they hit a number of buildings in the area, the radar towers were not damaged. Even today, ground attack aircraft miss their targets completely. A report done after WWII completed by the US Army Air Corps (the forerunner to the Air Force) showed that at the end of the war, aerial bombing, including low-level bombing, more often missed their targets than hit them. This is one reason the Allies switched to carpet bombing from 1943 onward; if you cover an entire area, you're bound to hit your target.

Another four planes attacked the station at Dunkirk (this one in England at the mouth of the Thames Estuary). This raid was more successful and destroyed some important equipment, although it was replaced quickly. The station went quiet for only a very short time. The most important part of the installation, the tower, went unscathed.

At the next station, located farther west at Rye, a number of buildings were destroyed, as well as some equipment, which caused the station to go dark. The next station at Pevensey was then hit by the last four planes of the Erprobungsgruppe. The result was the same; no towers were hit, and the station continued uninterrupted operations.

Later that morning, a formation of eighty Ju 88 bombers, one hundred Me 110s, and twenty-five Me 109s headed northwest to attack the port city of Portsmouth and the radar station at Ventnor on the Isle of Wight. The numbers proved the deciding factor, for the group that attacked the Ventnor station destroyed not only important buildings and communications but also did serious damage to the radar masts.

These relatively simultaneous attacks and their numbers threw the British defense system into disorder for a time. Assuming this would be the case, the Luftwaffe sent more sorties over the Channel. The large airfield at Manston was severely damaged, and the fighter stations at Hawkinge and Lympne were damaged as well. While this was taking place, flights of Stuka bombers attacked convoys in the Channel and sank two ships. The 109s protecting the dive bombers destroyed four Hurricanes that came to disrupt the raid.

Though it seemed to the Germans they had scored a victory on the first day of the battle, they overestimated the damage they had caused. The buildings and the ships were not the most important targets; the radar stations were. The only serious damage was done at the Ventnor radar station. It would take weeks before it was fully functional again. Stop-gap measures and overlapping radar signals would fill in for Ventnor. As for the other four stations the Germans attacked, all were up again within six hours at the most. This so-called victory cost the Germans twenty-seven planes.

The British observation corps, its radar system, and the men and women behind them were very good. Because the Germans made the erroneous assumption that British radar was only as good as theirs or worse, they were constantly surprised to find RAF fighters lying in wait for them on the exact flight path they were taking to their targets.

Believing they had done more damage to the radar systems than they really had and not knowing that the British could tell when a raid was forming by the radio signals that were intercepted when large numbers of

German aircraft came together and that they were reading many of the messages being sent to and from Luftwaffe High Command and its units in France, Göring was confident the next week or so would see the elimination of RAF Fighter Command as an effective fighting force. This would allow Hitler to move forward with his planned invasion, Operation Sealion. It would also put Göring in even better stead with Hitler and see an increase in his power and influence, which were already substantial.

August 13th, 1940

Things began badly for the Germans on the morning of August 13th. There was bad weather and poor visibility. Most units received orders to stand down, but a number did not and took off for their assigned targets in England. The original plan called for masses of coordinated attacks with bombers escorted by large numbers of fighters. Two separate flights of German bombers flew their raids with no fighter cover at all and paid the price for it.

By the afternoon, the weather had cleared, and German planes began to take off in the hundreds. The RAF challenged a large number of them in the area of Southampton, one of Britain's most important ports. Just west of Southampton, the Isle of Portland, home to a Royal Navy base, was attacked.

A flight of Heinkel 111 bombers on their way to England, 1940.[57]

The majority of the 30 Me 110s, 30 Bf 109 fighters, and 120 Ju 88 bombers attacked Southampton and inflicted heavy damage. A section of Ju 88s went on to drop their bombs on the naval base in Portland. The British launched elements of four squadrons to meet them.

The next German attack consisted of seventy-seven Ju 87 Stukas escorted by a large number of Bf 109s. Their destination was an RAF airbase north of the Isle of Portland at Middle Wallop. The formation was attacked from the rear by a Spitfire squadron returning from defending the base at Portland. Nine of the Stukas were blown out of the sky.

Near the Straits of Dover, a mixed group of 109s and 110s were on their way to attack a bomber factory at the mouth of the Thames when they were surprised, this time by a large flight of Hurricanes, which forced the 109s and the slower 110s to turn home. Another group of German planes was launched immediately after this group and attacked RAF Coastal Command airfield at Detling, where the Operations Block (what we would call the "command and control center" of the base) and every hangar were flattened. Sixty-seven civilians and military staff were killed.

The actions of the first day of German attacks on British bases and airfields were just a foretaste of what was to come, but thirty-four German planes were destroyed, fifteen of which managed to crash on the French coast. The RAF suffered the loss of twelve Hurricanes and one Spitfire, along with four planes that were forced to crash-land, suffering serious damage in the process. There was good news for the RAF, though; only four pilots were killed, and two were seriously injured. The British also lost planes on the ground, but of the nearly fifty that were destroyed, only one was an important fighter plane. That luck would not hold every day. The Luftwaffe flew over 1,400 sorties over England, and the RAF launched more than 700 to meet them.

On August 14th, the RAF had a chance to recoup due to bad weather over France, but on the 15th, the Luftwaffe came again, this time with every available plane. They flew more than 1,800 sorties in an attempt to stretch British defenses thin over a wide area of southern England. The Germans' attempt to catch all of Britain's fighters in the air failed for two reasons. First, their intelligence services let them down. Luftwaffe intelligence officers believed the RAF only had three hundred fighters on hand. That was less than half of what the British put in the sky. Second, the Germans had no insight into Dowding's strategy of only sending what he believed to be enough planes to deter the Germans from their target.

Early in the morning, one hundred Stukas and 109s flew across the Straits of Dover and attacked RAF fighter bases at Lympne and Hawkinge, doing severe damage. The base at Lympne was put out of action for three days. These were followed by twenty-five Me 110s that attacked another RAF airfield nearer the Thames Estuary at Manston.

While all of that was happening on the southeast coast, northern England was "welcomed" to the war by a large German attack aimed at airfields near York and Northampton on the northeastern coast of the country.

Luftflotte 5, which flew over the North Sea, was in charge of this attack. A flight of Heinkel 115s, biplane/seaplane fighters, flew ahead of the main attack to draw any British fighter cover away. In actuality, the Germans believed that most, if not all, of the RAF fighters had been moved to the south and expected little resistance. These outdated German planes were met by Hurricanes from the 605 Squadron. They were being chased from the scene by the British when bad German navigation led the following sixty-three bombers and their twenty-one Me 110 fighter escorts right into the assembled Hurricanes. What's more, the planes of the 605 Squadron were soon joined by elements of three other British squadrons. The Germans suffered heavy losses, with a number of them facing the miserable death of bailing out into the very cold North Sea in heavy clothes. Twenty percent of *Luftflotte* 5 had been either severely damaged or lost permanently. It was a serious blow, though it was the smallest of the German air fleets deployed against Britain. The Germans would launch no further daylight raids from Norway for the rest of the battle.

A German flight of fifty Ju 88 bombers headed from Denmark to the northern English coast and was bounced by another squadron of RAF fighters, suffering heavy losses as well. Fourteen bombers from *Luftflotte* 5 were shot down, and seven Me 110s were destroyed. It was early in the battle, but the Germans were getting the idea that their vaunted Me 110s, which Göring loved, could not safely engage in drawn-out dogfights with the RAF. Before the battle was over, the 110s were being used in more of a dive bomber role and had to be escorted by flights of 109s.

This did German morale no good, and as the Battle of Britain wore on, Göring began to get much of the blame for his "sponsorship" of the 110s. One of the men who had a poor opinion of Göring was Adolf Galland, who became one of the best-known and respected pilots of WWII by his comrades and enemies.

Galland is the one gesturing. Sperrle is to his right, with fellow pilots Mölders and von Osterkamp to his left. The occasion was Osterkamp's birthday in 1941. Galland had shot down three Hurricanes on his way to the party, carrying a lobster dinner crammed behind his seat.[58]

Adolf Galland

The results of the second day's raids told some of the *Jagdflieger* (fighter pilots, literally "hunters of the air") that there was something or perhaps many things that Luftwaffe intelligence was missing. The men had been told the British only had three hundred fighters and that they were all located in the south of the country. The German pilots could not count the number of RAF planes for themselves, but the fact there were plenty of them in the sky over the north coast and North Sea was an indication that either the British had more fighters than was being reported or that the British had an inside line on German movements and shifted planes from the south to the north to meet them. The British did not have to shift more fighters north. They already had them there, although they also had an inside line to German movements through the breaking of German codes.

Galland was one of the men who began to see that the Battle of Britain was not going to be the "cakewalk" that some of his comrades and most of his countrymen and women seemed to think it would be.

Galland, who was born in 1912, was one of those young men you occasionally read about who fell in love with flying from a young age. He was only two when WWI began, and he, like many other German boys, was brought up on tales of the famous German pilots of WWI, like the Red Baron and his successor, Hermann Göring. Galland was also one of the young men who learned the basics of flying at one of the gliding schools that popped up all over Germany between the wars.

In 1932, he gained a rare commercial pilot license. He applied to join the army that same year (remember, the German Army had been limited in size by the Treaty of Versailles; there were only 100,000 slots to fill). He was accepted but chose to remain a commercial pilot for the government-run Lufthansa for another year before he was transferred to the new German air force in 1934.

In 1937, Galland went to Spain with the Condor Legion and flew ground attack missions in the Spanish Civil War. When he returned the next year, he was sent to Berlin to write about his experiences in Spain and to help formulate better ground attack tactics for the Luftwaffe. His writings became part of German air combat doctrine in WWII.

Very few people who wanted to fly in their nation's air forces sit by their bedroom window looking up at the sky, saying, "I want to fly a bomber." No, most look up at the clouds and imagine blowing through them in a fighter plane. It was the same for Galland, as it was for many of the pilots of the Luftwaffe and the RAF. In early 1940, Galland switched over to fighter planes. By the end of the year, he had scored fifty-seven victories over France and England. By late 1941, Galland had shot down ninety-six planes. In November 1941, Galland's friend Werner Mölders died in a plane crash, and Galland took his place as general until January 1945. In 1942, Galland was the planner of a highly technical yet successful operation in which the Luftwaffe escorted important and much sought-after (by the British) German battleships and cruisers through the Straits of Dover.

For all of his gallantry in battle and service during the war, at the war's end, Galland earned the Knight's Cross of the Iron Cross with Golden Oak Leaves, Swords and Diamonds, which was only given to twenty-seven men during WWII, Werner Mölders being one of them. When the war ended, Galland was only thirty-three years old.

By 1944, the air superiority the Germans had in 1939 and early 1940 was a dream. The United States, with its immense industrial capacity, had entered the war. German bombing raids over England had ground to an almost complete halt by this time. The British were making thousands of planes a year. Attacks on German cities were growing in intensity, and

Göring, many of whose decisions were faulty, looked around for someone to blame for the increasing number of Allied planes flying over Germany. He blamed Galland, who had been very vocal about what he needed to defend Germany but whose suggestions had fallen on deaf ears. In January 1945, Galland and a number of his supporters were removed from command for what is known as the Fighter Pilots' Mutiny, in which they came face to face with Göring and criticized him, his decision-making, and his leadership style in front of others.

By the time the Fighter Pilots' Mutiny broke out, Göring had lost much of his power and his influence with Hitler, having made promise after promise but never following through on them. Most notably, he vowed to fly in over one thousand tons of supplies each day to the encircled German 6th Army at Stalingrad in late 1942/early 1943. He was unable to do so.

By 1945, Göring was spending most of his time at his estate Carinhall, named for his first wife, who had died in 1931. The wedding to his second wife, Emmy, with Hitler as Göring's best man, was the Nazi event of the year in 1935. In the latter part of the war, Göring was high on morphine virtually all the time and cared less and less about the Luftwaffe unless it affected him personally. Even before this, Hitler had begun to grow tired of his company, which he had once enjoyed, pointing to Göring at a dinner party and telling the people present to watch the Luftwaffe chief "eat like a pig." Likely due to a combination of Göring's apathy, his growing irrelevance, and Galland's popularity among the men, Galland and the others were only removed from their posts rather than jailed or worse.

As you just learned, Göring's and Galland's opinions of each other grew worse and worse as the war went on, but it may have taken its first turn for the worse during the Battle of Britain. Galland and many other German fighter pilots during the battle were growing frustrated with the role in which Göring put them. Close escorts of the bombers at slower speeds put the Bf 109 at risk, for its pilots would then have to accelerate. At the lower speeds, the 109 lacked the maneuverability for which it was famous. At a meeting on the coast of France, Galland told Göring, "If you demand I fight at these ineffective speeds, give me a squadron of Spitfires." The "Spit" was respected and feared by the German pilots, and it was much more maneuverable at slower speeds than the 109. Galland had a lot of guts, for he said this to Göring in front of others, most of whom were pilots that had agreed with his assessment of German tactics.

In March 1945, a month and a half before the end of the war, Galland formed and commanded a squadron of the famous Me 262s, the world's first operational jet fighter. By the war's end, Galland had claimed one hundred kills, six of them in the Me 262, becoming one of the world's first jet fighter aces.

After the war, Galland was kept in British custody as a high-ranking officer of the Luftwaffe and was interrogated (not tortured) many times about Luftwaffe tactics. He spent two years as a prisoner of war, most of it in England. After his release, Galland, who had never been accused of war crimes, went to Argentina, where there had been a large German immigrant population before the war. There, he became an instructor for the air force. He then returned to Germany and wrote his autobiography, which was popular not only in Germany but also in the US and Great Britain, making him a rich man. He also ran an aircraft consultancy firm and was a consultant for the epic English movie, *The Battle of Britain.*

One of the other consultants was English fighter ace Robert Stanford-Tuck, with whom Galland became fast friends. At one point during the movie, Galland's character was supposed to give Göring the Hitler salute. Galland became angry and threatened to walk off the set. Stanford-Tuck supported him, and the movie was made without it. Another consultant was Polish squadron commander Boleslaw Drobinski, one of two men to have shot down Galland during the war.

Galland died in 1996 and was a commentator for the famous WWII documentary *World at War* and was the subject of or a participant in many other documentaries about the Battle of Britain, his other experiences during the war, and life in WWII Germany.

Back to the Battle

As the battle on England's northern coast was ending, the German forces in France were gathering for yet another attack. The formations massing over the French coast were so big that British radar was not able to show individual units but instead showed one massive blob gathering over the Channel.

At 3 p.m., twenty-five Me 110s of Erprobungsgruppe 210 and a slightly smaller number of 109s made their way to an airfield on the north side of the Thames Estuary and damaged it badly, despite being challenged by a dozen Hurricanes.

Eighty-eight Dornier "Flying Pencils" launched off Cap Gris-Nez, the closest French territory to England. They were escorted by an astounding

130 Bf 109s and a follow-on group of 61 Bf 109s from Galland's 26th Fighter Group, which flew high above the main flight to clear the way or bounce any British fighters rising to meet them. Parts of five British squadrons, totaling thirty-nine fighters, rose up to meet them, but the Germans' advantage in numbers was too great for any appreciable damage to be done to them. The bombers split up and hit a series of targets on the south side of the mouth of the Thames.

After refueling and gathering intelligence, Erprobungsgruppe 210 launched another raid. This time, their target was the important sector station at Kenley, northeast of the Isle of Wight, but they made an error and hit another sector station at Croydon, which was home to a famous civilian airfield in peacetime. The sector stations were extremely important, for vital information came to these stations from RAF Fighter Command. They were also home to varied numbers of fighters.

The next attack came in the form of twenty-four German bombers, which also made an error. The German bombers were meant to strike the large sector station at Biggin Hill, south of the Thames River, but struck a smaller satellite airfield to the northeast, which wasn't even operational yet.

Sixty Ju 88 bombers and forty-one 110s launched from Normandy flew through three RAF squadrons and bombed three airfields in south-central England, causing some damage. The men and women in the operations rooms plotting German attacks were busy on August 15th, and they weren't done yet.

A group of thirty Stukas launched from the Brittany Peninsula on the far west French Channel coast, escorted by a large mixed group of 109s and 110s. They attacked Portland, the Royal Navy base, just days after the previous attack. Eighteen British fighters rushed to intercept them.

August 15th was the most intense day of the battle, even though September 15th is remembered today as Battle of Britain Day for the RAF's actions over London and other cities. Fourteen RAF squadrons had planes in the air at one time or another, and some of those fighters took to the air more than once. One thousand RAF sorties took place that day. Seventy-one German planes were shot down, while the RAF only lost thirty-one.

During two of the next three days, the Luftwaffe launched one massive attack after another. The radar station at Ventnor, which was recovering from a previous raid, was hit again. Another radar station was also badly damaged. Many RAF airfields were attacked, as were three sector stations.

Over the course of those three days, the Germans lost one hundred planes to fifty-three downed British planes.

The Military Situation One Week after the *Adlerangriff* Began

In the one week since the start of the Eagle Offensive, the Germans lost 284 planes; they were either destroyed, crash-landed over England or France in various states of disrepair, or were in the Channel. This was 10 percent of Germany's available strength. The Germans could not understand why there seemed to be a steady or growing number of British planes in the air while they were losing theirs at an increasing rate. German planes that went down over England were carefully picked over for intelligence information and airplane performance. Surviving Luftwaffe crew were taken prisoner or went to hospitals.

Though a number of German pilots were roughed up by locals rushing toward their falling parachutes, there was only one confirmed case of German pilots being killed by English civilians. Though the Battle of Britain was fought for the survival of the British nation and system, many pilots and politicians have noted that, much like in WWI, RAF and German pilots had a respect for each other that was not often seen in other theaters of war. There were cases of British planes escorting parachuting Germans to the ground to prevent other RAF planes or air defense guns from shooting at them, though not all British pilots were so sanguine.

In the famous documentary series *World at War*, one British pilot spoke about feeling sorry for German pilots whom he had killed or witnessed being shot down. The next RAF veteran said, "I didn't feel sorry for them, no. Not a bit. They were trying to enslave us."

Bf 109 that ran out of fuel over England and was forced to land, 1940.[59]

It became clear to the Germans that their famous Stukas were completely obsolete except over uncontested skies. Thirty had been destroyed in one day alone. Göring's favorite, the Me 110, the only German long-range fighter with ranges between 480 miles and 565 miles depending on speed, load, and wind, was much too slow to engage with the Spitfires and found the older Hurricanes a challenge as well. These planes, which were designed to fly on their own, now had to be escorted by 109s. The performance of both planes suffered because of another one of Göring's mistakes, as he promoted the plane as being the best of the German fighters. Almost eighty were blown out of the sky in one week.

This left the 109s as the Germans' primary fighter, and though it was the best German fighter of the time, it was only able to stay above England for twenty minutes at the most since there were no drop tanks designed specifically for the 109 available at the time. Obviously, this meant a limited range for the fighters, and any German raids flying farther inland were either escorted by the 110s, which worked out badly, or flew at night, hoping to evade British radar and fighter patrols. As you can imagine, these limitations further increased the odds against a successful German invasion of Britain before hard weather set in.

Chapter 10 – Göring Changes Plans, and the British Grit Their Teeth

Göring finally admitted changes would have to be made in how the Luftwaffe attacked its ground targets and engaged with the British fighters. On August 19th, he pulled all of the Stukas out of the battle. *Luftflotte* 3 would now concentrate on night bombing missions, and the 109s of *Luftflotte* 3 would be transferred to *Luftflotte* 2, which would put them closer to England, slightly increasing the time they were able to stay in enemy territory.

Furthermore, the Reichsmarschall had German attacks focus on the southeastern coast nearest France instead of attacking all along the English coastline. The prime targets would continue to be RAF airfields and sector stations, which were becoming less and less functional with each passing day, despite the incredible work of British ground crews to get them back in business after each raid. However, the British caught a break, for Göring ordered another change to German plans. He ceased the raids on radar stations since they were proving too costly and difficult to destroy. This was true, but it gave the British a decided advantage because, at least before Göring's order, some radar stations were put out of action for a day or more. The RAF would soon realize that they did not have to patrol the areas over their radar stations and could concentrate on German attacks elsewhere.

Adolf Galland's complaint to Göring and his sarcastic request for Spitfires, which we talked about in the prior chapter, happened around this time. In addition to the changes described above, the 109 pilots were ordered to stay close to the bombers, which were taking heavy damage. Göring also ordered that from that point forward, every bomber would be escorted by three fighters, which limited their roles and missions even further. It also meant the number of bombing raids over England would be cut down since there were not enough fighters to escort the current number of raids.

We already mentioned some of the disadvantages the 109 pilots experienced when this order was given, but Göring's order also meant that because the Bf 109's stall speed (the point at which the plane would lose lift and fall toward the earth) was about the same as the bomber's cruising speed, the fighters would have to zig-zag behind them to keep close to them, which used more fuel without covering more ground.

Cities, Churchill, and the Royals

From August 19th to August 23rd, bad weather restricted German daytime raids to just a few probing attacks. Fighter pilots on both sides got a much-needed rest, and some of the British pilots were able to go on a short leave, perhaps to homes nearby. The German pilots sat around soggy airfields in France and slept.

The weather at night during those four days was relatively clear, and the British began to get a taste of what was to come in September: the bombing of cities and civilians. Over these four days, Liverpool, Sheffield, Coventry, Darby, and Hull were all attacked.

Coventry is a name you might recognize from WWII history. Though it was first bombed on August 3rd and again on August 19th, the most infamous attack on the city occurred after the Battle of Britain was over, on November 14th, 1940. Nearly six hundred civilians were killed, and much of the city center, including its famous cathedral, was destroyed. After the war, a former member of the secret British code-breaking and intelligence effort (codenamed "ULTRA") asserted that Winston Churchill had been told that Coventry was the target for that evening but that he had ordered RAF Fighter Command not to defend the city because it might tip off the Germans that their codes had been broken. This assertion was later proved to be incorrect. Churchill gave no such order, as he and RAF Fighter Command were actually under the impression that London was going to be the main target that evening.

Churchill (center) reviewing the damage to Coventry Cathedral, November 1940.[60]

As we mentioned earlier, Winston Churchill became the symbol of British resilience and defiance during the Battle of Britain, the Blitz (which would follow the battle), and the war itself. He seemed to be everywhere, sometimes even showing up unexpectedly at RAF Fighter Command or various sector stations. His presence was not always welcome in the operations rooms, for he tended to be a meddler, but for the most part, Churchill's presence did wonders for the spirits of the pilots, ground crews, WAAFs, and civilians who were suffering from German attacks. He visited damaged parts of London and other cities, and as you likely know, his speeches, especially during the Battle of Britain, electrified the nation and provided an immeasurable boost to morale.

He was not the only one. His wife Clementine toured damaged cities and organized various drives to help those affected by German attacks. Most importantly, the royal family remained at Buckingham Palace. King George VI knew that for the sake of the country and the future of the monarchy, he had to remain in London and share the trials and tribulations of his people. When he told his wife and children that they had to leave, he received a resounding no. They all remained, including the future Queen Elizabeth II, and they contributed to the war effort in any way they could.

Support for the royal family greatly increased. Elizabeth was only fourteen when the Battle of Britain raged, but she made her first public speech during the Blitz, addressing the many children of England's cities who had been evacuated to the countryside for their safety, torn apart from their parents and friends. She told them, among other things, that "We are trying to do all we can to help our gallant sailors, soldiers, and airmen, and we are trying, too, to bear our own share of the danger and sadness of war. We know, every one of us, that in the end all will be well."

On September 13th, 1940, Buckingham Palace was hit by a number of German bombs, which caused considerable damage. Afterward, the Queen Mother, also named Elizabeth, said, "Now, we can look the East End in the face." The East End was the hardest-hit area of London, and after the bombing of the palace, the royals didn't feel embarrassed when visiting the worst-hit areas.

Airfields

When the weather cleared on August 24th, German raids began in earnest on the airfields in southeastern England, all of which were the responsibility of the RAF's 11 Group under Vice Marshal Keith Park. This period of the battle would be perhaps the toughest for RAF Fighter Command.

The first of the daylight raids on 11 Group's sector hit five sector stations east of London on both sides of the Thames, another upriver farther toward the city, and another on the south coast. These happened over the course of a few days, and a number of the sector stations were heavily damaged or hit more than once.

While the British covered the important sector stations with airborne patrols, the satellite airfields of the sector were hit. On August 31st, the same sector stations and smaller airfields were all attacked again.

When September began, the German attacks on the same sector stations and airfields continued. After each attack and sometimes literally as the Germans were flying away, crews began to try to repair the damage. At the airfields, the runways, which could be dirt or asphalt, were the priority. At the sector stations, key command and control equipment and buildings were restored as best they could under the circumstances. Some key airfields were so badly damaged that it was considered a minor miracle that planes were able to take off from them at all.

The after-battle report at Manston airbase after one of these raids read, "At 1250 hrs the aerodrome was heavily attacked by approximately fifteen Me110's and some Heinkel's and bombed at low altitude; some 150 HE bombs were dropped; the aerodrome was pitted with approximate 100 craters and rendered temporarily unserviceable; two hangars were damaged, and workshops were destroyed; in the latter building a civilian clerk was killed, this being the only fatal casualty; the raid lasted approximately five minutes."

For a brief period of time, Hermann Göring had done the right thing, at least for Germany. Bomber raids escorted by huge numbers of fighters made it very hard for the British Spitfires and Hurricanes to penetrate enemy formations and attack the bombers. However, the fighting spirit and resilience of the RAF and the British were at their height. At times, one RAF squadron would get the order to "scramble" (get to their planes) and find they'd been sent against a formation of thirty bombers escorted by more than one hundred fighters. They attacked anyway. As Churchill said in his speech after France was defeated, "Upon this battle depends the survival of Christian civilization ... if we fail, then the whole world, including the United States, including all that we have known and cared for, will sink into the abyss of a new Dark Age."

Both experienced and novice RAF pilots were being shot down at an alarming rate, though they were taking a toll on the Germans as well. The problem for the RAF was not a lack of planes but a lack of pilots. In peacetime, fighter training was considered complete after about eight months. Though this was shortened considerably, and though there was no shortage of volunteers, it still took time to train men to become fighter pilots. It only took a second to shoot one down. These men would have had a decent amount of time for flight training, but training on actual fighters was cut radically. Some of the men coming to the front lines of the Battle of Britain were facing the best the Luftwaffe could offer with only spending *nine* hours in a Hurricane or Spitfire.

One of the interesting aspects of the battle was that many British fighter pilots and other RAF personnel were beginning to harbor private doubts as to whether the RAF could survive more of the punishment the Germans were dealing out. However, many German pilots, who were very rarely, if ever, given leave during the battle, were losing heart as well. During August, 18 percent of the Luftwaffe's strength had been lost.

Friends were being shot down or captured by the hundreds. Many of the bombers that did return were heavily damaged and contained dead and wounded men. The insides of the bombers resembled the inside of a destroyed tank. There was blood pooled on the floor, and guts and limbs were strewn about. Many men who crashed were seriously burned and disfigured for life if they survived. The Luftwaffe lost 229 men, killed or taken prisoner. Eighty were seriously wounded, and 264 were missing—and that was in August alone. The Luftwaffe had more experienced pilots than the RAF did, but their numbers were rapidly dwindling.

During this time, the debate over tactics, which would later cost Hugh Dowding his job, began to heat up as RAF losses mounted. The opposition to Dowding's tactic of only meeting the Luftwaffe with what was deemed the minimal strength necessary came from 12 Group commander Trafford Leigh-Mallory, who was backed by the popular squadron commander Douglas Bader. Bader advocated launching three or four squadrons at a time at the German formations as they flew over the Channel. Supporting Dowding was the New Zealander 11 Group's commander Keith Park. The debate between the two groups grew quite intense, and for a time, it caused cooperation between the two sector groups to suffer. Leigh-Mallory finally grew so frustrated that he went over his commander's head and met with Winston Churchill, who, for the moment, stood with Dowding.

The German effort in the last week of August and the first part of September seemed to be working. Not only was the strain showing in RAF command, but it was also showing in the tired pilots of the RAF (who, you must remember, numbered only half the number of the Luftwaffe). The practice of rotating pilots out of high combat areas to areas that were seeing less action was being brought to a halt. The damage done to the airfields of southeastern England, which were the most important in the country, was getting so great that crews could not keep up with repairs. Worse was the fact that the RAF's losses were, for the first time, greater than what British factories could produce. New RAF pilots were thrown immediately into the fight, and there was no rest. Men landed their planes and sometimes had to be lifted out of their cockpits due to exhaustion. They would head into barracks, sit down on the edge of their beds in their combat gear, and sometimes fall asleep sitting down. Things were quite grim.

Attacks against civilians happened throughout the battle but increased after the Germans lost their bid to invade England. The Britons' spirit was never broken. Here, a young woman plays music during an air raid.[61]

The fighters were not the only British pilots getting tired. Throughout the Battle of Britain, RAF Bomber Command was hitting targets behind enemy lines with varying degrees of success. In many cases, they were targeting Germany itself. These sorties were flown at night and were very costly. Many people do not know this, but RAF Bomber Command lost more men and aircraft during the battle than RAF Fighter Command did.

On the evening of August 24th, German bombers were separated from their formation and missed their target. Not wanting to return to base with a load of bombs, which would not be seen in a very good light by their fellow pilots and commanders, not to mention the dangers of landing on a rough, unpaved runway with heavy bombs on board, the Germans dropped their payload over a civilian area of London. This had not been done before, though civilians had been killed throughout the battle in other locations. Today, we would call them "collateral damage," as they hadn't been specifically targeted.

To the British, the bombs dropped on London, the capital of the British Empire, required revenge. They did not know and had no reason to believe that the "raid" over London had been accidental. Ironically, when Göring was told of the raid on London, he flew into a rage. He had specifically ordered that no bombs were to be dropped on London. The stray pilots who had done so were drummed out of the Luftwaffe.

Churchill called a meeting of the War Cabinet early the next morning and unanimously agreed that retribution was called for. They must raid Berlin. The chief of RAF Bomber Command, Air Marshal Charles Portal, put together a group of just over one hundred bombers (a significant percentage of Bomber Command at the time) to go on a mission that night, August 25th, 1940. The bombers were assigned to strike an aircraft factory, a power station, and two airfields. Other attacks were sent against targets around other German cities farther to the west of Berlin, as well as in France and Holland. These were to serve as decoys to distract German air defenses from the raid on Berlin, which amounted to sixty-seven planes. They arrived near Berlin in the early morning hours of August 26th.

Unfortunately for the British pilots, their target was largely obscured by fog. Only twenty-six of the bombers dropped their payloads, and virtually none of the bombs hit their targets. They did cause light damage to residences in the Berlin suburbs, but it's not clear if there were any German civilian deaths. Over the next ten days, five more British raids hit Berlin.

Adolf Hitler grew angrier by the day, as he was said to be out of his mind with rage. He issued a *Führerbefehl* ("Führer's order"), which stated that from that point forward, Luftwaffe attacks should focus on British cities, especially London. Just when the RAF was on the ropes, Hitler "saved" them.

On September 7th, Göring and Kesselring watched from the cliffs opposite England as a huge formation assembled for the first massed daylight attack on the British capital. The first wave of German planes consisted of three hundred bombers and six hundred fighters.

Looking at their radar screens, the British saw the German formation mass on the other side of the Channel, then fly over the water. They had every reason to believe this was an attempt to strike a massive blow against the vital sector stations, which were almost at the end of their ropes. Twenty-one RAF squadrons, over 250 fighters, were scrambled to cover the sector stations in the southeast. By the time they realized what was happening, the Germans were over the city.

The German raid, all nine hundred planes, targeted the docks of the East End of London. These docks were an important part of London's lifeline to the outside world. The area was densely populated and poor and consisted of many wooden buildings. Not only were the buildings flammable, but the warehouses in the East End also contained things like sugar, rum, rubber, and other items that burned easily and intensely.

The daylight raid caused much of the East End to go up in flames. That evening, the flames were so intense and so bright that the next wave of German bombers, some three hundred, easily found their way to their target from the English Channel coast. Though the British had suffered civilian losses during the battle, the toll for that night exceeded them all: 448 people were killed.

Over the next four days and nights, bad weather reduced the number of raids, but on September 11th, another large German daylight raid on London took place. There were mixed feelings in RAF Fighter Command and in the Cabinet as they realized the Germans had switched tactics. Raids on British airfields decreased greatly and gave the RAF time to strengthen their defenses and repair them. The fighter pilots also got some much-needed rest. Not only did the rest boost the RAF's effectiveness and morale, but the raids over London also motivated them more than any nap could. Though many British fighter pilots knew it at the time, it was only after the battle that most others realized the turning point in the battle had been reached. RAF Fighter Command would survive, and Hitler would not be able to launch his invasion, at least not in 1940. From that point forward, the RAF would increase in strength, and it would inflict a terrible toll on the Luftwaffe, even as London began to burn.

Adlertag

On September 15th, now known as Battle of Britain Day in Great Britain, the Luftwaffe began forming once again over France. Many British radar operators watched their screens in astonishment as more and more German planes joined the formation. Once again underestimating British radar, the German planes massed inland, hoping to avoid detection as they formed up, but on the other side of the water, the British knew the Germans were coming.

Not only did the RAF know the Germans were coming, but they were also almost 100 percent certain the incoming raid would head to London. This gave RAF Fighter Command time to organize its defenses. The men of the Luftwaffe had been told by their intelligence services that the RAF had no more than 150 fighters left. That was wrong. Both 11 Group and 12 Group formed around London to give the Germans a shock.

Throughout the day, the Luftwaffe sent over 1,000 planes to London: 500 bombers and 620 fighters. Meeting them were 630 RAF Spitfires and Hurricanes. This was the day Churchill decided to visit RAF Fighter Command. There, he asked how many reserves there were. The answer was zero.

The day was costly for both sides. The RAF lost twenty-nine planes, with twenty-one being damaged. Fifteen pilots had been killed. The Germans lost around sixty planes, with twenty severely damaged. Since German pilots who bailed out over England were captured, Germany's losses for the day were around eighty killed and sixty-five captured. A further twenty-one were listed as missing. The Germans had lost 166 highly trained men.

With RAF airfields back in business, aircraft production again exceeding losses, and the men rested and well motivated, the Luftwaffe's continuing but gradually decreasing daylight raids became more and more costly for the Germans. For the next ninety days, Göring launched nighttime bombing raids over London and England, hoping to break English morale and cause a civilian uprising. The raids of 1940/41 killed tens of thousands of people all over the country, but British morale wasn't weakened at all. In fact, it was strengthened.

On September 15th, the RAF broke the back of the Luftwaffe. Though the German air force would go on to achieve great victories over the Soviet Union after Germany's invasion the following summer and would continue its night raids on London and other population centers, its attempt to control the skies over England had failed. Hitler, whose main goal was to grab "living space" for the German people in Russia, committed the same error he had always criticized the German Army of WWI. He was fighting a two-front war.

"The gratitude of every home in our Island, in our Empire, and indeed throughout the world, except in the abodes of the guilty, goes out to the British airmen who, undaunted by odds, unwearied in their constant challenge and mortal danger, are turning the tide of the World War by their prowess and their devotion. Never in the field of human conflict was so much owed by so many to so few." - Winston Churchill, August 20th, 1940.

A poster from WWII featuring Churchill's words.[62]

Conclusion

The RAF prevented Hitler from invading the United Kingdom in 1940. Its victory and the spirit of the British people changed other people's minds about the war's outcome. This was especially true in the United States.

Many people in the United States believed that the country's entry into WWI had been a mistake. Around 100,000 Americans had died in just a few months of combat in 1917/18, and most Americans wanted their government to keep out of another European war.

Franklin Roosevelt knew that Britain's survival was paramount, and he began to send increasing amounts of weapons and supplies to the UK. However, these actions received criticism, both in Congress and from the American people.

The majority of Americans sided with Britain and were motivated by Churchill's speeches, even before the battle, but most of these people still believed the US should stay neutral and not get involved in the conflict. Also, by June 1940, Hitler looked invincible.

Many Americans, a great many of them from Ireland or with Irish roots, were decidedly anti-British in outlook. Many German immigrants hated Hitler, but others did not.

One of the factors in changing the American public's opinion was the reports from American reporters on the ground in London. Though there were many reporters, the most famous of them all was Edward R. Murrow, whose live radio reports, sometimes with bombs exploding and sirens wailing audibly in the background, brought the terror of the

German attacks into living rooms all over the United States. He would begin each broadcast with the now-famous words: "This is London."

Murrow's broadcasts and interviews with undaunted Londoners and the occasional British pilot swayed public opinion. As the Battle of Britain went on, more and more Americans were awed by the British people's spirit and fight. Churchill's speeches were listened to as eagerly as speeches by Roosevelt. On December 26th, 1941, just weeks after the Japanese attack on Pearl Harbor, Churchill delivered one of the first speeches by a foreign leader to a joint session of the US Congress. Even members who had been strongly against America's entry into the war and had viewed Churchill as a militarist throughout his long career stood and gave him one of the longest-standing ovations in congressional history.

Hitler declared war on the United States on December 11th, sealing his fate, but he began to lose the war in Europe on September 15th, 1940.

Roosevelt and Churchill aboard the HMS *Prince of Wales*, August 10th, 1941.[63]

If you enjoyed this book, a review on Amazon would be greatly appreciated because it would mean a lot to hear from you.

To leave a review:

1. Open your camera app.
2. Point your mobile device at the QR code.
3. The review page will appear in your web browser.

Thanks for your support!

Here's another book by Captivating History that you might like

Free Bonus from Captivating History (Available for a Limited time)

Appendix A: Further Reading and Reference

Part 1

Dyer, Christopher. *Everyday Life in Medieval England.* 1994.

Hunter, Peter. *Roman Britain and Early England: 55 BC-871 AD.* 1966.

Levine, Philippa. *The British Empire: Sunrise to Sunset.* 2007.

McCourt, Malachy. *Malachy McCourt's History of Ireland.* 2001.

Schama, Simon. *A History of Britain.* 2000. (TV series)

Part 2

Chapter 1

"First Britons" https://www.nhm.ac.uk/discover/first-britons.html Accessed: December 7, 2023.

"Neolithic Britain: where did the first farmers come from?" https://www.nhm.ac.uk/discover/news/2019/april/neolithic-britain-where-did-the-first-farmers-come-from.html#:~:text=The%20introduction%20of%20farming%20across,has%20been%20providing%20some%20answers Accessed: December 7, 2023.

"Why was Stonehenge Built?" https://www.history.com/news/why-was-stonehenge-built Accessed: December 7, 2023.

"Stunning Sacred Megalithic Sites of Britain" https://www.ancient-origins.net/ancient-places-europe/megalithic-sites-0017711 Accessed: December 7, 2023.

Chapter 2

"Ancient DNA study reveals large scale migrations into Bronze Age Britain" https://www.york.ac.uk/news-and-events/news/2021/research/ancient-dna-study-migration-bronze-age/ Accessed: December 9, 2023.

"Who were the Celts?" https://museum.wales/articles/1341/Who-were-the-Celts/ Accessed: December 9, 2023.

"Study Finds Huge Undetected Migration Wave to Prehistoric Britain" https://www.ancient-origins.net/news-history-archaeology/prehistoric-britain-0016211 Accessed: December 9, 2023.

"What was the Society of the Celts Like?" https://www.thecollector.com/the-celts-society-celtic/ Accessed: December 9, 2023.

"Early Celtic Social Structures" https://exploringcelticciv.web.unc.edu/early-celtic-social-structures/ Accessed: December 9, 2023.

"The Iron Age Tribes of Britain" https://www.heritagedaily.com/2021/01/the-iron-age-tribes-of-britain/136847 Accessed: December 9, 2023.

"Druids: The Ancient Celtic Class That Did It All" https://historycooperative.org/druids/ Accessed: December 9, 2023.

"Sacred Sites & Rituals in the Ancient Celtic Religion" https://www.worldhistory.org/article/1710/sacred-sites--rituals-in-the-ancient-celtic-religi/ Accessed: December 9, 2023.

"Celtic Mythology: Myths, Legends, Deities, Heroes, and Culture" https://historycooperative.org/celtic-mythology/ Accessed: December 14, 2023.

"History of Chysauster Ancient Village" https://www.english-heritage.org.uk/visit/places/chysauster-ancient-village/history/ Accessed: December 9, 2023.

"Clothing of the Ancient Celts" https://reconstructinghistory.com/blogs/blog/clothing-of-the-ancient-celtsla-tene-500-bc-1-ad-late-iron-age Accessed: December 9, 2023.

Chapter 3

"Why did Julius Caesar invade Britain?" https://www.historyskills.com/classroom/ancient-history/caesar-in-britain/ Accessed: December 11, 2023.

"Invasion of Britain" https://www.unrv.com/julius-caesar/invasion-of-britain.php Accessed: December 11, 2023.

"Julius Caesar's Expedition to Britannia" https://warfarehistorynetwork.com/article/julius-caesars-expedition-to-brittania/ Accessed: December 11, 2023.

"Julius Caesar's First Landing in Britain" https://www.historytoday.com/archive/julius-caesar%E2%80%99s-first-landing-britain Accessed: December 11, 2023.

"Julius Caesar's Description of the Britons" https://elfinspell.com/PrimarySource55BCBritons.html Accessed: December 11, 2023.

"Roman Britain" https://www.britannica.com/place/Roman-Britain Accessed: December 11, 2023.

"The Roman Invasions of Britain" https://warwick.ac.uk/fac/arts/classics/warwickclassicsnetwork/romancoventry/resources/interactions/invasion/ Accessed: December 11, 2023.

"What Caused Boudica's Great British Revolt Against Roman Rule?" https://www.historyhit.com/what-caused-boudiccas-great-british-revolt-against-roman-rule/ Accessed: December 11, 2023.

"The harrowing reason that drove Boudica to rise up against the military might of the Roman Empire." https://www.historyskills.com/classroom/ancient-history/boudicca/. Accessed: December 11, 2023.

"Boudica" https://englishhistory.net/romans/boudica/ Accessed: December 11, 2023.

"Boudica's Revolt: When Britannia's Warrior Queen Took On Rome" https://www.thecollector.com/bouddica-warrior-queen-iceni-revolt-rome/ Accessed: December 11, 2023.

Chapter 4

"Changing Landscape: Roman Infrastructure in the Early Middle Ages" https://www.medievalists.net/2020/07/roman-infrastructure-middle-ages/ Accessed: December 13, 2023.

"Roman Britain" https://www.britannica.com/place/Roman-Britain Accessed: December 13, 2023.

"The Romanization of English Law" https://openyls.law.yale.edu/bitstream/handle/20.500.13051/3928/Romanization_of_English_Law.pdf?sequence=2 Accessed: December 13, 2023.

"Romanization: The Process of Becoming Roman" https://www.bbc.co.uk/history/ancient/romans/romanisation_article_01.shtml Accessed: December 13, 2023.

"Roman Britain – villas, baths and daily life" https://www.britainexpress.com/History/Life_in_Roman_Britain.htm Accessed: December 13, 2023.

"Life in Roman Britain" https://www.britannica.com/place/Roman-Britain/Life-in-Roman-Britain Accessed: December 13, 2023.

"The Rural Settlement of Roman Britain: an online resource" https://archaeologydataservice.ac.uk/archives/view/romangl/ Accessed: December 13, 2023.

"Economic Changes the Romans Brought to Britain" https://www.romanobritain.org/rcb_econonic_changes.php Accessed: December 13, 2023.

"Roman Society" https://www.britannica.com/place/United-Kingdom/Roman-society Accessed: December 13, 2023.

"Why did the Romans abandon Britain in AD 410?" https://www.historyskills.com/classroom/ancient-history/romans-leave-britain/ Accessed: December 14, 2023.

"Why did the Romans Leave Britain?" https://www.historyhit.com/why-did-the-romans-leave-britain-and-what-was-the-legacy-of-their-departure/ Accessed: December 14, 2023.

"The Decline of Roman Britain" https://www.historytoday.com/archive/decline-roman-britain Accessed: December 14, 2023.

"Uncovering the Secrets of Hadrian's Wall" https://www.english-heritage.org.uk/visit/places/birdoswald-roman-fort-hadrians-wall/history-and-stories/the-secrets-of-birdoswald/ Accessed: December 14, 2023.

Chapter 5

"The Roman 'Brexit': how life in Britain changed after 409AD" https://www.heritagedaily.com/2018/10/the-roman-brexit-how-life-in-britain-changed-after-409ad/121937 Accessed: December 15, 2023.

"The Evolution of Post-Roman Kingdoms: Anglo-Saxons, Welsh, and Picts in Britain" https://history-of-europe.com/the-evolution-of-post-roman-kingdoms-anglo-saxons-welsh-and-picts-in-britain/ Accessed: December 15, 2023.

"The Historical King Arthur" https://www.worldhistory.org/article/1068/the-historical-king-arthur/ Accessed: December 15, 2023.

"How Did the Fall of Roman Britain Create King Arthur?" https://www.thecollector.com/roman-britain-and-king-arthur/ Accessed: December 15, 2023.

"The Origins of King Arthur" https://www.arthurian-legend.com/origins-king-arthur/ Accessed: December 15, 2023.

Chapter 6

"Who were the Druids? A history of druidism in Britain" https://britishheritage.com/history/history-druids-britain Accessed: December 17, 2023.

"Druids: The Ancient Celtic Class That Did It All" https://historycooperative.org/druids/ Accessed: December 17, 2023.

"The Druids and Druidism" https://www.roman-britain.co.uk/the-celts-and-celtic-life/the-druids-and-druidism/ Accessed: December 17, 2023.

"The Romans in Britain: The Druids and Druidism" https://romanobritain.org/4-celt/clb_religion_druidism.php Accessed: December 17, 2023.

"The Consequences Roman Contact Had on British Religion" https://druidry.org/resources/the-consequences-roman-contact-had-on-british-religion Accessed: December 17, 2023.

"How did Christianity come to England?" https://archaeology.co.uk/articles/features/christianity-come-england.htm Accessed: December 17, 2023.

"Christianity and the Romans" https://www.romanobritain.org/2-arl_life/arl_religion_christianity.php Accessed: December 17, 2023.

"Forgotten faith? Tracing early Christianity in western Britain and Ireland" https://the-past.com/feature/forgotten-faith-tracing-early-christianity-in-western-britain-and-ireland/ Accessed: December 17, 2023.

Chapter 7

"Pre-Roman Britain" https://elizabethanenglandlife.com/roman-britain/pre-roman-britain.html Accessed: December 19, 2023.

"Rites before romanitas: Reconstructing Britain's Iron Age beliefs" https://archaeology.co.uk/articles/features/rites-before-romanitas-reconstructing-britains-iron-age-beliefs.htm Accessed: December 19, 2023.

"Brit History: Britain Before the Romans" https://anglotopia.net/british-history/brit-history-britain-romans/ Accessed: December 19, 2023.

"The Early Middle Ages" https://human.libretexts.org/Bookshelves/Art/Art_History_(Boundless)/16%3A_Early_Medieval_Europe/16.01%3A_The_Early_Middle_Ages Accessed: December 19, 2023.

"The 5 Greatest Treasures of the Anglo-Saxons" https://www.thecollector.com/5-greatest-anglo-saxons-treasures/ Accessed: December 19, 2023.

"Celtic Languages" https://www.britannica.com/topic/Celtic-languages Accessed: December 19, 2023.

Charles-Edwards, T.M. "The Britons and their Languages" in *Wales and the Britons, 350-1064.* (Oxford, 2012: online edn, Oxford Academic, 24 Jan. 2013.)

"What is Oral Tradition and Why Was It Useful in Ancient Times?" https://historydisclosure.com/what-is-oral-tradition-and-why-was-it-useful-in-ancient-times/ Accessed: December 19, 2023.

"Oral Tradition: Definition, Significance, Examples" https://blog.daisie.com/oral-tradition-definition-significance-examples/ Accessed: December 19, 2023.

Chapter 8

"Briton People" https://www.britannica.com/topic/Briton Accessed: December 21, 2023.

"Ancient Celtic Society" https://www.worldhistory.org/article/1720/ancient-celtic-society/ Accessed: December 21, 2023.

"Briton: Indigenous Celtic Peoples of Ancient Britain" https://brewminate.com/briton-indigenous-celtic-peoples-of-ancient-great-britain/ Accessed: December 21, 2023.

"Romans: Daily Life" https://www.english-heritage.org.uk/learn/story-of-england/romans/daily-life/ Accessed: December 21, 2023.

"Migration in Roman Britain" https://www.historytoday.com/migration-roman-britain Accessed: December 21, 2023.

"Brit History: Britain Before the Romans" https://anglotopia.net/british-history/brit-history-britain-romans/ Accessed: December 19, 2023.

"Becoming Boudica: How Celtic Female Warrior Culture Challenged Rome" https://classicalwisdom.com/people/leaders/becoming-boudica-how-celtic-female-warrior-culture-challenged-rome/ Accessed: December 21, 2023.

"Gender and Celtic Religions" https://www.encyclopedia.com/environment/encyclopedias-almanacs-transcripts-and-maps/gender-and-religion-gender-and-celtic-religions Accessed: December 21, 2023.

"Powerful women in late Iron Age London: the Harper Road burial" https://www.museumoflondon.org.uk/discover/powerful-women-late-iron-age-london-harper-road-burial Accessed: December 21, 2023.

"Gendered Violence in Iron Age and Roman Britain: Summary" https://www.cambridge.org/core/books/abs/cambridge-world-history-of-violence/gendered-violence-in-iron-age-and-roman-britain/82968DF0745DEE5E3DCD20E52AC21B65 Accessed: December 21, 2023.

"Women in Roman Britain: Diversity and Religion" https://warwick.ac.uk/fac/arts/classics/warwickclassicsnetwork/romancoventry/resources/diversity/women/ Accessed: December 21, 2023.

Moore, Tom. "Britain, Gaul, and Germany: Cultural Interactions", in Martin Millett, Louise Revell, and Alison Moore (eds), *The Oxford Handbook of Roman Britain,* Oxford Handbooks, 2016.

"The Romans in Britain: 100BC to 450AD" https://romanobritain.org Accessed: December 21, 2023.

Chapter 9

"Ancient British Weapons and Armour" https://www.historic-uk.com/HistoryUK/HistoryofEngland/Arms-Armour-up-to-1066/ Accessed: December 23, 2023.

"Celtic Warfare" https://www.roman-britain.co.uk/the-celts-and-celtic-life/celtic-warfare/ Accessed: December 23, 2023.

"The British Ware-Chariot" https://penelope.uchicago.edu/~grout/encyclopaedia_romana/britannia/boudica/chariot.html Accessed: December 23, 2023.

"The War Chariots of the Celtic Elite" https://warfarehistorynetwork.com/article/the-war-chariots-of-the-celtic-elite/ Accessed: December 23, 2023.

"Britons, Saxons & Vikings" https://www.battlefieldstrust.com/resource-centre/viking/ Accessed: December 23, 2023.

"Roman Britain" https://www.roman-britain.co.uk Accessed: December 23, 2023.

Davies, Sean, 2010. "The Battle of Chester and Warfare in Post-Roman Britain" *History.* Vol. 95(2). Pp. 143-158.

"The Romans in England" https://www.historic-uk.com/HistoryUK/HistoryofEngland/The-Romans-in-England/ Accessed: December 23, 2023.

"Boudica's Revolt: When Britannia's Warrior Queen Took On Rome" https://www.thecollector.com/bouddica-warrior-queen-iceni-revolt-rome/ Accessed: December 11, 2023.

"The Battle of Mons Graupius" https://penelope.uchicago.edu/~grout/encyclopaedia_romana/britannia/monsgraupius/monsgraupius.html Accessed; December 23, 2023.

"10 British Iron Age Hill Forts" https://www.heritagedaily.com/2021/03/10-british-iron-age-hill-forts/118900 Accessed; December 23, 2023.

"Iron Age Hill Forts in Britain" https://www.englishmonarchs.co.uk/celts_19.html Accessed: December 23, 2023.

"Inside Britain's biggest Iron Age fortress" https://www.cam.ac.uk/research/news/inside-britains-biggest-iron-age-fortress Accessed: December 23, 2023.

Chapter 10

"Ancient Celts" https://www.worldhistory.org/celt/ Accessed: December 26, 2023.

Jones, Michael E., 1998. *The End of Roman Britain.* Cornell University Pres.

"Who were the Picts, the early inhabitants of Scotland?" https://www.livescience.com/who-were-picts-scotland Accessed: December 26, 2023.

"Picts offer historians a picture of non-Roman Briton culture" https://www.psu.edu/news/research/story/picts-offer-historians-picture-non-roman-briton-culture/ Accessed: December 26, 2023.

"The Anglo-Saxon Invasion" https://englishhistory.net/middle-ages/the-anglo-saxon-invasion/#:~:text=During%20the%20first%20half%20of,the%20Battle%20of%20Mount%20Badon. Accessed: December 26, 2023.

"The Anglo-Saxon invasion and the beginnings of the 'English'" https://www.ourmigrationstory.org.uk/oms/anglo-saxon-migrations Accessed: December 26, 2023.

"How did the Anglo-Saxon Invasion of Britain Really Happen?" https://www.thecollector.com/did-the-anglo-saxon-invasion-happen/ Accessed: December 26, 2023.

"Saxons Invasion of Britain" https://www.heritage-history.com/index.php?c=resources&s=war-dir&f=wars_saxonbritain Accessed: December 26, 2023.

"DNA study reveals fate of ancient Britons" https://www.abc.net.au/science/articles/2015/03/18/4200057.htm Accessed: December 26, 2023.

Part 3

Admin. "German Military in the Soviet Union 1918-1933." Feldgrau. Last modified December 11, 2020. https://www.feldgrau.com/WW2-German-Military-Soviet-Union/.

Bauer, Eddy. *Illustrated World War II Encyclopedia.* Stuttman, 1978.

Churchill Archives Centre. Last modified May 23, 2022. https://archives.chu.cam.ac.uk/

Corum, James S. *The Luftwaffe: Creating the Operational Air War, 1918-1940.* 1997.

Dear, Ian, and Michael R. Foot. *The Oxford Guide to World War II.* New York: Oxford University Press, USA, 2007.

Donnelly, Larry. *The Other Few: The Contribution Made by Bomber and Coastal Aircrew to the Winning of the Battle of Britain.* Red Kite / Air Research, 2004.

"Galland's Briefcase." Tangmere Museum | Tangmere Military Aviation Museum. Last modified April 22, 2012. https://www.tangmere-museum.org.uk/artefact-month/gallands-briefcase.

Gates, Carrie. “Historian Offers First Deep Dive into Secret German-Soviet Alliance That Laid Groundwork for WWII.” Notre Dame News. Last modified July 14, 2021. https://news.nd.edu/news/historian-offers-first-deep-dive-into-secret-german-soviet-alliance-that-laid-groundwork-for-wwii/

“Hitler Pledges Respect for Versailles Borders; Suggests Limiting Arms; Backs Collective Peace (Published 1935).” The New York Times - Breaking News, US News, World News and Videos. Last modified May 22, 1935. https://www.nytimes.com/1935/05/22/archives/hitler-pledges-respect-for-versailles-borders-suggests-limiting.html .

Holmes, Richard, Hew Strachan, Chris Bellamy, and Hugh Bicheno. *The Oxford Companion to Military History*. New York: Oxford University Press, USA, 2001.

Hooton, E. R. *Phoenix Triumphant: The Rise and Rise of the Luftwaffe*. 1999.

Hope and Glory. Directed by John Boorman. Columbia Pictures, 1987. Film. Excellent movie about civilian life during the Blitz, told from the perspective of a young boy

Imperial War Museums. Accessed August 11, 2022. https://www.iwm.org.uk/

Koester@vektorpunkt.de, Dirk. “Katschmarek.” Kunstworte – Dein Wörterbuch Für Wortkreationen. Accessed September 17, 2022. https://www.kunst-worte.de/archaismen/archaismus-4015-katschmarek/

“The London Blitz described by Edward R. Murrow.”
YouTube. n.d.
https://www.youtube.com/watch?v=O7e3G2WUhD4&ab_channel=KD

“Luftwaffe Fighter Aces: General Adolf Galland.” YouTube. Accessed September 21, 2022. https://www.youtube.com/watch?v=Y-nAVhtnHQM&ab_channel=LuftwaffeFighterAces.

“Luftwaffe Pilots and Crew Exhaustion in the Battle of Britain.” Weapons and Warfare. Last modified November 22, 2018. https://weaponsandwarfare.com/2018/11/27/luftwaffe-pilots-and-crew-exhaustion-in-the-battle-of-britain/

“Mr. Winston Churchill: Speeches in 1936 (Hansard).” Accessed August 11, 2022. https://api.parliament.uk/historic-hansard/people/mr-winston-churchill/1936

Osprey Publishing. *Dogfight: War in the Skies*. Oxford: Osprey Publishing, 2010.

Thorburn, Jacob. “Battle of Britain Pilot, 103, Reunites with WW2-era Hurricane Fighter.” Mail Online. Last modified July 23, 2022. https://www.dailymail.co.uk/news/article-11041529/Sole-surviving-Battle-Britain-pilot-103-reunites-World-War-2-era-Hurricane-fighter-plane.html

Winston S. Churchill. *Their Finest Hour, 1949.* New York: RosettaBooks, 2010.

Wood, Derek, and Derek Dempster. *The Narrow Margin: The Battle of Britain and the Rise of Air Power, 1930–1940.* Barnsley: Pen and Sword, 2010.

Image Sources

---

[1] myself, CC BY-SA 3.0 <https://creativecommons.org/licenses/by-sa/3.0>, via Wikimedia Commons https://commons.wikimedia.org/wiki/File:Britain.circa.540.jpg

[2] https://en.wikipedia.org/wiki/File:LindisfarneFol27rIncipitMatt.jpg

[3] Hel-hama, CC BY-SA 3.0 <https://creativecommons.org/licenses/by-sa/3.0>, via Wikimedia Commons; https://commons.wikimedia.org/wiki/File:England_878.svg

[4] https://commons.wikimedia.org/wiki/File:Odo_bayeux_tapestry.png

[5] https://commons.wikimedia.org/wiki/File:Henry_II_Plantagenet.jpg

[6] https://en.wikipedia.org/wiki/File:Magna_Carta_(British_Library_Cotton_MS_Augustus_II.106).jpg

[7] https://commons.wikimedia.org/wiki/File:HenryIII.jpg

[8] https://commons.wikimedia.org/wiki/File:Edward_I_-_Westminster_Abbey_Sedilia.jpg

[9] https://commons.wikimedia.org/wiki/File:Edward-III-king-England.jpg

[10] https://commons.wikimedia.org/wiki/File:Henry_Seven_England.jpg

[11] https://commons.wikimedia.org/wiki/File:1491_Henry_VIII.jpg

[12] https://commons.wikimedia.org/wiki/File:Mary1_by_Eworth_3.jpg

[13] https://commons.wikimedia.org/wiki/File:Elizabeth_I_in_coronation_robes.jpg

[14] This file is licensed under the Creative Commons Attribution-Share Alike 2.5 Generic, 2.0 Generic and 1.0 Generic license; https://commons.wikimedia.org/wiki/File:English_civil_war_map_1642_to_1645.JPG

[15] https://commons.wikimedia.org/wiki/File:Charles_II_by_John_Michael_Wright.jpg

[16] https://commons.wikimedia.org/wiki/File:British_Empire_1921.png

[17] Kjetil Bjørnsrud, CC BY-SA 3.0 <http://creativecommons.org/licenses/by-sa/3.0/>, via Wikimedia Commons; https://commons.wikimedia.org/wiki/File:Braveheart_edinburghcastle.jpg

[18] https://commons.wikimedia.org/wiki/File:SA_4973-Anno_1689._De_kroning_van_Willem_III_en_Maria_Stuart.jpg

[19] AlexD, CC BY-SA 3.0 <https://creativecommons.org/licenses/by-sa/3.0>, via Wikimedia Commons; https://commons.wikimedia.org/wiki/File:Wales_1039-63_(Gruffudd_ap_Llywelyn).svg

[20] Maximilian Dörrbecker (Chumwa), CC BY-SA 2.5 <https://creativecommons.org/licenses/by-sa/2.5>, via Wikimedia Commons; https://commons.wikimedia.org/wiki/File:Northern_Ireland_-_Counties.png

[21] Free to use; https://www.pexels.com/license/. https://www.pexels.com/photo/landscape-photo-of-stonehenge-2716774/

[22] By ianproc64; https://pixabay.com/photos/northumberland-hadrian-wall-7482851/. Free for use: https://pixabay.com/service/license-summary/

[23] By krystianwin; https://pixabay.com/photos/cross-cemetery-grave-religion-3235879/. Free for use: https://pixabay.com/service/license-summary/

[24] https://en.wikipedia.org/wiki/File:Lord_Randolph_Churchill.jpg

[25] This work is licensed under the Creative Commons Attribution-ShareAlike 2.5 License; <https://creativecommons.org/licenses/by-sa/2.5/> via Wikimedia Commons https://en.wikipedia.org/wiki/File:Casematedambachnord.jpg

[26] This file is licensed under the Creative Commons Attribution-Share Alike 3.0 Germany license; < https://creativecommons.org/licenses/by-sa/3.0/de/deed.en> via Wikimedia Commons https://en.wikipedia.org/wiki/File:Bundesarchiv_B_145_Bild-F051620-0043,_Hitler,_G%C3%B6ring_und_v._Schirach_auf_Obersalzberg.jpg

[27] https://en.wikipedia.org/wiki/File:It_is_far_better_to_face_the_bullets.jpg

[28] This file is licensed under the Creative Commons Attribution-Share Alike 3.0 Germany license; <https://creativecommons.org/licenses/by-sa/3.0/de/deed.en> via Wikimedia Commons, https://en.wikipedia.org/wiki/File:Bundesarchiv_Bild_183-H25224,_Guernica,_Ruinen.jpg

[29] This file is licensed under the Creative Commons Attribution-Share Alike 3.0 Germany license;< https://creativecommons.org/licenses/by-sa/3.0/de/deed.en> via Wikimedia Commons, https://en.wikipedia.org/wiki/File:Bundesarchiv_Bild_146-1971-116-29,_Werner_M%C3%B6lders.jpg

[30] Muddywaters; This file is licensed under the Creative Commons Attribution-Share Alike 3.0 Unported license; < https://creativecommons.org/licenses/by-sa/3.0/deed.en> via Wikimedia Commons, https://en.wikipedia.org/wiki/File:Der_Adler_magazine.jpg

[31] https://commons.wikimedia.org/wiki/File:Hugh_Dowding.jpg

[32] https://commons.wikimedia.org/wiki/File:Sir_Winston_Churchill_-_19086236948.jpg

[33] https://en.wikipedia.org/wiki/File:OperationSealion.svg

[34] https://www.awm.gov.au/collection/C99009

[35] This file is licensed under the Creative Commons Attribution-Share Alike 3.0 Unported license; < https://creativecommons.org/licenses/by-sa/3.0/deed.en> via Wikimedia Commons, https://commons.wikimedia.org/wiki/File:Messerschmitt_Bf_109E.jpg

[36] Bundesarchiv, Bild 101I-363-2258-11 / Rompel / CC-BY-SA 3.0, CC BY-SA 3.0 DE <https://creativecommons.org/licenses/by-sa/3.0/de/deed.en>, via Wikimedia Commons; https://commons.wikimedia.org/wiki/File:Bundesarchiv_Bild_101I-363-2258-11,_Flugzeug_Junkers_Ju_88_(cropped).jpg

[37] Alan Wilson from Stilton, Peterborough, Cambs, UK, CC BY-SA 2.0 <https://creativecommons.org/licenses/by-sa/2.0>, via Wikimedia Commons; https://commons.wikimedia.org/wiki/File:Hawker_Hurricane_I_%27R4118_UP-W%27_(G-HUPW)_(41455530471).jpg

[38] https://commons.wikimedia.org/w/index.php?curid=5838617

[39] https://commons.wikimedia.org/w/index.php?curid=4495685

[40] Bundesarchiv, Bild 101I-404-0521-19A / Koster / CC-BY-SA 3.0, https://creativecommons.org/licenses/by-sa/3.0/; https://www.warhistoryonline.com/world-war-ii/42-stunning-photos-of-the-battle-of-britain.html?chrome=1

[41] Bundesarchiv, Bild 101I-344-0741-30 / Röder / CC-BY-SA 3.0, https://creativecommons.org/licenses/by-sa/3.0/; https://www.warhistoryonline.com/world-war-ii/42-stunning-photos-of-the-battle-of-britain.html?chrome=1

[42] https://en.wikipedia.org/wiki/File:Battle_of_britain_air_observer.jpg

[43] https://en.wikipedia.org/wiki/File:Chain_Home_radar_installation_at_Poling,_Sussex,_1945._CH15173.jpg

[44] https://en.wikipedia.org/wiki/File:Chain_home_coverage.jpg

[45] https://en.wikipedia.org/wiki/File:The_Operations_Room_at_RAF_Fighter_Command%27s_No._10_Group_Headquarters,_Rudloe_Manor_(RAF_Box),_Wiltshire,_showing_WAAF_plotters_and_duty_officers_at_work,_1943._CH11887.jpg

[46] https://en.wikipedia.org/wiki/File:Barrage_balloons_over_London_during_World_War_II.jpg

[47] https://commons.wikimedia.org/wiki/File:Corporal_J.D.M_Pearson,_GC,_WAAF_(1940)_(Art._IWM_ART_LD_626).jpg

[48] https://commons.wikimedia.org/w/index.php?curid=7379762

[49] https://commons.wikimedia.org/wiki/File:Air_Marshal_Sir_Keith_Park.jpg

[50] Bundesarchiv, Bild 183-J16050 / CC-BY-SA, CC BY-SA 3.0 DE <https://creativecommons.org/licenses/by-sa/3.0/de/deed.en>, via Wikimedia Commons; https://commons.wikimedia.org/wiki/File:Junkers_Ju_87Ds_in_flight_Oct_1943.jpg

[51] Rolf Süssbrich, CC BY-SA 3.0 <http://creativecommons.org/licenses/by-sa/3.0/>, via Wikimedia Commons; https://commons.wikimedia.org/wiki/File:France_manche_vue_dover.JPG

[52] https://commons.wikimedia.org/wiki/File:British_and_German_aircraft_a_dog_fight.jpg

[53] https://en.wikipedia.org/wiki/File:Douglas_Bader_by_Cuthbert_Orde.JPG

[54] Bundesarchiv, Bild 146-2006-0107 / CC-BY-SA 3.0. This file is licensed under the Creative Commons Attribution-Share Alike 3.0 Germany license < https://creativecommons.org/licenses/by-sa/3.0/de/deed.en> via Wikimedia Commons,; https://en.wikipedia.org/wiki/File:Bundesarchiv_Bild_146-2006-0107,_Albert,_Kesselring,_Wilhelm_Speidel,_Hermann_G%C3%B6ring.jpg

[55] Bundesarchiv, Bild 146-1987-121-30A / CC-BY-SA 3.0. This file is licensed under the Creative Commons Attribution-Share Alike 3.0 Germany license; < https://creativecommons.org/licenses/by-sa/3.0/de/deed.en> via Wikimedia Commons, https://en.wikipedia.org/wiki/File:Bundesarchiv_Bild_146-1987-121-30A,_Hugo_Sperrle.jpg

[56] https://en.wikipedia.org/wiki/File:Dywizjon_303_4.jpg

[57] https://en.wikipedia.org/wiki/File:Heinkel_He_111_during_the_Battle_of_Britain.jpg

[58] Bundesarchiv, Bild 183-B12018 / CC-BY-SA 3.0 This file is licensed under the Creative Commons Attribution-Share Alike 3.0 Germany license;< https://creativecommons.org/licenses/by-sa/3.0/de/deed.en> via Wikimedia Commons,

https://en.wikipedia.org/wiki/File:Bundesarchiv_Bild_183-B12018,_Geburtstag_Theo_Osterkamp,_G%C3%A4ste.jpg

[59] https://commons.wikimedia.org/wiki/File:The_Battle_of_Britain_HU67704.jpg

[60] https://en.wikipedia.org/wiki/File:Churchill_CCathedral_H_14250.jpg

[61] https://en.wikipedia.org/wiki/File:A_young_woman_plays_a_gramophone_in_an_air_raid_shelter_in_north_London_during_1940._D1631.jpg

[62] https://en.wikipedia.org/wiki/File:Never_was_so_much_owed_by_so_many_to_so_few.jpg

[63] https://en.wikipedia.org/wiki/File:President_Roosevelt_and_Winston_Churchill_seated_on_the_quarterdeck_of_HMS_PRINCE_OF_WALES_for_a_Sunday_service_during_the_Atlantic_Conference,_10_August_1941._A4816.jpg

Made in the USA
Columbia, SC
24 February 2025